Third Edition

CORPORATE GOVERNANCE

The Prentice Hall Series in Finance

* denotes **myfinancelab** titles   **Log onto www.myfinancelab.com to learn more**

Third Edition

CORPORATE GOVERNANCE

Kenneth A. Kim
State University of New York at Buffalo

John R. Nofsinger
Washington State University

Derek J. Mohr
State University of New York at Buffalo

Boston Columbus Indianapolis New York San Francisco Upper Saddle River
Amsterdam Cape Town Dubai London Madrid Milan Munich Paris Montreal Toronto
Delhi Mexico City Sao Paulo Sydney Hong Kong Seoul Singapore Taipei Tokyo

Editor in Chief: Donna Battista
Editorial Project Manager: Kerri McQueen
Managing Editor: Jeff Holcomb
Production Manager: Kathy Sleys
Director of Marketing: Patrice Jones
Marketing Manager: Elizabeth A. Averbeck
Marketing Assistant: Ian Gold
Manager, Rights and Permissions: Charles Morris
Creative Director: Jayne Conte
Cover Designer: Margaret Kenselaar
Media Director: Susan Schoenberg
Media Project Manager: Nicole Sackin
Full-Service Project Management, Composition, and Illustration: Joseph Malcolm
   GGS Higher Education Resources, PMG
Printer/Binder: STP Bind Rite Robbinsville
Text Font: 10/12 Palatino

Credits and acknowledgments borrowed from other sources and reproduced, with permission, in this textbook appear on appropriate page within text.

10 9 8 7 6 5 4 3 2 1—BBR—14 13 12 11 10 09

Prentice Hall
is an imprint of

ISBN-10:   0-13-510158-1
ISBN-13: 978-0-13-510158-2

CONTENTS

PREFACE

Corporate Governance, Third Edition, is the perfect textbook to supplement:

a. any corporate finance class;
b. an accounting class;
c. a variety of management courses such as strategy, ethics, and/or especially business and society; and
d. a business law class.

In addition, this text is sufficiently self-contained so that it can be used as the sole textbook in a business administration module specifically focusing on corporate governance. The book can also be used for executive training programs and can serve as an important reference for executive and academic libraries.

A little more than a decade ago, the term "corporate governance" was largely academic jargon. Today, the term is familiar to almost everyone. Unfortunately, its familiarity in our society comes about due to two major calamitous periods in our recent history: several shocking corporate scandals at the turn of the century (e.g., WorldCom and Enron) and the recent failures of financial firms (e.g., Bear Sterns) and the ensuing global economic crisis.

At the turn of the century, numerous revelations came to light, such as executives expropriating wealth from their firms; accountants helping companies doctor their financial numbers; and analysts irresponsibly hyping Internet stocks. Meanwhile, boards of directors, lenders, credit rating agencies, shareholder activists, and regulators seemed almost absent or ineffective in staving off the corporate governance crisis. As a result, the market lapsed into a meltdown during the early 2000s. With investor confidence down, and with the flaws of our corporate governance system revealed, everyone responded with calls for regulatory reform and corporate governance improvements. Subsequently, reforms were made (e.g., Sarbanes-Oxley Act).

Recently, the revelations have been about financial firms taking excessive risk. Many mortgages were issued to people who were not creditworthy. These mortgages were backed by financial firms. Eventual defaults on mortgages and subsequent foreclosures led to what is now known as the subprime mortgage crisis. The crisis has exposed pervasive weaknesses in the financial industry. Obviously, financial firms were poorly monitored and/or the regulation of these firms fell short. This serves as a wake-up call. Our corporate governance system still needs fixing.

Why is corporate governance important? The goal of every firm is to increase its shareholders' wealth. However, the firm's value diminishes when it does not have the trust of its shareholders. The goal of a well-functioning capital market system is to foster economic stability and growth so that its citizens can prosper. This too requires the trust of the average investor. Without the trust of investors, firms will not be able to obtain new capital and grow. Thus, the system breaks down. *The entire economy suffers when trust is broken.*

Effective corporate governance can instill confidence, and thus trust, in our companies, in our markets, and in our economy.

Believe it or not, we already have an extensive system of corporate governance. The system has never been perfect, but we have only begun to notice the extent of its weaknesses. Now the media regularly discusses corporate governance. Business and law schools have begun incorporating the topic of corporate governance into classrooms and curricula. Just when the lessons of the corporate governance crisis at the turn of the century had started to fade, it is now painfully obvious how important is a strong corporate governance system.

NEW TO THIS EDITION

- Brand new chapter!

  - **Chapter 10, Moral Hazard, Systemic Risk, and Bailouts:** Discusses the current economic crisis, excessive risk-taking by financial firms that eventually led to the crisis, the role of government as a de facto rescuer of last resort, and the government's bailouts of troubled firms.
- The Securities and Exchange Commission and the New Governance Rules chapters are now combined into one chapter (Chapter 9, The Securities and Exchange Commission and the Sarbanes-Oxley Act).
- Reports on latest research findings!

  - Some chapters now contains a box that outlines **recent research** from scholars.

HIGHLIGHTS

In **Chapter 1**, we provide an overview of the U.S. corporation. Then we lay out the reasons why effective corporate governance is needed. In general, we believe there are many mechanisms in which corporations can be effectively monitored.

After Chapter 1, the **rest of the book** is organized into chapters that discuss *each* corporate governance mechanism.

Every chapter is organized in the same way, and each chapter is self-contained. Each chapter begins with a detailed overview of the monitor or monitoring mechanism, and then highlights potential problems.

In key chapters, **real-world examples** are used to illustrate the outlined problems. Almost all of these examples are recent.

Every chapter provides an **international perspective** and a **list of Web sites** so that students can have access to the latest developments in corporate governance.

At the end of each chapter, we provide **Review Questions** that are based on the chapter reading and **Discussion Questions** that can facilitate class discussions. We also offer **Exercises** that students can do to further their understanding of the chapter material. Lastly, we provide **Exercises for**

Non-U.S. Students to help them dig into corporate governance issues in their own country.

FOR INSTRUCTORS

The following supplements are available for download for adopting instructors on the Instructor's Resource Center (IRC) online. For detailed descriptions, please visit *www.pearsonhighered.com/irc*.

> *PowerPoint slides (created by the authors):*   The extensive set of PowerPoint slides contains figures from the text and is available on the online catalog page for this book.
>
> *Instructor's Manual (plus Test Bank):*   The Instructor's Manual, prepared by the authors, includes ideas on how to structure your course, with a sample syllabus. The test-bank portion includes an array of both true/false and multiple-choice questions and answers. PowerPoint slide printouts follow the test-bank chapters.

INSTRUCTOR'S RESOURCE CENTER

Register. Redeem. Login.

Instructors can access a variety of print, media, and presentation resources available with this text in downloadable, digital format at *www.pearsonhighered.com/irc*. For most texts, resources are also available for course management platforms, such as Blackboard, WebCT, and Course Compass.

It gets better. Once you register, you will not have additional forms to fill out or multiple usernames and passwords to remember to access new titles and/or editions. As a registered faculty member, you can log in directly to download resource files and receive immediate access and instructions for installing Course Management content to your campus server.

Need help? Our dedicated Technical Support team is ready to assist instructors with questions about the media supplements that accompany this text. Visit: *http://247pearsoned.custhelp.com/* for answers to frequently-asked questions and toll-free user support phone numbers.

ACKNOWLEDGMENTS

This book could not have been written without the guidance and support we have received from many people throughout our careers. We acknowledge all of our former teachers and professional colleagues, and our former and current research collaborators, for shaping the way we think about corporate governance. We also readily acknowledge our friends who continue to work in the "real world" as they keep us grounded in reality, thus preventing us from getting carried away with our theories. We also appreciate our former students for letting us try out most of the material used in this textbook in our own classrooms. We appreciate our publisher, Prentice Hall (especially Kerri

McQueen), for working with us, and for all of the reviewers who have given us such valuable feedback:

Tim Michael—University of Houston Clear Lake

Armand Picou—Texas A&M University–Corpus Christi

Cindy Schipani—University of Michigan

Betty Simkins—Oklahoma State University

Sudhir Singh—Frostburg State University

Curt H. Stiles—University of North Carolina at Wilmington

Diane Swanson—Kansas State University

Melissa Williams—University of Houston–Clear Lake

Finally, we are deeply indebted to our close friends and family for their support. They help us maintain our sanity.

FEEDBACK

The author and product team would appreciate hearing from you! Let us know what you think about this book by writing to *finance@pearson.com*. Please include "Feedback about Kim/Nofsinger/Mohr 3e" in the subject line.

You can also contact the author team directly. They would also be happy to receive your comments and questions:

Ken Kim—*kk52@buffalo.edu*

John Nofsinger—*john_nofsinger@wsu.edu*

Derek Mohr—*dmohr@buffalo.edu*

If you have questions related to this product, please contact our customer service department online at *http://247pearsoned.custhelp.com/*.

ABOUT THE AUTHORS

Kenneth A. Kim, Ph.D., is associate professor of finance at the State University of New York (SUNY) at Buffalo. Kim is coauthor of the CFA Institute's "body of knowledge" material pertaining to corporate governance. During 1998 and 1999, as a senior financial economist at the U.S. Securities and Exchange Commission in Washington, DC, he worked on a wide variety of corporate finance and governance issues, including mergers and acquisitions regulations. His primary research interests include corporate finance and corporate governance. His research has been highlighted in the financial press including the *Wall Street Journal*, the *Financial Times*, and *BusinessWeek*. He has been published in the *Journal of Finance*, the *Journal of Business*, the *Journal of Corporate Finance*, and the *Journal of Banking and Finance*, among other leading journals. He recently coauthored a review paper on international corporate governance for the journal *Corporate Governance: An International Review*. Kim is also coauthor of *Infectious Greed* and the textbook, *Global Corporate Finance*.

John R. Nofsinger, Ph.D., is associate professor of finance at Washington State University and author of *Investment Madness*, *The Psychology of Investing*, and *Investment Blunders*, and coauthor of *Infectious Greed*. Widely acknowledged as one of the world's leading experts in investor psychology and behavioral finance, he is frequently quoted in financial media including the *Wall Street Journal*, *Fortune*, *BusinessWeek*, *SmartMoney*, *Bloomberg*, and *CNBC*, as well as other media from the *Washington Post* to *Wired.com*. Nofsinger has published more than 30 articles in leading scholarly and professional journals. His research has won awards from the Financial Management Association, Chicago Quantitative Alliance, and PACAP conferences. He has also done advanced research for private firms, the New York Stock Exchange, and the CFA Institute. He posts on a blog called "Mind on My Money" at the *Psychology Today* blog site, *http://www.psychologytoday.com/blog/mind-my-money*.

Derek J. Mohr, J.D., is visiting assistant professor of finance at the State University of New York (SUNY) at Buffalo where he codeveloped the MBA course in ethics and corporate governance. Before SUNY Buffalo, he worked for six years as a corporate attorney advising clients on forming, buying, and selling businesses, as well as securities and tax issues. He conducts research and provides consulting and legal advice on corporate governance and related legal matters.

Corporations and Corporate Governance

Capitalism is an economic system of business based on private enterprise. Individuals and businesses own land, farms, factories, and equipment, and they use those assets in an attempt to earn profits. Capitalism provides rewards for those who work hard and who are inventive and creative enough to figure out new or improved products and services. One potential reward for creating value in an economy is the accumulation of personal wealth. The wealth incentive provides the fuel to generate new ideas and to foster economic value that provides jobs and raises our standard of living.

The main goal of a company is to create an environment conducive to earning long-term profits, which stem from two main sources. First, a large portion of a firm's value derives from the current and future profits of the products and/or services it provides to its customer base. Finding ways to increase profits from these core operations can increase economic value. Second, increased profits can come from growth in the sales of an existing product or from introducing new products. The ability to access capital and to control risk is important in the success or failure of a firm. Expansion usually requires additional money, or capital, that must be raised by the company. Business activities also entail risk as there is no guarantee that new products will be successful or that existing products will continue to be successful. As these are important attributes for companies, capital requirements and risk sharing affect the manner in which a company or firm is organized. A small part-time business may operate as a sole proprietorship (i.e., one owner), while a major international business is more likely to be a publicly traded corporation.

In this chapter, we first describe different forms of business, with emphasis on the publicly traded corporation. We then describe the structure of publicly traded corporations, including the separation of owners and managers that is required to effectively run such a company. As this separation means that the owners of the company do not control day-to-day operations, there is a potential for managers to take actions other than those that the owners would prefer.

An integrated system of checks and balances known as corporate governance has evolved to address this potential conflict. Throughout this chapter, we outline the parties who have some impact on the governance of corporations. Then, in the following chapters, each of the parties involved in corporate governance is analyzed individually.

FORMS OF BUSINESS OWNERSHIP

In general, a business can be a sole proprietorship, a partnership, or a corporation. Other forms exist,[1] but we will focus on these three as this is the most general distinction. Each organizational form involves different advantages and disadvantages. A **sole proprietorship** is a business owned by a single person. These businesses are relatively easy to start up and business tax is computed at the personal level. Due to its simplicity, sole proprietorships are ubiquitous, representing more than 70 percent of all U.S. businesses.[2] However, there are several significant drawbacks. Such firms often have a limited lifespan (they die with the owner's death or retirement), they have a limited ability to obtain capital, and the owner bears unlimited personal liability for the firm.

A **partnership** is similar to a sole proprietorship but there is more than one owner. As such, a partnership shares the advantages and disadvantages of the sole proprietorship. While one obvious advantage of a partnership is the ability to pool capital, this advantage may not be as important as combining service-oriented expertise and skill, especially for larger partnerships. Examples of such partnerships include accounting firms, law firms, some investment banks, and advertising firms. The biggest disadvantage to partnerships is that each partner bears unlimited personal liability for the activities of the partnership.

This book focuses on the third business form, the **corporation**. Fewer than 20 percent of all U.S. businesses are corporations but they generate approximately 90 percent of the country's business revenue.[3] The corporation is its own legal entity, as if it were a person. This means the corporation can sue and be sued in court, and that the corporation is a taxpayer that must pay taxes regardless of the fact that its owners already pay taxes.[4] Even though it exists as a legal person that has unlimited life, real individuals are required to act on behalf of the corporation. This is the role of the corporate officers who act as agents for the corporation.

A corporation is formed by filing a document with the state government that sets forth how many shares of stock are authorized for issuance to shareholders. Once the corporation is formed, shareholders contribute capital in exchange for shares of stock. The shareholders then elect a board of directors to run the corporation and the board appoints officers to handle the day-to-day operations. While these corporate officers (also known as "executives" or "management") control the activities of the corporation, the board of directors and the shareholders each retain some power to govern the corporation.

One of the primary reasons for choosing the corporate form of organization is to limit the liability of the owners of the company. Shareholders' investment in a corporation is limited to the amounts they paid for their shares. If the company fails and owes large amounts to creditors, the creditors can only collect from the corporate assets. The shareholders, as owners of the corporation, are not required to put any additional funds into the company to cover the losses of the creditors.[5]

The other important reasons for choosing to operate as a corporation are the ability to raise capital and to share risk. Issuing shares of stock in a corporation is an efficient method for raising capital. As new shares of stock can be created by fiat by the corporation, there is no limit to the amount of shares that can be issued. These new shares also have the effect of an increased sharing of risk because the new shareholders have effectively taken over some of the risk of the corporation's failure.

Examples of the benefits of a corporation can be seen in the history of large companies such as Apple and Google. Each was started by two individuals and operated initially as a partnership. Apple was started in a garage by Steven Jobs and Steve Wozniak; Google was started at Stanford University by Larry Page and Sergey Brin. As the potential for success of these companies readily became apparent, there was a need for capital to expand. Each did this expansion in the same way—they found a large investor to bankroll their startup and converted the business to a corporation. Soon after, both companies became public corporations and sold shares of stock to the general public. In this way, the growing companies took advantage of the corporation's ability to raise capital as Apple sold $65 million in stock in 1980 and Google sold $1.6 billion worth in 2004. The risk of expanding their businesses into wide distribution was also spread across a large number of shareholders.

The advantages of the corporate business form are appealing, but there are also major disadvantages. Corporate profits are subject to business taxes before any income goes to shareholders in the form of dividends.[6] Subsequently, shareholders must also pay personal taxes on dividend income. Therefore, shareholders are exposed to double taxation. In addition, running a public corporation can be expensive. For example, the costs of hiring accountants and legal experts, the costs of communicating with all shareholders, the costs of complying with regulations, and so forth, can cost millions of dollars per year. Finally, and perhaps the most important disadvantage, large corporations suffer from potentially serious governance problems. The separation of ownership from management results in a situation where many investors own only a small stake of a large public corporation, so they consequently do not have much of an incentive to get involved in monitoring the activities of mangers of the firms in which they own stock. Management may also not be as careful in spending money when managers are not major shareholders because they are effectively spending someone else's money.

SEPARATION OF OWNERSHIP AND CONTROL

In 1932, Adolf Berle and Gardiner Means wrote what was to become a famous book about the corporate form of business.[7] They pointed out that corporations were becoming so large that the ownership and control was separated. The stockholders own the firm and managers (technically, officers or executives) control the firm. This situation comes about because the thousands, or even hundreds of thousands, of investors who own public firms cannot collectively make the daily decisions needed to operate a business. Hence the need for specialized management.

Most shareholders do not wish to take part in a firm's business activities. These shareholders act like passive investors, not active owners. The difference is subtle but important. An active owner is like a sole proprietor who is focused on the business performance of the firm. In contrast, a passive investor is an investor who does not have the time or desire to get involved in running the company and instead focuses on the risk and return of the investment. While diversifying reduces risk for the investor, ownership of many companies also makes participation and influence in those companies less likely. Therefore, investors tend to be inactive shareholders of many firms.

Hence, there is a problem with this separation of ownership and control. Why would the managers care about the owners? Berle and Means pointed out that with managers being freed from vigilant owners, managers would only pursue enough profit to keep stockholders satisfied while managers sought self-serving gratification in the form of perks, power, and/or fame. In academic terms, this situation is known as the principal-agent problem or the agency problem. The owners are the principal and the manager is the agent who is supposed to work for the owner. If shareholders cannot effectively monitor the managers' behavior, then managers may be tempted to use the firm's assets for their own ends, all at the expense of shareholders. This should not be hard to imagine. Secretaries may take home office supplies. When traveling, mid-level managers may order as much food as allowed for on their expense accounts. Executives might prefer fancy oak furniture for their offices and the use of corporate jets when traveling. All of these actions are at the expense of shareholders. If people feel they can get away with these minor offenses, what else might they try?

Among all employees, the agency problem is the greatest with the executives of a corporation because they have the most power and control in the corporation. Mid-level managers have bosses who look at expense reports. But who watches the executives? The primary monitor of the executives is the board of directors of the corporation who are appointed by the shareholders to run the corporation on behalf of the shareholders. It is the board that appoints the executives and removes them if they take actions that harm the corporation. However, if the shareholders are passive investors without an incentive to monitor closely, will the shareholders make sure the board does its job? If not, then what is to stop the executives from including the directors in the activities that personally benefit them at the expense of the shareholders?

Solutions to this problem tend to come in two categories: incentives and monitoring. The incentive solution attempts to tie the wealth of the executive to the wealth of the shareholders, so that executives and shareholders want the same thing. This is called aligning executive incentives with shareholder desires. Managers would then act and behave in a way that is also best for the other shareholders. How can this be done? For most U.S. companies, executives are given stock, restricted stock, stock options, or combinations of these as a significant component of their compensation. A similar approach is frequently considered with directors as well. If all directors own stock or have options on stock, then directors will personally benefit if the firm does well. The advantages and disadvantages of this incentive solution for executives are explored in Chapter 2. The incentive problem with the board of directors is covered in Chapter 4. Suffice it to say, there are troubles with incentives as a solution to the agency problem.

The second solution is to address the weaknesses in the monitoring by the board and to set up additional monitoring mechanisms for monitoring the behavior of managers. Several monitoring mechanisms are discussed shortly in this chapter, and they are importantly discussed throughout this book.

CAN SHAREHOLDERS INFLUENCE MANAGERS?

Theoretically, managers (executives) work for owners (shareholders). In reality, because shareholders are usually inactive and the board does as management asks, the firm actually seems to belong to management. Some active shareholders have tried to influence management and/or change the directors on the board, but they are often met with defeat. Recent evidence of unsuccessful outcomes of shareholder proposals is quite telling. Shareholders of public corporations have the power to make proposals that can be voted on at the annual shareholders meeting. There are generally two types of proposals, those related to governance (e.g., suggesting changes in board structure) and those oriented to social reform (e.g., proposing to stop selling chemicals to rogue countries). About half of all shareholder-initiated proposals progress far enough in the process to reach the voting stage. When there is a vote, such proposals usually are defeated.[8]

A huge factor in whether a proposal is successful depends on management's opinion. Without management approval, proposals have little chance of succeeding. The reason for this is that management is permitted to ask shareholders who will not be able to attend a meeting to return proxy statements voting as management suggests. Traditionally, shareholders have trusted management to know what is best for the firm, so most passive shareholders will go along with whatever management wants. The result is that management effectively controls a large block of votes due to the proxies of uninvolved shareholders and it is unlikely that activist shareholders will prevail. The same issue arises in shareholder voting to replace directors. It is difficult for outside shareholders to mount a serious challenge to the directors nominated by the company.

Monitors

There are a variety of potential monitors of the actions of corporate executives that jointly make up the current system of corporate governance.

EXAMPLE 1.1   Carly Fiorina's Takeover of Compaq

For an illustration of management control and influence, consider the 2002 merger between Hewlett-Packard (HP) and Compaq.[9] Carly Fiorina, the CEO of Hewlett-Packard, announced on September 4, 2001, that HP would acquire Compaq for $25.5 billion. The stock markets, industry experts, and the business media reacted negatively to the news. Hewlett-Packard stock was down 18 percent following the announcement, and even Compaq's stock declined by 10 percent, which is rare for a target firm. Of particular note, David W. Packard and Walter Hewlett, both significant shareholders (when including the Packard Foundation, the pair owned 18 percent of HP stock) and sons of HP's founders, were also strongly opposed to the acquisition. In fact, they took out newspaper ads asking other HP shareholders to vote against the merger.

However, Fiorina went ahead with her plan, despite attacks from both Packard and Hewlett, and on March 19, 2002, the plan was approved by the shareholders. Despite the controversy and the drop in stock prices, most shareholders voted with management's wishes and approved the acquisition. This example reinforces the idea that even though some investors may want to influence business strategy and direction, management controls the firm.

Figure 1.1 illustrates the separation of ownership and control between stockholders and managers. In addition, the figure shows that monitors exist inside the corporate structure, outside the structure, and in government.

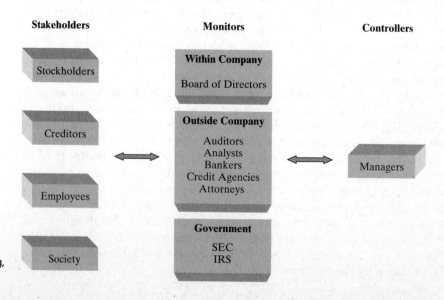

FIGURE 1.1 Separation of Ownership, Monitoring, and Control

The monitoring role inside a public corporation falls on the board of directors who oversee management and are supposed to represent shareholders' interests. The shareholders elect directors at the annual meeting each year. These directors have a legal obligation to represent the shareholders' interests in running the corporation. One of the most important roles the board carries out is to appoint the executives who will actually run the day-to-day operations of the company. The board hires the executives and can replace them if the board is unhappy with management for any reason. The board can also design compensation contracts to tie management's salaries to the firm's performance.

You may remember that Apple Computer was cofounded by Steve Jobs. When the firm became a public corporation, Jobs was the largest shareholder, and he also became CEO, which is the highest executive at a corporation. However, the Apple board of directors felt that Jobs was not experienced enough to steer the firm through its rapid expansion. Therefore, they hired John Sculley as CEO in 1983. In 1985, a power struggle ensued for control of the firm, and the board backed Sculley. Jobs was forced out of Apple and no longer had a say in business operations even though he was the largest shareholder. (Interestingly, when Apple Computer experienced difficulties in the late 1990s, the board hired Jobs back as CEO!)

As shown in the figure, outsiders—including auditors, analysts, investment banks, credit rating agencies, and outside legal counsel—all interact with executives and the board and monitor manager activities (as well as the actions of the board). Auditors examine the firm's accounting systems and comment on whether financial statements fairly represent the financial position of the firm. Investors and other stakeholders use these public financial statements to make decisions about the firm's financial health, prospects, performance, and value. Even though investors may not have the ability or opportunity to validate the firm's activities, accountants and auditors can attest to the firm's financial health and verify its activities.

Investment analysts who follow a firm conduct their own, independent evaluations of the company's business activities and report their findings to the investment community. Analysts are supposed to give unbiased and expert assessments. Investment banks also interact with management by helping firms access the capital markets. When obtaining more capital from public investors, firms must register documents with regulators that show potential investors the condition of the firm. Investment banks help firms with this process and advise managers on how to interact with the capital markets.

The U.S. government also monitors business activities through federal laws covering securities, taxes, antitrust, foreign trade, and other aspects that affect large corporations. Federal laws have created the Securities and Exchange Commission (SEC), the Internal Revenue Service (IRS), and other federal agencies with jurisdiction over publicly traded companies. The SEC regulates public firms for the protection of public investors, and it makes policy and prosecutes violators. The IRS enforces the tax rules to ensure corporations comply with the tax code in paying its taxes. Violations of federal law by executives can lead to large fines and even jail time.

In response to corporate and investment community scandals, the U.S. government enacted the Sarbanes-Oxley Act of 2002. Overall, the act created a new oversight body to regulate auditors, created laws pertaining to corporate responsibility, and increased punishments for corporate white-collar crime. Similarly, the two largest stock exchanges, the NYSE and NASDAQ, both developed and adopted their own governance-focused listing standards to address the problems.

More recently, the government has impacted corporate governance in the firms asking for financial help during the 2008 and 2009 economic recession. In formulating a bailout package for the big three American auto companies, Congress first demanded the three CEOs accept compensation of only $1. Later, as the government helped GM navigate through the bankruptcy court process quickly, it demanded CEO Rick Wagoner's resignation. Also, U.S. Treasury is providing capital to financial firms from the Troubled Asset Relief Program (TARP) in exchange for debt and equity stakes in the firms. This makes the government an investor stakeholder in these firms. It is unclear how this new relationship will impact the corporate governance of the firms and what incentives might have been created. However, we have already seen Congress interfere with compensation bonus payments at American International Group, Inc., (AIG).

Another monitor of management is market forces. If a manager is not doing a good job, either because he is bad at managing or because he is abusing his managerial discretion, then his firm might get taken over and he is subsequently fired. On the contrary, an executive who avoids agency problems and is successful in increasing the value of shareholders' investments at one firm will be in demand in the marketplace by other firms who are looking for an effective leader. In this sense, the fear of a potential takeover and the reward of a CEO position at a more prestigious company each might represent powerful disciplinary mechanisms to make sure that managers perform to the best of their abilities and to make sure that managerial discretion is controlled.

Other potential monitors include: stockholders, such as large institutional investors like pension funds, who are active monitors; creditors and credit rating agencies who analyze whether the firm can handle its current debt level; employees, such as internal auditors, who monitor the firm to make sure it is healthy; and others in the corporation's community who can instill a sense of corporate citizenship to the firm so that firm executives feel a sense of responsibility toward their community.

As a group, this is a pretty impressive set of monitors. Unfortunately, all of these mechanisms can fail at one time or another. An important purpose of this book is to describe each of these corporate monitors and the problems that may exist with each of them.

AN INTEGRATED SYSTEM OF GOVERNANCE

The corporate governance system is integrated and complicated. The potential incentives for executives, auditors, boards, banks, and so on, to misbehave are intertwined. By focusing on one part of the system, readers

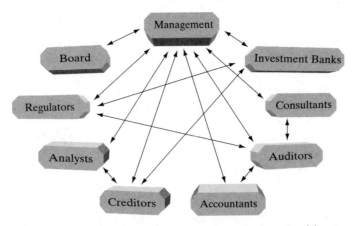

FIGURE 1.2   Interlinking Relationships among Business Participants

might not fully understand how the governance system can break down. Consider the diagram of corporate participants in Figure 1.2. The arrows show the relationships between the groups. Note that these relationships are interconnected.

For example, analysts talk to management to gauge the prospects of the firm. Managers want to paint a rosy picture so that analysts will recommend a "buy" rating and the stock price will rise. However, this situation may also cause analysts to predict a high profit forecast for the company, and the managers may struggle to meet the high profit forecast. If the business activities of the firm do not merit the high profit forecast, managers might then pressure their accounting department to help. In some cases, consultants are hired who recommend aggressive accounting techniques to help show increased profits.

The public auditors for the firm may have had a long and fruitful relationship with the company, auditing the books for many years. The auditors are proud to have a prestigious corporation as a client and do not want to end this relationship; consequently they may not press too hard on limiting aggressive accounting methods. Why are managers so obsessed with pushing hard for smooth and increasing profits? Why are they obsessed with gaining analyst favor? It is because a board (which is largely picked by the managers) awards them stock options and stock incentives. If managers can increase the price of the stock, then they can cash in their options and stock and earn far more than their base compensation level.

Government regulators also monitor managers' behavior. However, regulators often have experience as partners in the consulting firms, auditing firms, or law firms that are an integral part of the system. By participating in the corporate system, regulators know how it works. Unfortunately, they might also have their own conflicts of interest.

This book describes the following monitors or monitoring mechanisms:

- incentive contracts that supposedly align executive incentives with shareholder interests;
- accountants and auditors who check the firm's financial statements;
- boards of directors who represent shareholders;
- investment banks and analysts who bring securities to the public for sale and evaluate them;
- creditors and credit rating agencies who monitor the firm's ability to handle debt;
- shareholders themselves;
- the corporate takeover market where supposedly good firms take over bad firms;
- the Securities and Exchange Commission who are the official regulators of the securities industry;
- government and the governance of international firms;
- the government's role in the survival of firms; and
- corporate citizenship that should instill a sense of corporate responsibility to the executives.

INTERNATIONAL MONITORING

Other capitalist countries use the types of monitoring and incentives used in the United States to align the interests of executives and shareholders. However, important differences do occur. Some countries use different compensation contracts and have different accounting standards. Many countries do not have the same institutional investing environment as the United States. Some countries are bank oriented rather than capital markets oriented. A country's legal environment can explain some of the differences. However, corporate scandals can occur in every country. In this book, every chapter contains an international perspective on that chapter's topic.

Summary

The corporate form of business allows firms that need capital to obtain it and expand, thereby helping the economy. This form also allows people with money to provide those funds and profit from having ownership in business. The disadvantage of public corporations lies in the relation between ownership and control. Managers who control the firm can take advantage of the investors who own the firm. To inhibit poor managerial behavior, boards of directors try to align the executives' interests with shareholders' interests through incentive programs involving stock and stock options. In addition, the corporate system has several different groups of people that monitor managers. Unfortunately, both alignment incentives and monitoring groups bring to the table their own set of problems. The corporate system has interrelated incentives that combine to create an environment where people might act unethically. The following chapters discuss each aspect of the incentive and monitor system of corporate governance.

Review Questions

1. What are the three basic forms of business owner-ship? What are the advantages and disadvantages of each?
2. How can executive compensation align managers interests with shareholders interests?
3. Name and describe the different groups that moni-tor a firm.
4. Describe the separation of ownership and control. Explain how that separation comes about and why it leads to problems.

Discussion Questions

1. Figure 1.1 shows monitors and stakeholders. In your opinion, which group is in the best position to monitor the firm? Explain why. Which group has the potential to be the weakest monitor? Explain why.
2. Figure 1.2 shows how business participants are in-terlinked. In your opinion, which links potentially create the greatest problems for stockholders? Explain why.
3. In your opinion, how do you think U.S. corpora-tions became as important and as large as they are today?
4. In general, and in your personal experience, which has been the most effective way to get people to do what you want:
   (i) provide incentives for good behavior;
   (ii) closely monitor them; or
   (iii) give punishments for bad behavior?

From what you have seen, read, and heard from the mass media, journalists, politicians, and so on, what do these people think is the best way to get executives to behave ethically? If your answers to these two ques-tions are different, then try to reconcile the differences.

Exercises

1. This chapter described how Carly Fiorina exerted control over Hewlett-Packard despite objections from large shareholders. Find another example of how management went against shareholders' wishes and describe what happened.
2. Do some research and explain how U.S. corpora-tions became as important and as large as they are today. Some academics have discussed the "theory of the firm" or the "nature of the firm." To what extent, and how, do these theories explain U.S. corporations today? How do agency problems play a role in these theories?

Exercises for Non-U.S. Students

1. Figure 1.2 shows how business participants are interlinked in the United States. Create a figure showing the interlinkages among business partici-pants in your country. Explain the interlinkages.
2. How severe is the agency problem in your coun-try? Explain. Also, provide real examples.
3. In your country, which ideology seems to be used in resolving agency conflicts:
   (i) providing incentives to executives for good behavior;
   (ii) closely monitoring the executives; or
   (iii) giving punishments to executives for bad behavior?

Do you think it is working? Explain why or why not.

Endnotes

1. There are other common forms of business organizations, such as the Limited Liability Company (LLC) and limited partnership (LP). These are "hybrids" that combine the limited liability of corporations with the tax benefits of partnerships. Depending on the size and structure of LLCs and LPs, they could be managed similar to large corporations or to sole proprietorships.

2. William J. Megginson, *Corporate Finance Theory* (Reading, MA: Addison-Wesley, 1997), p. 40.

3. Ibid.

4. In contrast, the sole proprietor and partnership are not taxpayers. Income from the companies are charged directly to the owners on their tax returns.

5. In contrast, the owner of the sole proprietorship or a partner in a partnership would be legally liable for paying off the creditor in full. Note, also, that the limitation of liability is not absolute in corporations, as there are rare cases where a court "pierces the corporate veil" and assigns personal liability to shareholders in cases where the court finds the corporate form was abused for personal gain.

6. Corporations with small numbers of shareholders can elect to become "S" corporations where the only tax is at the shareholder level. Public corporations, however, are required to be "C" corporations with double taxation.

7. Adolf Berle and Gardiner Means, *The Modern Corporation and Private Property* (New York, MacMillan, 1932).

8. See, for example, Stuart Gillan and Laura Starks, "A Survey of Shareholder Activism: Motivation and Empirical Evidence," *Contemporary Finance Digest* 2, no. 3 (1998):10–34; Cynthia Campbell, Stuart Gillan, and Cathy Niden, "Current Perspectives on Shareholder Proposals: Lessons from the 1997 Proxy Season," Financial Management 28, no. 1 (1999):89–98; and Gordon and Pound, "Information, Ownership Structure, and Shareholder Voting: Evidence from Shareholder-Sponsored Corporate Governance Proposals," *Journal of Finance* 47, no. 2 (1993):697–718.

9. Larry Magid, "Many Would Lose in Hewlett-Packard, Compaq Merger," *Los Angeles Times*, *www.larrysworld.com/articles/synd.hpmerger. htm;* Mike Elgan and Susan B. Shor, "Gloves Are Off in Merger Fight," *HP World* 5, no. 2, *www. interex. org/hpworldnews/hpw202/01news.html.*

Executive Incentives

The introductory chapter described the agency problems that can arise in a large corporation where there is a separation of ownership and control. A corporation's ownership and control are separated between three parties—shareholders (owners), the board of directors, and executives (managers). The shareholders own the firm, the board of directors controls major decisions on behalf of the shareholders, and executives have day-to-day control over the firm's decisions. This separation of ownership and control creates the potential for managers to use the firm's assets to enhance their own lifestyles.[1] In other words, the managers can capture the benefit of actions such as buying a corporate jet and using it for personal trips while leaving the cost to fall on the shareholders.

Solutions to agency problems tend to fall in two categories: incentives and monitoring. The board of directors, auditors, and other components of the governance system serve to monitor managers; this is discussed in later chapters. The incentive solution, covered in this chapter, ties an executive's wealth to the wealth of shareholders so that everyone shares the same goal. This is called aligning executive incentives with shareholders'. To align manager and shareholder interests, most executives receive stock options or restricted stock as a significant component of their compensation. The idea is that managers should then act in ways to benefit shareholders. In this chapter, we focus on the incentives of modern executive compensation.

POTENTIAL MANAGERIAL TEMPTATIONS

A manager has a variety of stakeholders that are affected by her actions. These include investors such as stockholders (owners) and lenders, the firm's customers and suppliers, the firm's employees, and of course herself. A good manager should put the needs of other stakeholders before her own, but human nature may cause her to put her needs first. Examples of self-serving managerial actions include:

- shirking (i.e., not working hard);
- hiring friends;
- consuming excessive perks (e.g., purchasing extravagant office furniture, using company cars, enjoying large expense accounts);
- building empires (i.e., making the firm as large as possible even though it may hurt the firm's per share value);
- taking no risks or chances to avoid being fired; and
- having a short-run horizon if near retirement.

One way to make sure that managers will not behave in these ways is to give them the right monetary incentives to act in the interests of their other stakeholders. We discuss various types of executive compensation that are aimed at accomplishing this task.

TYPES OF EXECUTIVE COMPENSATION

Company executives are compensated in many different ways. They receive a basic salary that also includes pension contributions and perquisites (company car, club memberships, and so on). In addition, top executives might receive a bonus that is usually linked to accounting-based performance measures. Lastly, managers might receive additional wealth through long-term incentive programs, usually in the form of stock options, which reward the manager for increasing the company's stock price. Restricted stock grants are another common form of long-term awards.

Base Salary and Bonus

As with most jobs, CEOs are promised a specific annual salary. The base salary of a company CEO is often determined through the benchmarking method. This method is where the compensation committee of the board of directors surveys peer CEO salaries for comparison.[2] Salaries less than the 50th percentile are considered under market, while salaries in the 50th to 75th percentile are considered competitive. CEO base salary has continuously drifted upward because CEOs typically argue for competitive salaries and if each CEO receives a salary above the median, the median salary will go up each year. So each year, we often see CEOs getting nice raises and we also see new CEOs making more than current CEOs. Interestingly, this basic pay results more from characteristics of the firm (e.g., industry, size) than from characteristics of the CEO (e.g., age, experience). This means the CEO of a large firm often gets a salary higher than a CEO of a smaller firm, regardless of the person's past success, age, and experience. Mercer Human Resource Consulting annually surveys proxy statements for 350 of the Fortune 1,000 U.S. companies to examine CEO compensation trends.[3] They examine 50 of the largest firms, 150 large firms, and 150 mid-size firms. In 2007, the median base salary for CEOs of the large firms was about $1.15 million.

At the end of every year, CEOs often receive cash bonuses. The size of the payment is based on the performance of the firm over the past year and is typically based on the accounting profit measurements of earnings per share (EPS) and earnings before interest and taxes (EBIT). Measures of economic value added (or EVA) are also common. These value-added measures are usually variations on earnings minus the cost of capital. The idea is to measure the value added to the firm in relation to the firm's costs of using different sources of money to conduct its business activities.

Whether EBIT or EVA is used, most CEO contracts have a low threshold that needs to be reached in order to qualify the CEO for a bonus. Higher levels of firm performance merit higher bonus amounts up to a specific maximum or cap. An advantage of awarding bonuses, as opposed to giving large raises, is that bonuses are one-time rewards for past *realized* performance, while raises are permanent additions to salaries for future unrealized performance. For these reasons, bonuses are a popular component of the overall compensation package. The median bonus payment for CEOs in large firms was about $2.17 million in 2007.

Stock Options

Executive stock options are the most common form of market-oriented incentive pay. Stock options are contracts that allow executives to buy shares of stock at a fixed price, called the exercise or strike price. Therefore, if the price of the stock rises above the strike price, the executive will capture the difference as a profit. For example, if the stock of a company trades at $50 per share, the CEO may be given options with a strike price at $50. Over the next few years, if the stock price rises to $75 per share, then shareholders would receive a 50 percent return on their stockholdings. The CEO could buy stock for $50 per share by exercising the option and sell it for $75 per share, thus making a $25 profit on each option owned. If the executive has options for 1 million shares, then he could pocket $25 million. If the stock price reaches $100 per share, the executive could cash in for $50 million. In contrast, if the stock price were to drop to less than $50 per share, then the options have no exercisable value and are said to be underwater. Executives treat stock options as compensation; they nearly always exercise the options to buy the stock and then sell the stock for the cash. Only rarely will an executive keep the stock.

Stock options give the executives of the firm the incentive to manage the firm in such a way that the stock price increases, which is precisely what the stockholders want as well. Therefore, stock options are believed to align managers' goals with shareholders' goals. This alignment helps to overcome some of the problems with the separation of ownership and control. The typical executive option contract assigns the strike price of the options to the prevailing stock price when the option is granted. The most common length of an option contract is 10 years. That is, the CEO has 10 years to increase the price of the stock and exercise the options. After 10 years the options expire. Executives cannot sell or transfer their options during the 10-year period and are discouraged from hedging the stock price risk. The median long-term incentive compensation for CEOs in large firms was $6.09 million in 2007, of which about 34 percent was realized option-based awards.

OPTIONS AND ACCOUNTING   The popularity of stock options as incentive compensation in the United States partly came from its favorable tax treatment for both the executive and the company. When options were granted, the company only needed to report an accounting cost when the strike price was less than the current stock price. Then the cost was amortized over the life of the option. Because most options were granted with the strike price equal to the current stock price, the firm never had to report an accounting cost. The favorable tax treatment for executives comes from the ability of the manager to pick the year in which she will exercise the options and thus determine when the tax liability occurs. In addition, the compensation is treated as a capital gain, not as income, which is an advantage to the CEO because capital gains tax rates are lower than regular personal income tax rates.

EXAMPLE 2.1   Ten Highest Paid CEOs in 2007 (Includes Salary, Bonus, and Stock Options)

Lawrence J. Ellison, Oracle	$192,920,000	Nabeel Gareeb, MEMC Electronic Mats	$79,560,000
Frederic M. Poses, Trane	$127,100,000	Daniel P. Amos, Aflac	$75,160,000
Aubrey K. McClendon, Chesapeake Energy	$116,890,000	Lloyd C. Blankfein, Goldman Sachs Group	$73,720,000
Angelo R. Mozilo, Countrywide Financial	$102,840,000	Richard D. Fairbank, Capital One Financial	$73,170,000
Howard D. Schultz, Starbucks	$98,600,000	Bob R. Simpson, XTO Energy	$72,270,000

Source: http://www.forbes.com/lists/2008/12/lead_bestbosses08_CEO-Compensation_Rank.html

---

If an executive cashes in for $100 million, this cost does not appear on the firm's income statement; the firm does not have to report an accounting cost. However, the economic cost to the firm is real. Consider this simple example. A firm has 100 million shares outstanding and has given the executives options for 10 million shares. The firm currently has earnings of $100 million, or $1 per share. If the executives exercise their options, then they would buy 10 million shares from the firm at the strike price and sell them on the stock market. At that point, there would be 110 million shares outstanding, which means that the $100 million in earnings becomes only $0.91 per share. The earnings per share have fallen by 9 percent as each share of stock is diluted in value by the newly issued stock.

Since July 2005, firms have been required to expense executive stock options (this is referred to as FAS 123(R)). Even though stock options may have exercise prices at or below the current stock price when they are granted, they are still valuable. This value, which is estimated using a variation of a formula known as the Black-Scholes option pricing model, is now required to be deducted from reported income. This regulation makes the granting of executive stock options less attractive. We discuss this regulation in more detail later in this chapter.

Stock Grants

Because of the perception that executive options may have contributed to the governance failures in the late 1990s and early 2000s, many companies have been looking for alternative forms of long-term incentive compensation. Two types have gained in popularity; restricted stock grants and performance shares.

RESTRICTED STOCK is common stock of the company that includes a limitation that requires a certain length of time to pass or a certain goal to be achieved before the stock can be sold. Executives may receive a grant of shares that require 10 years to pass before the executive may sell them. Restricted stock has an advantage over options in that its value does not go to zero when the stock price falls. Therefore, it does not have the asymmetric incentives that options cause. (Options are asymmetric because their exercisable value could end up being worth a lot or worth nothing.) Restricted stock grants have increased from 12 percent of total long-term incentives in 2002 to 30 percent in 2007. The median restricted stock grant for CEOs of large companies in 2007 was just over $1.8 million.

PERFORMANCE SHARES refer to a company's stock given to executives only if certain performance criteria are met, such as earnings per share targets. In one sense, these shares could be viewed as bonuses for past realized performance. If the firm's stock price has increased, then these performance shares are more valuable to the CEO when he receives them. Performance share plans increased to 36 percent of the long-term incentive pay mix in 2007 and was just shy of $2.2 million for CEOs of large firms.

DOES INCENTIVE-BASED COMPENSATION WORK IN GENERAL?

There are two ways to examine whether or not incentive-based compensation works. First, one could try to see if there is a positive relation between firm performance and management compensation. This would be defined as *ex post* evidence. In other words, have managers been properly rewarded for increasing the firms' value? If the answer is "yes," then we could surmise that incentive compensation works. Professors Michael Jensen and Kevin Murphy provide the most well-known evidence that the answer is pretty much "no."[4] They examined the total compensation of over 2,000 CEOs and they found that when the value of the firm increased by $1,000, then those CEOs were paid $3.25 more on average. Imagine a CEO who takes over a large firm. This CEO would have to increase the firm's value by over $300 million to increase their compensation by a mere $1 million. In academic jargon, we would say that the pay-for-performance sensitivity is very low.

Another way to assess the efficacy of incentive-based compensation is to see if those firms that enacted these compensation mechanisms subsequently experienced superior performance. This could be defined as *ex ante* evidence. In other words, once managers are given incentives, then did the firms subsequently perform well? Intuitively we might expect the answer to be "yes" but surprisingly the evidence is mixed. Perhaps some managers are risk-averse. Their salaries are already large so why should they take risks? Or if a firm relies heavily on executive stock option incentives, then perhaps those managers are excessive risk-takers where the risk sometimes pays off and sometimes does not. In addition, note that it is difficult to relate firm performance to management compensation contracts. If firms perform well, how can we be reliably sure that the incentive-based compensation contract had anything to do with the firm's success?

POTENTIAL "INCENTIVE" PROBLEMS WITH INCENTIVE-BASED COMPENSATION

Problems with Accounting-Based Incentives

The use of accounting profits to measure performance has several potential drawbacks. First, to boost accounting profits, a CEO has an incentive to forego costly research and development that might make the firm more profitable in the future than in the present. Second, accounting profits may be manipulated (see Chapter 3). Third, the bonus plan is developed anew each year and, if the threshold cannot be met one year, the CEO has an incentive to move earnings from the present year to the future. This would lower expectations while the next year's bonus plan is being created and artificially increase the executive's chance of receiving that bonus in the future. In short, CEOs may place too much focus on manipulating short-term earnings instead of focusing on long-term earnings and shareholder wealth.

Problems with Stock Option Incentives

There is a good possibility that stock options do not align managerial incentives with shareholders goals. The following list cites potential incentive problems that executive options create:

1. Shareholder returns combine both stock price appreciation and dividends. The stock option is only affected by price appreciation. Therefore,

the CEO might forego increasing dividends in favor of using the cash to try to increase the stock price.

2. The stock price is more likely to increase when the CEO accepts risky projects. Therefore, when a firm uses options to compensate the CEO, she has a tendency to pick a higher risk business strategy.

3. Stock options lose some incentive for the CEO if the stock price falls too far below the strike price. In this case, the options would be too far underwater to motivate the manager effectively because the increase in value required to cash in the options would be essentially unattainable.

4. CEOs may try to manipulate earnings and thus maximize profits in one target year to make the stock price more favorable for exercising options. This manipulation can reduce earnings (and consequently the stock price) after the target year. In other words, managers may try to do what they can to time stock price movements to match the time horizons of their stock options.

ANOTHER PROBLEM WITH EXECUTIVE STOCK OPTIONS   The very advantage that stock options have of aligning manager incentives with stockholders goals also constitutes a major problem. Stock options are tied to the firm's stock price, which helps align incentives but executives only have partial influence on stock prices. Stock prices are affected by company performance but also by many other factors beyond its control, particularly the strength or weakness of the economy. When the economy thrives, stock prices rise. Even the stock price of a poorly run company may rise, although not as much as its more successful competitors. This occurrence may richly reward executives of poorly run firms through their options when they do not deserve them. Alternatively, the stock market may fall because of poor economic conditions or investor pessimism. A company whose management outperforms its competitors may still find that its stock is falling. In that case, managers should be rewarded, but they are not because their options go underwater when the market falls.

Options lose their effectiveness when the stock price falls too far below the strike price. To re-establish motivation for the executives, boards sometimes reprice previously issued options and lower the strike price. Consider the incentives listed above and how they create interesting dynamics for CEO behavior. Executives may choose risky company projects that have a chance of dramatically increasing the stock price. If the projects succeed, the CEO becomes rich and the stockholders experience increased wealth. However, if the projects fail, the stockholders lose money. Meanwhile, the CEO simply asks the board to reprice the options and the CEO can then repeat the strategy. Proponents of option repricing claim that it is necessary to keep executives at the firm. This argument has some truth, but that does not change the skewed incentives it causes.

Examples like that of O'Neal and Merrill Lynch are not fraudulent or illegal. Boards of directors freely give executives stock options and, therefore, accept the possibility that the options may have value based on circumstances

Real-World Examples

Using stock options can be a powerful way to align the interests of managers and shareholders. But is it an effective way? Consider the compensation of former Merrill Lynch CEO Stanley O'Neal. He was CEO during the financial crisis that began in 2007. After a $2.24 billion unexpected loss for the third quarter, the board forced O'Neal to retire in November 2007 instead of firing him.[5] In addition to presiding over the largest loss in Merrill's history (to that date), it was reported that O'Neal also managed to play 20 rounds of golf while the company was losing this record amount of money.[6] This is not the profile of the type of CEO shareholders like to see in charge.

After being forced out in such circumstances, O'Neal was not particularly deserving of an extremely large payday. O'Neal's compensation package at Merrill included a large number of options, grants of restricted stock and performance bonuses, so it seemed that instead of "pay for performance" there might be "no pay for no performance." Yet when the value of his options and performance bonuses was added up, O'Neal walked away from Merrill with $161.5 million. Less than a year later, as the financial crisis worsened, Merrill's losses mounted and it was forced to sell itself to Bank of America, a larger, better capitalized firm.

How could an executive who was performing so poorly be forced out by the board and yet still earn so much? In O'Neal's case, the big payday came from a combination of his options increasing in value before the stunningly bad performance at the end of his tenure and from restricted stock he was granted regardless of the company's operating results. Essentially, regardless of O'Neal's poor performance, the terms of his employment contract were not designed to punish an executive who lost the company a record amount of money.

unrelated to the performance of the executive. However, in other cases managers seem to mislead the public in order to enrich themselves. Consider the recent actions of companies in backdating options.

EXAMPLE 2.2 Backdating Options

How can executives increase the value of options they receive as part of their compensation? One way is to retroactively issue options on dates where the stock price was lower than today. As there is no way to verify when option grant documents are actually signed, many boards and executives conspired to falsify dates to ensure the options had a built in value when issued. Hence, an option could be issued with an exercise price equal to "fair market value" using the value from a month or two before. This scheme allows executives and board members to receive options with an exercise price of $25 on a day when the stock was selling for $30, adding $5 in value to every option granted.

At least 130 companies were discovered to be "backdating" options in a review at the end of 2006.[7] The scandal that ensued led to at least 50 executives and directors being fired or resigning as shareholders vented their anger at those involved. At Apple, its General Counsel Nancy Heinen left the firm in May 2006 after it was alleged that she was responsible for a series of backdated options issued to executives, including herself and CEO Steve

Jobs. In April 2007, the SEC brought charges against Heinen alleging she participated in the fraudulent backdating of options that resulted in Apple underreporting its expenses by almost $40 million. She ended up settling the charges by paying $2.2 million in a settlement where she did not admit or deny the SEC's allegations.[8]

The Debate over Expensing Executive Options

Even though the Financial Accounting Standards Board (FASB) regulations have required the expensing of stock options since 2005, this requirement remains controversial. On behalf of the requirement, proponents argue that the cost of stock options issued to employees and executives is a real cost to the firm and it should be treated as an expense on the granting firm's financial statements. Options are valuable even when option exercise prices are at or above current stock prices. Hence, because the option has value and because it has a real effect on the firm through the additional shares outstanding upon option conversion, this is the kind of thing that should be included as an expense on the income statement.

Parties opposed to expensing options argue that the requirement of expensing options now even though they might not be cashed in for 10 years has the effect of lowering earnings. While lower earnings may not matter as much for large firms, for high growth firms in new industries it may be a struggle to earn positive earnings at all. Hence, the requirement to expense options hurts these companies because the added expense makes it less likely the companies will show positive profits. For this reason, many technology firms are adamantly opposed to the new FASB regulation.[9]

It is also common for start-up companies to partially pay employees in stock options to help compensate for low salaries. Using this type of pay system, the young company can conserve one of its most precious resources, cash, and motivate employees to work hard. What happens to these compensation systems if options are expensed? The reduction in reported earnings may cause the companies to curtail option programs. This could inhibit the growth of new companies. It could even have an impact on the economy since new companies are an important source of new jobs.

Another argument is that it does not matter if options are expensed because the details of the options are readily available on the SEC Web site and it is easy for investors to adjust earnings to either reflect options or exclude them. In other words, the issue is irrelevant for sophisticated investors and expensing options will not have an effect one way or the other.

Overall it is not yet clear whether the requirement of expensing options has had an effect on executive compensation or small firms' behavior. Academic studies are beginning to address this question now that there are two years of operating results after the new rule was passed. These studies will begin to roll out shortly and hopefully resolve this debate.

OTHER COMPENSATION

Executives often receive other forms of compensation that are sometimes not reported to the SEC on official documents. The old style perk of a company paying for a CEO's club membership may come to mind, but that is passé compared to modern perks. The company will frequently pay for financial advisors, luxury cars and chauffeurs, personal travel, Manhattan apartments, and more.

Retirement compensation is also popular. For example, former CEO of FleetBoston, Terrence Murray, was promised a retirement package with a pension payment of $5.8 million per year and the use of corporate jets for his travel (and that of his guests) for up to 150 hours per year.[10] Louis Gerstner retired as CEO of IBM (though he continued for a time as chairman) in March 2002. In addition to his $2 million yearly pension, he has access to corporate jets, cars, and apartments for 20 years. If IBM wants Gerstner's advice, he will be paid $600 per hour.[11]

Retirement compensation is one type of severance. When a CEO leaves a firm (which might happen because of retirement, the firm being bought out, or other reason), the outgoing manager often receives any performance shares owed him and can sell any options or restricted stock accumulated. In all, this can add up to tens or even hundreds of millions of dollars and is referred to as a **golden-parachute**. For example, when Capital One Financial announced its purchase of North Fork Bancorp in 2006, the North Fork CEO John Kansas was set to receive a total of $135 million through $66 million in restricted stock, $15 million in severance that he will receive when he retires, $6 million in stock options, and $4 million in stock-based units. Interestingly, the U.S. Congress wanted to limit these golden-parachutes, so in the 1980s they enacted a law that taxes these benefits. It appears that the opposite has occurred. The severance compensation got larger so that the executives could better afford to pay the taxes and then companies started paying the taxes for the executive, known as a *gross-up*. John Kansas' contract had a gross-up. So his $44 million in taxes would be paid by shareholders of North Fork and ultimately Capital One.

Another benefit is obtaining a company loan. Executives commonly borrow hundreds of thousands, or even millions of dollars at extremely low interest rates—sometimes even interest free. These loans may be used to purchase expensive homes: Wells Fargo CEO Richard Kovacevich borrowed $1 million for a house down payment. The savings on low-interest loans can quickly add up to tens or hundreds of thousands of dollars. Frequently, executives do not even pay back the loans. Mattel, Inc. absolved ousted CEO Jill Barad from repaying a $7.2 million loan and then paid her an additional $3.3 million to cover the cost of resulting additional taxes.[12] The replacement CEO of Mattel, Robert Eckert, received a $5.5 million loan that would not have to be repaid if he stayed with the firm for two years. A similar arrangement existed with Compaq Chairman and CEO Michael Capellas for his $5 million loan.

CRIME AND PUNISHMENT

Earlier in this chapter, we stated that managers will work hard on behalf of shareholders if they are carefully monitored and if they have the right incentives. Most of this book discusses monitoring. This chapter has discussed managerial incentives. However, perhaps a third way to align the incentives of managers with shareholders is to increase the penalty for managers who intentionally and knowingly mislead and behave in ways that are not beneficial to shareholders.

Under the Sarbanes-Oxley Act, the firm's CEO and chief financial officer (CFO) have to certify the appropriateness of the financial statements. The effect is that they are now subject to criminal penalties if they certified fraudulent results. In addition, the act increased the scope and penalties for white-collar crimes. The intent of these changes is to increase the available criminal penalties for executives who commit fraudulent acts.

Even without the act, however, there are numerous criminal acts like fraud, larceny and securities law violations that have sent executives to jail. In July 2005, Bernie Ebbers, founder and former chief executive of WorldCom, was sentenced to 25 years in prison for his involvement in WorldCom's $11 billion accounting fraud. Dennis Kozlowski, former CEO of Tyco, was sentenced to a prison term of between 8 and 25 years following his guilty verdict of grand larceny against Tyco. Both former executives remain in prison at the time of this writing.

INTERNATIONAL PERSPECTIVE—CEO COMPENSATION AROUND THE WORLD

Paying the top officer in the company with long-term incentive awards is most common in the United States. Figure 2.1 shows the compensation of CEOs around the world, split into three categories. These categories are fixed pay (base salary and benefits), variable pay (incentive-type instruments like stock options), and perquisites. The data comes from surveys conducted by Towers Perrin.[13] The figure shows that 62 percent, on average, of a U.S. CEO's pay is variable in nature.

The variable component of CEO pay is much higher in the United States than most other countries. Only Singapore and Shanghai of China (56 percent each) have similar fractions of variable pay. In contrast, CEOs from many countries earn most of their compensation from fixed pay. For example, for CEOs in Sweden, 80 percent of their compensation is fixed. The percentages for Taiwan and Japan are 72 percent and 71 percent, respectively. Variable pay is at least 50 percent of total compensation for only 5 of the 23 countries. India, one of those five countries, pays an extraordinary 33 percent of total compensation in perquisites. From these statistics it is clear that there is a large variation in how top executives are paid throughout the world.

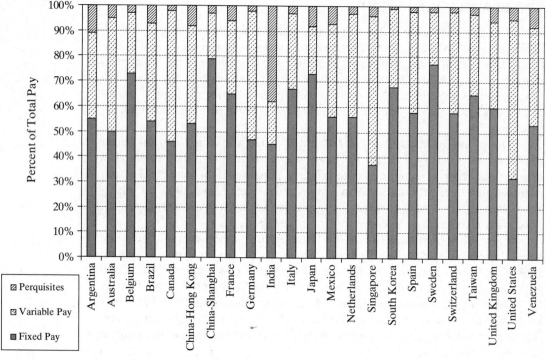

FIGURE 2.1 Components of CEO Compensation around the World, 2003

Summary

Managers who control public corporations are supposed to act in the firms' shareholders' best interests. But they may be tempted to take advantage of their control power to satisfy their own needs and desires, often to the detriment of the stockholders. To inhibit poor managerial behavior, shareholders and the board of directors try to align the executive's interests with their own through incentive programs involving bonuses, restricted stock and stock options. Many people believe that stock and option incentives reduce conflict between those who own the firm and those who control it. When executives work hard to increase the firm's stock price over the long term, both the shareholders and the executives reap the benefit.

However, whether or not the incentives work results in much debate. For example, stock options create an economic cost to the firm and sometimes do not create the correct rewards for good and poor managers.

In addition, Incentive-based compensation tied to reported earnings or stock prices creates the temptation for managers to manipulate or even falsify earnings. Overall, incentive compensation is not a perfect fix for the agency problem of managers not always acting to increase firm value. The rest of this book describes and discusses how monitors can also be an important way to reduce managerial opportunism.

WEB Info about Executive Compensation

Towers Perrin
www.towersperrin.com

AFL-CIO Corporate Watch
www.aflcio.org/corporatewatch/

Mercer Human Resource Consulting
www.mercerhr.com

Review Questions

1. In what ways can managers harm stockholders?
2. What is the rationale behind firms using executive stock options?
3. What potential misalignments do stock options create?
4. When might options fail to reward good managers?
5. List the pros and cons of compensating a CEO with stock options.
6. How does the repricing of stock options affect a manager's incentives?
7. How does executive pay in the United States compare to pay internationally?

Discussion Questions

1. How would you design an executive compensation contract to ensure managers have the right incentives? Do you think managers will like it?
2. Do you think executive options should be expensed? Why or why not?
3. What do you think CEO compensation will be like in the near future? Maybe it will be more conservative, but then do you think this will help or harm the future growth of corporate America? Discuss the cost-benefit trade-offs.
4. Do you think firms should force executives to own the firm's stock? This might create a near-perfect alignment between managers and shareholders, but do not forget that executives already have their entire personal wealth (i.e., their salaries) staked to the firm.

Exercises

1. KPMG was the auditing firm for Xerox during the time it was accused of manipulating its accounting figures (look up the Xerox details). To what degree is KPMG to blame for fraud? Like Xerox, should it be held accountable? What has the SEC done about KPMG's role?
2. The former CEO of Tyco, Dennis Kozlowski, has been accused of many abuses of the stockholders' money; describe some of these. John and Michael Rigas were sent to prison for perpetrating massive financial fraud and looting Adelphia Communications. Look up the details of what happened and describe how the corporate governance system failed in this case.
3. Obtain the total compensation of five CEOs of companies (of different sizes and in different industries). Compare and contrast their compensation and comment on the potential alignment or misalignment of incentives.
4. For the five CEOs you researched for Exercise #3 above, argue that they deserved their pay. Then argue that they did not deserve their pay.
5. Find a real-world U.S. example of what you think is a fair executive option. Describe the details of the option and explain why you think it is fair.

Exercises for Non-U.S. Students

1. Does your country use executive stock options? If so, do some research and describe its experience with them. If not, then do you think it should? Why or why not? Is there anything unique about your country that makes executive options more or less attractive than in the United States?

2. What are the primary ways in which CEOs are rewarded in your country? Do you think they are effective? Why or why not?

3. Obtain the total compensation of five CEOs of companies in your country (of different sizes and in different industries). First, argue that they each deserved their pay. Then argue that they each did not deserve their pay.

Endnotes

1. There is also an incentive for the board of directors to take actions to personally benefit the board at the expense of the shareholders. This agency problem is discussed in the chapter on the board of directors.

2. Much of the compensation description in this section is summaries from Kevin Murphy, "Executive Compensation," in *Handbook of Labor Economics*, eds. O. Ashenfelter and D. Card, Vol. 3B. Amsterdam: North-Hollan Publishers, 1999.

3. Mercer Human Resource Consulting, "2007 CEO Compensation Survey and Trends," May 2008.

4. Michael Jensen and Kevin Murphy, "Performance Pay and Top Management Incentives," *Journal of Political Economy* 98 (1990):225–263.

5. *www.aflcio.org/corporatewatch/paywatch/ retirementsecurity/case_merrilllynch.cfm.*

6. *http://money.cnn.com/galleries/2007/fortune/0712/ gallery.101_dumbest.fortune/5.html.*

7. *http://en.wikipedia.org/wiki/Options_backdating.*

8. *www.sec.gov/litigation/litreleases/2008/lr20683.htm.*

9. Donald P. Delves, Stock Options and the New Rules of Corporate Accountability, McGraw-Hill Professional, New York, 2003.

10. Joann Lublin, "As CEOs' Reported Salaries and Bonuses Get Pinched, Many Chiefs Are Finding Hidden Ways to Increase Their Compensation," *Wall Street Journal*, April 11, 2002, B7.

11. Joann Lublin, "How CEOs Retire in Style," *Wall Street Journal*, September 13, 2002, B1.

12. Gary Strauss, "Many Execs Pocket Perks Aplenty," *USA Today*, May 1, 2001, B1.

13. Specifically, the data are from 2005–2006 Worldwide Total Remuneration study by Towers Perrin.

Accountants and Auditors

Accountants and auditors are an important part of any corporate monitoring system. Accountants keep track of the quantitative financial information of the firm. Because mistakes and other problems (such as intentional fraud) may occur with accounting, there are auditors who review the financial information. As such, auditors may be in the best position to monitor companies. In this process, auditors obtain private information about the company that others cannot obtain. They use this information to determine whether the company's public financial statements reflect the true level of business being conducted. Banks, creditors, and others rely on these statements to get an accurate picture of the firm's business activities and financial health. Investors use these public statements to assess the value of the company. Therefore, the auditor's candid evaluation of those statements is crucial. This chapter first provides an overview of accounting and auditing. Then it discusses how accountants and auditors might contribute to financial fraud and how they might expose fraud.

ACCOUNTING FUNCTIONS

Historically, accounting has been the function of gathering, compiling, reporting, and archiving a firm's business activities. This accounting information helps individuals in many roles who depend on it to make decisions. For convenience, those who need accounting information are categorized as either insiders or outsiders of the firm.

Accounting for Inside Use

Management accounting is the development of information for insiders, such as company managers. Managers use this information to measure the progress toward their goals and highlight any potential problems in advance. For example, managers want to know which products have the best sales and which are selling poorly. Which products tend to sell together? How is inventory being managed? What about cash? Will the firm have enough cash to pay its upcoming debt payments?

Accountants answer these questions with budgets, variance reports, sensitivity analysis, revenue reports, cost projections, and even analysis of competitors. When firms consider how to expand products and services, managerial accountants help formulate profit projections from revenue and cost projections. In short, managerial accounting has historically played a large part in the control and evaluation of the business and its performance.

Accounting for Outside Use

Outsiders of the firm also use accounting information. Investors, banks, the government, and other stakeholders have a keen interest in the financial health of the firm. Banks and other creditors want to know if the firm will be able to pay its debts. Shareholders want to know how profitable the firm is and how profitable it may be in the future. Employees might have a double interest because they have their careers and employment at stake and they might be investors through their retirement plans as well.

Financial accounting provides information for outsiders. Whereas managerial accounting reports may break down performance for managers by individual products or regions of the country, financial reports summarize the business as a whole, although they can be broken into business segments and regions. In the case of publicly held companies, these reports are the quarterly and annual financial statements that they must file with the SEC.

The three main **financial statements** (income statement, balance sheet, and statement of cash flows) and other pieces of important information (e.g., popular press articles and analyst recommendations) are used by outsiders to determine the firm's value, profits, and its risk. Outsiders want to be able to compare firms easily. Thus the SEC requires that these accounting statements adhere to a uniform set of standards known as generally accepted accounting principles (GAAP) for public companies. These statements are prepared by the accountants of the firm and reviewed by independent accountants from an auditing firm (more on auditors later in the chapter).

The Internal Revenue Service (IRS) also requires accounting information for tax purposes. The accountants of the firm report profits or losses to the IRS and determine the tax liability. Interestingly, accounting methods and business record-keeping can be very different for reports to managers, for public financial statements, and for the IRS. For example, there are ambiguities regarding how to record some transactions in GAAP. When reporting business activities in an annual report, choices might be made that maximize earnings in order to make them appear stronger than they would otherwise be, in the hope of driving up the firm's stock price. When IRS forms are being completed, choices might be made to minimize earnings in order to minimize tax expenditures.[1]

PROBLEMS THAT MAY OCCUR IN ACCOUNTING

As with any kind of record-keeping there are potential problems. First, unintentional errors are possible. Sometimes these errors are due to miscalculations or due to applying an expense to the wrong accounting ledger. Another potential problem occurs when judgments are required. For example, should firms count all receivables when they know that some clients and customers might never pay for goods or services rendered? Finally, accountants could perpetuate fraud. For example, they could overstate income, understate liabilities, or overstate assets such as receivables. Or they could be tricked by a manager to inadvertently commit fraud on his behalf. Accounting fraud is probably the largest potential problem with accounting, as it is intentional (either by a manager or by an accountant) and hurts the firm's stakeholders, including its shareholders. Because of these potential accounting problems, the role of auditors is important, which we discuss next.

AUDITING

Internal Auditors

Many firms have **internal auditors**. Their responsibility is to oversee the firm's financial and operating procedures, to check the accuracy of the financial record-keeping, to implement improvements with internal control, to ensure compliance with accounting regulations, and to detect fraud. Firms are not required to have internal auditors but many firms have them to enhance their accounting and internal control efficiency. In fact, the people who initially detected financial fraud at WorldCom were the company's own internal auditors.

EXAMPLE 3.1   Excerpted from the *Wall Street Journal*[2]

Sitting in his cubicle at WorldCom Inc. headquarters one afternoon in May, Gene Morse stared at an accounting entry for $500 million in computer expenses. He could not find any invoices or documentation to back up the stunning number.

"Oh my God," he muttered to himself. The auditor immediately took his discovery to his boss, Cynthia Cooper, the company's vice president of internal audit.

By June 23, they had unearthed $3.8 billion in misallocated expenses and phony accounting entries. It all added up to an accounting fraud, acknowledged by the company, which turned out to be the largest in corporate history. Their discoveries sent WorldCom into bankruptcy, left thousands of their colleagues without jobs, and roiled the stock market.

External Auditors

External auditors are accountants from outside the firm, who review the firm's financial statements and its procedures for producing them. Their job is to attest to the fairness of the statements and that they materially represent the condition of the firm. Often the external auditor will assess the system and procedures used by internal auditors to see if they can rely on the internally-generated reports when conducting their own audit.[3] To conduct their external audit, the auditors might:

1. conduct interviews with the firm's employees to assess the quality of the internal audit system;
2. make their own observations of the firm's assets such as inventory levels;
3. check sample balance-sheet transactions;
4. confirm with the firm's customers and clients to check the accuracy of short-term assets and liabilities; and
5. conduct their own financial statements analysis such as comparing the firm's financial ratios from one period to the next.

Once they have completed their audit, they will generate a report (see Lehman Brothers' example in the following text).

Because external auditors are supposed to be independent of the firm being audited and because their explicit job is to check for financial misstatements and adherence to GAAP, it is they who must ensure the accuracy of the firm's financial information for shareholders. Today, the four largest accounting firms, known as the "Big Four," that provide external audits, are PriceWaterhouseCoopers, Deloitte Touche Tohmatsu, Ernst & Young, and KPMG.

EXAMPLE 3.2   Independent Auditors Report for Lehman Brothers[4]

The following audit report was issued by the external auditors of Lehman Brothers eight months before the company went bankrupt. You will notice that this is an unqualified opinion which means that the auditors did not find anything material concerning the ability of the company to survive as a going concern. Is it a failure of the auditors to point out that the company could suddenly become insolvent? This example shows what a typical audit report looks like and also provides a cautionary example that auditor reports do not catch everything going on at the company.

LEHMAN BROTHERS HOLDINGS INC.
Report of Independent Registered Public Accounting Firm

To the Board of Directors and Stockholders of Lehman Brothers Holdings Inc.

We have audited Lehman Brothers Holdings Inc.'s (the "Company") internal control over financial reporting as of November 30, 2007, based on criteria established in Internal Control—Integrated Framework issued by the Committee of Sponsoring Organizations of the Treadway Commission (the COSO criteria). The Company's management is responsible for maintaining effective internal control over financial reporting, and for its assessment of the effectiveness of internal control over financial reporting included in the accompanying *Management's Assessment of Internal Control over Financial Reporting*. Our responsibility is to express an opinion on the Company's internal control over financial reporting based on our audit.

We conducted our audit in accordance with the standards of the Public Company Accounting Oversight Board (United States). Those standards require that we plan and perform the audit to obtain reasonable assurance about whether effective internal control over financial reporting was maintained in all material respects. Our audit included obtaining an understanding of internal control over financial reporting, assessing the risk that a material weakness exists, testing and evaluating the design and operating effectiveness of internal control based on the assessed risk, and performing such other procedures as we considered necessary in the circumstances. We believe that our audit provides a reasonable basis for our opinion.

A company's internal control over financial reporting is a process designed to provide reasonable assurance regarding the reliability of financial reporting and the preparation of financial statements for external purposes in accordance with generally accepted accounting principles. A company's internal control over financial reporting includes those policies and procedures that (1) pertain to the maintenance of records that, in reasonable detail, accurately and fairly reflect the transactions and dispositions of the assets of the company; (2) provide reasonable assurance that transactions are recorded as necessary to permit preparation of financial statements in accordance with generally accepted accounting principles, and that receipts and expenditures of the company are being made only in accordance with authorizations of management and directors of the company; and (3) provide reasonable assurance regarding prevention or timely detection of unauthorized acquisition, use, or disposition of the company's assets that could have a material effect on the financial statements.

Because of its inherent limitations, internal control over financial reporting may not prevent or detect misstatements. Also, projections of any evaluation of effectiveness to future periods are subject to the risk that controls may become inadequate because of changes in conditions, or that the degree of compliance with the policies or procedures may deteriorate.

In our opinion, the Company maintained, in all material respects, effective internal control over financial reporting as of November 30, 2007, based on the COSO criteria.

We also have audited, in accordance with the standards of the Public Company Accounting Oversight Board (United States), the consolidated statement of financial condition of the Company as of November 30, 2007 and 2006, and the related consolidated statements of income, changes in stockholders' equity, and cash flows for each of the three years in the period ended November 30, 2007 of the Company and our report dated January 28, 2008 expressed an unqualified opinion thereon.

ERNST & YOUNG LLP
New York, New York
January 28, 2008

How the Nature of External Auditing Has Evolved Since the Late 1930s

While banks and other creditors have always wanted independent verification of a firm's financial health, the role of monitoring a firm's financial statements was cemented by the Securities Act of 1933 and the Securities Exchange Act of 1934. During the Great Depression, after the corporate spending excesses of the late 1920s, the country was reeling from business scandals. Congress reacted with legislation that called for stronger oversight and regulation and required annual independent audits of all public companies.

Because of this legislative requirement, in the late 1930s and 1940s accounting firms flourished with the increased demand for auditing services. Initially the high demand resulted from the new laws that required independent verification of a firm's financial books. The demand for auditing services continued to grow as the economy eventually picked up and the number of public firms increased. There was plenty of business for auditing firms and the environment was such that they could play an effective role as independent monitors—even becoming adversarial with the firm if necessary.

In the 1970s and 1980s, however, the auditing business began to change. The number of new companies that needed auditing services was no longer expanding. If auditing firms wanted to grow, they had to steal clients away from other auditing firms. The code of ethics was changed to permit advertising and other competitive practices. Auditing firms began to advertise and cut their prices to lure new clients. The relationship between the auditing firm and the audited company also began to change; with other audit firms courting them and corporate managers no longer tolerating adversarial auditors. Because of the prestige associated with having Fortune 500 companies as clients, auditing firms may have become less confrontational in order to keep them as clients. During this period, auditing firms also developed consulting services to advise companies on how to improve their accounting methods and business activities. This provided both another source of income for accounting firms and a way to solidify their relationships with company management. The consulting role also created a potential conflict of interest because a company's auditor might now be trying to sell tax shelter strategies to the same client they are auditing.

ACCOUNTING OVERSIGHT

Accountants are responsible for the firm's financial information and auditors are supposed to monitor and check the financial information for accuracy. However, both accountants and auditors are governed by regulations and regulatory bodies. The **Financial Accounting Standards Board (FASB)**, a non-government entity made up of members of the accounting, business, and academic professions, sets accounting standards known as **generally accepted accounting principles (GAAP)**. The SEC recognizes FASB as authoritative, which means that the SEC recognizes FASB decisions on creating and amending GAAP, though the SEC and the U.S. Congress have been known to influence FASB accounting policies. Associations in the accounting profession sponsor FASB and, to promote independence, its seven board members are required to serve full time and divest their interests in their former employers. Even non-CPAs (certified public accountants) serve on the FASB board.

External auditors are required by the SEC to make sure the financial statements adhere to GAAP. An organization called the **American Institute of Certified Public Accountants (AICPA)** had set auditing standards and had governed external audits. However, with the passage of the 2002 Sarbanes-Oxley Act, a new board called the **Public Company Accounting Oversight Board (PCAOB)** was established that would, in effect, replace AICPA's role as the regulatory body overseeing the auditing profession. Under the 2002 Act, all public firms have to be registered with PCAOB and meet its standards. The PCAOB also oversees public accounting firms. The example of Lehman Brothers' audit report indicates that the auditor conducted its report in accordance to PCAOB standards. In Chapter 9, we discuss the relationship between the SEC and the accounting profession and also the 2002 Act.

While the PCAOB now sets auditing standards, the AICPA still remains an active organization. It is the largest association for CPAs, with over 330,000 regular members. In order to promote a high ethical standard for association members, the AICPA maintains and distributes the AICPA Professional Code of Conduct. The Code provides Principles and Rules that govern the professional behavior of members.

EXAMPLE 3.3   Insolvent IndyMac Bank Meets Capital Requirements

Is it possible for auditors following PCAOB standards to miss companies in serious financial distress? The recent case of IndyMac Bank suggests that the answer is yes. Under federal rules, banks are required to maintain minimum capital requirements to remain solvent. As part of the audit, auditors are charged with making sure that banks comply with applicable regulations such as capital standards. In the case of IndyMac, a large bank that was heavily involved in the residential mortgage business, the real estate crash of 2007 and 2008 created a situation where the bank's capital position was shaky. However, under applicable federal rules, the bank's 2007 annual report was issued on February 29, 2008 showing the company met the capital requirements.[5] The auditors, Ernst & Young, issued an unqualified opinion on this report. But on July 11, 2008, the FDIC (Federal Deposit Insurance Corporation) placed the bank in receivership due to insolvency. What happened in that short time?

The collapse of IndyMac was apparently due to a flaw in the regulations governing bank capital and not to a failure of auditing. Banks are required to maintain capital to cover against loans that go bad. Tier 1 capital, or deposits by customers, must be at least 5 percent of loans made by the bank. Beyond customer deposits, banks are allowed to include other assets in their capital (Tier 2 assets) such as a large amount of mortgage backed bonds held by IndyMac. The combination of Tier 1 and Tier 2 must be at least 10 percent of outstanding loans. In the 2007 annual report, IndyMac reported its Tier 1 and Tier 2 capital at 10.26 percent of loans, qualifying the bank as "well capitalized" under the accounting rules. Hence, Ernst & Young was following the rules when they decided that IndyMac was well capitalized.

The problem with the 10.26 percent capital figure is that it relied heavily on the market value of the Tier 2 assets owned by IndyMac. By the end of 2007, the market for mortgage backed bonds had collapsed due to high foreclosure rates and falling housing prices. This led to reduced trading in the bonds and difficulty in figuring out a current market value. As IndyMac barely met its capital when the bonds were fully valued, any decrease would put the bank below minimum capital requirements. Hence, signs in the troubled mortgage market were suggesting IndyMac might be insolvent already at the end of 2007. Note that the audit rules and bank regulations did not require the auditor to speculate as to the true value of these hard to value bonds. Only when there was no doubt that this capital had fallen significantly in value, did the FDIC step in and take over the bank.

THE CHANGING ROLE OF ACCOUNTING— MANAGING EARNINGS

During the last two decades, the role of accounting departments within companies has changed. Instead of simply providing information to insiders and outsiders, accounting departments have begun the transition into being profit centers. Instead of simply reporting the quarterly profits of the firm, accounting departments are asked to increase profits through application of accounting methods. In some areas, the ambiguity in GAAP and the subjectivity of business activities provide for different ways of accounting for the same transaction. Different methods often lead to different levels of reportable profits. The reporting of profits, therefore, can be both an art and a science. This process is known as **managing earnings**.

For example, accountants may feel pressure to **meet internal targets**. Managers may want to show their employees and the board of directors that they were able to increase revenue and decrease costs. As discussed in Chapter 2, when firms meet internally set targets, such as target ROAs (return on assets) or ROEs (return on equity), it may lead to a raise or a bonus for the CEO and other managers.

Recent Research

Do companies with smooth earnings have higher values? If smooth operating results increase firm value, then, holding other effects constant, firms with smooth cash flows and/or earnings will have a higher value than firms with volatile cash flows and earnings.

Professors Rountree, Weston, and Allayannis analyze approximately 4,000 firms over three five-year periods: 1988–1992, 1993–1997, and 1998–2002. For each company, the authors measure the volatility of the earnings and of the cash flow. As volatility is a measure of fluctuation in a data series, low volatility implies a smoother data series than high volatility. The authors also look for artificially smoothed earnings under the accounting rules that permit managers to vary accruals and effectively move income from one period to another.

One result of the study is that, evaluated separately, investors do place a higher value on firms with smooth cash flow streams and on firms with smooth earnings streams. This result is determined using a multiple regression that controls for other possible effects and that attempts to isolate the relation between smooth cash

flows or earnings and the value investors place on the firm in the market. Based on this result, managers may be tempted to smooth earnings to increase firm value.

Next the authors compare earnings and cash flow volatility to see which influences investors more. Here, the authors find that investors value smooth cash flow more than smooth earnings. They attribute this to the fact that a smooth earnings stream can be artificially created by manipulating accruals. Separating these effects, the authors conclude that investors appear to value smooth earnings only to the extent the smoothness corresponds to smooth cash flows and does not arise from manipulating accruals.

Overall, this study concludes that using accounting accruals to artificially smooth earnings does not add value to firms. This is an important result given the temptations that managers have to use accruals to smooth earnings.

Brian Rountree, James P. Weston and George Allayannis, "Do investors value smooth performance?" *Journal of Financial Economics* 90, no. 3, (2008): 237–251.

Accountants may also feel pressure to **meet external targets**. Analysts make predictions about firms' profitability measured by earnings per share (EPS). If the firm fails to meet these expectations, then the share price may decline. Therefore, accountants might use whatever methods possible to meet these external expectations. In addition, accountants may be asked to **window dress** the firm's financial statements to improve its chances of getting a favorable external financing arrangement, such as a low interest loan. Accountants could stretch assumptions to increase reported income or reduce existing liabilities.

Another example of variations in accounting method applications relates to the desire of companies to exhibit a steady growth in profits, that is, to **smooth income**. If the profits generated by business activities grow, but at an erratic pace, then accountants are asked to smooth out the earnings over time. Smooth earnings give shareholders a sense of reduced risk. Accountants can defer or accelerate the recognition of some revenues to smooth reported income from year to year.

FROM MANIPULATION TO FRAUD

The accounting schemes that companies use can be either simple or complex. Indeed, companies can structure deals in a way that may not have any value in conducting business, but that spin off either profits or losses that can be reversed in the future to manage earnings. A question often asked is how much can companies manipulate accounting figures before they cross the line into fraud? Where is the line?

For example, a firm could sell an asset, such as a truck, to its own subsidiary (e.g., technically a special-purpose entity created as an offshore partnership) for an outrageously high price. The book value of the truck is low so the firm has a large capital gain and profits go up. The subsidiary capitalizes the cost of the truck, which means that the subsidiary will have to report lower earnings in each of the future years in which the truck cost is depreciated. In effect, the firm takes a profit now that it will have to offset as expenses in the future from to the sale of a truck it still owns!

The pressure on accounting departments to smooth earnings, or even produce earnings can be intense when the firm is not meeting investor (analyst) expectations. Because the role of accounting has changed and accounting departments are often viewed as profit centers, they may be pressed to make up shortfalls created by the business operations of the firm. Sometimes firms and their accountants and auditors cross way over the line to fraudulent practices. Recent examples of alleged accounting fraud are WorldCom, Enron, Rite Aid, Adelphia, and Tyco. For example, on June 25, 2002, WorldCom disclosed that roughly $3.8 billion had been improperly booked as capital investments instead of operating expenses over the previous five quarters. Specifically, WorldCom had to pay fees to other phone companies in order for them to transfer WorldCom customers' calls immediately.[6] By capitalizing these fees, contrary to GAAP, WorldCom pushed current expenses into the future, thereby boosting current earnings (at the expense of future earnings).

Enron used sophisticated and complicated methods to generate inflated reported earnings. For example, Enron would sell assets to its own subsidiaries for high prices in order to book huge capital gains and profits. Enron would also enter into contracts to sell energy to a customer for 30 years. Then they underestimated the cost of providing that energy, thereby overestimating the annual profit of the contract.[7] Enron would also book all 30 years of these inflated profits in the current year. This made Enron appear incredibly profitable over the short-term but was detrimental to its longer-term financial health. While these types of maneuvers help to manage earnings, doing so on a large scale probably crosses the line into fraud. Enron went even further across the line when it created complex partnership arrangements and foreign subsidiaries to hide liabilities from its balance sheet. For its role in Enron's questionable accounting and its subsequent conviction for obstruction of justice by destroying documents, Arthur Anderson, previously one of the big five public accounting firms, dissolved and no longer exists as an auditing firm.

So while managing earnings can be legal, there is a fine line between legal accounting maneuvering and accounting fraud. It is important to point out, however, that when accounting fraud does occur, accountants and auditors can claim that they were fooled by management. However, while accountants and auditors might not be engaged in fraudulent acts, it does not entirely absolve them from responsibility. A part of their job is to detect incorrect accounting numbers, whether they are a result of a mistake or a fraudulent act.

EXAMPLE 3.4 Rite Aid's Overstatement of Income

On June 21, 2002, a federal grand jury indicted four former and current executives of Rite Aid for conducting a wide-ranging scheme to overstate income.[8] The SEC noted in its investigation of the matter that Rite Aid reported false and misleading information in 10 different areas, ranging from reducing its costs and accelerating revenue to manipulating numbers between quarterly and annual reports.[9] Indeed, Rite Aid restated earnings for its fiscal year 1998 in a way that caused $305 million in net income to become $186 million in net losses. The restatement in fiscal year 1999 was from a $143 million profit to a $422.5 million loss, and a total of more than $1 billion in earnings disappeared.

Figure 3.1 shows the price of Rite Aid's stock during this period and its relationship to stated and restated earnings. Rite Aid stated that it earned $116.7 million in fiscal year 1997, which ended February 28, 1998. The stock price at this time was $21 per share. As indicated above, Rite Aid then stated earnings of $305 million in 1998 and the stock price rose to $34.25. The stock price reached its maximum of $50.94 on January 8, 1999. A few months later the firm reported fiscal year 1999 earnings of $143 million. However, investors started to realize that something was wrong. By July 10, 2000, the stock had slowly fallen to $7.85 per share. The stock price fell to $5 per share the next day when Rite Aid restated its earnings for 1998 to 2000. The stock spent the summer of 2002 at less than $2.50 per share.

Rite Aid's stock price was artificially inflated in the late 1990s because of fraud in financial reporting. The investors who purchased Rite Aid stock in 1999 did so based on false information, thinking the firm is profitable and growing. As a result they lost money. Existing investors should also have been

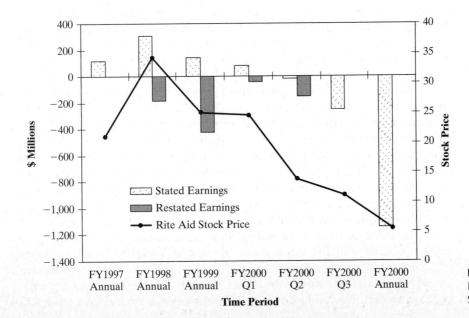

FIGURE 3.1 Rite Aid Earnings and Associated Stock Price

informed about the extent of the firm's losses so that they could decide whether to keep or sell their stock. After the truth finally became public, it was too late—shareholders had lost most of their investments.

AUDITORS AS CONSULTANTS

Business consulting firms typically advise firms on tactical issues, such as how to enter a new market, and strategic issues, such as acquiring or spinning off other firms. Accounting firms have aggressively expanded into the consulting business as the income from consulting exceeds the income from auditing. The problem for shareholders, however, is that there is a potential conflict of interest when auditors provide consulting services, and this can reduce the monitoring role of auditors.

When a consulting firm also conducts auditing services for a company, auditors may be pressured by their own accounting firm to overlook borderline practices, especially when their own consultants advocated those practices. This situation represents a serious conflict of interest for the auditors. Their responsibility should be effective monitoring for the shareholders but instead their inclination may be different because their bonuses will be affected by overall accounting firm profitability (which in turn depends heavily on consulting income).

The Sarbanes-Oxley Act of 2002 provided some protection from this conflict of interest. Under the Act, accounting firms are prohibited from providing both auditing and consulting activities to the same company. The result is that an accounting firm has to choose either auditing or consulting for each client.

INTERNATIONAL PERSPECTIVE

Compared to the accounting systems used in many countries, the system in the United States is quite rigorous. Characteristics of a high-quality system include many shareholder rights and strong protection of those rights. This protection comes from strong laws that are enforced and accounting standards that are unambiguous.

In a study of 31 countries, the United States was found to have the best legal environment to discourage earnings manipulations and smoothing.[10] Australia, Ireland, Canada, and the United Kingdom also have good investor protection and enforcement histories. Countries where earnings manipulations are more common include Austria, Italy, Germany, South Korea, and Taiwan. While some shareholders might question the quality of the financial statements in the United States, the accounting numbers of some firms that are not based in the United States could be of much lower quality. The scandals in some U.S. firms parallel some recent international scandals (see the Parmalat example that follows).

The **International Accounting Standards Board (IASB)** developed a single set of high-quality, understandable, and enforceable global accounting standards that require transparent and comparable information in general-purpose financial statements. In addition, IASB wants to encourage convergence in accounting standards of individual countries around the world. As of

2009, IASB standards are adopted in over 100 countries and non–U.S.-based companies can report to the SEC under IASB standards as well.[11]

EXAMPLE 3.5 Parmalat's Accounting Scandal

Apparently U.S. firms do not have a monopoly on fictitious revenue. On the heels of the Enron and Tyco scandals, a non-U.S. industry giant also experienced its own shocking accounting scandal. The eighth largest industrial firm in Italy, Parmalat, is perhaps best known in the United States for its pasteurized Parmalat milk, Archway cookies, and Black Diamond cheeses. The firm was exposed for a $10 billion accounting fraud. One of Parmalat's fraudulent accounting practices involved the setting up of numerous shell companies to generate fake profits. Parmalat's external auditor, up-and-coming firm Grant Thornton, might have assisted Parmalat with some of its accounting fraud. Under Italian law, a firm must change its external auditor every nine years. So when Grant Thornton's time was up, it suggested to Parmalat to spin off several of its businesses so that it could continue to keep various Parmalat concerns as clients. These spun-off subsidiaries made fake payments to Parmalat in the form of owed debt. Meanwhile, these subsidiaries created false accounts to make it look like they could pay the debt. However, not all of Parmalat's frauds were this complicated. Parmalat executives forged a document using Bank of America letterhead to claim that Parmalat had a $5 billion bank deposit. They ran this document through the fax machine a few times to make it look "authentic." Parmalat was declared bankrupt in 2003. Carlisto Tanzi, the founder of Parmalat, and his son and daughter, along with several other former Parmalat executives, were arrested for financial fraud.

Sources: www.wsws.org/articles/2004/jan2004/parm-j06.shtml; http://en.wikipedia.org/wiki/parmalat

---

Summary

Accountants keep track of the firm's financial records. Internal and external auditors review these records. Therefore auditors are an important part of the governance system. However, the role of accounting has changed in recent years. Aside from keeping financial records, they are asked to manage earnings to meet internal and external targets, to window dress the firm's financial statements, and to smooth reported income from year to year. Sometimes when accountants "work the numbers," they are treading a dangerous line between manipulating figures within the rules and outright fraud. External auditors might be fooled by the accounting tricks, which weakens their ability to detect errors. Further, auditors might even be tempted to participate in this dangerous treading. They want clients to be happy and they are subject to a possible conflict of interest problem if they are also the firm's consultants. With the passage of the Sarbanes-Oxley Act, auditors are no longer allowed to provide consulting services to the firms they are auditing and a new regulatory body has been created to oversee independent audits. Even before the passage of the act, the United States probably had, and probably still has, one of the strictest sets of accounting and auditing standards in the world.

WEB Info about Accounting and Auditing

Institute of Internal Auditors
www.theiia.org/

Public Company Accounting Oversight Board
www.pcaobus.org

American Institute of Certified Public Accountants
www.aicpa.org

International Accounting Standards Board
www.iasb.org

Review Questions

1. What is the role of management accounting, financial accounting, internal auditing, and external auditing?
2. What has weakened the ability of external auditors to conduct objective audits?
3. Who regulates accounting and auditing?
4. What is meant by "managing earnings"?
5. Give examples of how firms can manipulate earnings. Give examples of how firms commit accounting fraud.

Discussion Questions

1. Smoothing accounting earnings, from year to year, could make the stock price less volatile (i.e., less risky). So is smoothing, or managing earnings good or bad for shareholders? Compare and contrast the advantages versus disadvantages of smoothing earnings.
2. How would you improve the system of external auditing in the United States? Make sure you weigh the costs and benefits to your ideas. Also make sure you describe how your ideas are feasible.
3. Do you think the United States should adopt the International Accounting Standards that IASB has created? Do you think the rest of the world should adopt U.S. GAAP? For the latter question, first argue "no" and then argue "yes."

Exercises

1. Find a firm that has exhibited smooth earnings growth for the past decade or so. How do you think this firm was able to have such smooth earnings? Find another firm that exhibited erratic earnings. Why do you think this firm was unable to show smooth earnings? Do some research and try to figure out what the repercussions have been to the latter firm for having erratic earnings.
2. When firms report their income to their shareholders, they want to show high income. When firms report their income to the IRS, they want to report low income. Find and describe three legal ways in which accountants are able to report different incomes to shareholders and to the IRS.
3. Periodically a firm might decide that its recent past financial statements did not accurately reflect its financial condition. When the firm provides a new revised financial statement, it is said to have restated. The number of earnings restatements has dramatically changed over the past decade. Do some research and try to figure out how and why the number has changed.
4. WorldCom disclosed that roughly $3.8 billion had been improperly booked as capital investments instead of operating expenses. Describe how this affected its financial statements, stock price, and credit rating.
5. Find a recent restatement announcement by a firm not discussed in this chapter. Describe the restatement and describe how it changes the firm's overall financial condition.
6. Do some research and try to identify some key differences between International Accounting Standards and U.S. GAAP.

Exercises for Non-U.S. Students

1. Do some research and describe the accounting principles in your country. How are they different from U.S. GAAP?
2. Describe some details of the external auditing system used in your country. Is there a designation similar to CPA in your country? Does your country have problems with external auditing similar to those in the United States? Whether you answer "yes" or "no" to this last question, describe and explain why.
3. To what extent are financial statements important in your country? Who uses financial statements the most? Investors? Lenders? Government?
4. To what extent does accounting manipulation occur in your country? Do you trust the accuracy of financial statements in your country? Elaborate on your answer.
5. How is accounting and auditing regulated in your country? Describe the regulatory body and its composition and describe its powers.
6. How would you improve the auditing environment in your country? Make sure you weigh the costs and benefits of your ideas. Also make sure you describe how your ideas are feasible.

Endnotes

1. There are limitations on the differences between public reporting and IRS reporting.
2. Susan Pulliam and Deborah Solomon, "How Three Unlikely Sleuths Exposed Fraud at WorldCom," *Wall Street Journal*, October 30, 2002, 1.
3. Some of this discussion, along with some discussion in the section on managing earnings, comes from Steve Albrecht, James Stice, Earl Stice, and Monte Swain, *Accounting*, 9th edition, Thomson South-Western Publishing, 2005.
4. *www.sec.gov/Archives/edgar/data/806085/ 000110465908005476/a08-3530_110k.htm# IndexToConsolidatedFinancialState_005309.*
5. *http://idea.sec.gov/Archives/edgar/data/773468/ 000095014808000053/0000950148-08-000053- index.idea.htm.* Similarly, the 2008 first quarter results issued on May 12, 2008, also met the capital requirements.
6. Jesse Drucker and Henny Sender, "Sorry, Wrong Number: Strategy Behind Accounting Scheme," *Wall Street Journal*, June 27, 2002, A9.
7. Paul Krugman, "Flavors of Fraud," *New York Times*, June 28, 2002, A27, and "Everyone is Outraged," *New York Times*, July 2, 2002, A21.
8. Reuters, "SEC Charges Ex-Rite Aid Execs with Fraud" (June 21, 2002): 11:05 a.m.
9. Rite Aid Corporation, Accounting and Auditing Enforcement Release No. 1579, *Securities and Exchange Commission*, June 21, 2002.
10. Christian Leuz, Dhananjay Nanda, and Peter Wysocki, "Investor Protection and Earnings Management: An International Comparison," *Journal of Financial Economics* 69, no. 3 (2003): 505–527.
11. *www.iasb.org/About+Us/About+the+IASB/IFRSs+ around+the+world.htm.*

The Board of Directors

What are the responsibilities of a board of directors? In general, a board of directors acts as the shareholders' agent in charge of running the company. The board in a large corporation is not involved in running the day-to-day operations of the company. Instead, the board handles major decisions and delegates responsibility for everything else to corporate officers. Hence, the board is charged with the following five broad functions:

1. to hire, evaluate, and perhaps even fire top management, with the position of CEO being the most important to consider;
2. to vote on major operating proposals (e.g., large capital expenditures and acquisitions);
3. to vote on major financial decisions (e.g., issuance of stocks and bonds, dividend payments, and stock repurchases);
4. to offer expert advice to management; and
5. to make sure the firm's activities and financial condition are accurately reported to its shareholders.

In executing all of the above functions, the board provides an important corporate governance function. Because the board is a part of the firm's organizational structure at the top of the corporate hierarchy it might be considered the firm's most important internal monitor.

While the board's role in the corporation seems to ensure that shareholder interests are being attended to, there are some potentially serious problems. Among the issues are a lack of board independence from the CEO, directors who do not have the time or expertise to fulfill their roles adequately, and members who do not have a vested interest in the firm. In other words, there is an agency problem where the directors do not always act in the shareholders' best interest. This chapter provides an overview of corporate boards and their role in corporate governance and it also highlights potential problems with many of today's boards.

OVERVIEW OF BOARDS

The Board's Legal Duties

No federal law explicitly dictates that public corporations must have a board of directors. Instead, corporations must follow the statute of the state in which they are incorporated. State laws vary from one state to the other but every state requires that a corporation have a board of directors. The **Model Business Corporation Act** provides a guideline that states, "All corporate powers shall be exercised by or under authority of, and the business affairs of a corporation shall be managed under the direction of a board of directors." Further, all state laws require directors to act in good faith and with sincere belief that their actions are in the corporation's and shareholders' best interests. In order to abide by the spirit of this rule, directors have certain responsibilities, otherwise known as **duties**.

Because directors are supposed to represent shareholders' interests, directors have a **fiduciary duty** to conduct activities to enhance the firm's profitability and share value. Another way of saying this is that a fiduciary duty means that directors must act in furtherance of the shareholders' financial interests at all times. Related to their fiduciary duty, directors also have a **duty of loyalty and fair dealing**, where they must put the interests of shareholders before their own *individual* interests. In addition, directors must also exercise a **duty of care** by doing what an ordinary prudent person would do under the same position and circumstances. Exercising this duty involves being informed and making rational decisions. Finally, the board of directors has a **duty of supervision**, in which they should establish rules of ethics and ensure disclosure. In this regard the board should hold regular meetings to review the firm's performance, operations, and management, and it must make sure that accurate financial reporting and objective auditing are taking place.

As this is a daunting list of duties that may discourage individuals from agreeing to join a board, the law has developed the **business judgment rule** that protects directors from being sued for decisions that comply with the rule. Under the business judgment rule, a director will not be found liable for a decision that turns out poorly if that director took all reasonable measures to evaluate the decision. For example, if directors were well informed and researched the issues carefully, they will not be found legally liable to the shareholders for approving a merger that some shareholders believe is ill-advised.

Election of Directors

Directors are elected to serve on the board by a vote of shareholders. The right to vote in director elections is the primary way in which shareholders influence the control of the corporation. This vote depends on the voting power of each share of stock (which may differ between classes of stock and between preferred stock and common stock). All of the directors on the board can be removed and replaced by the shareholders for any reason or no reason, although the timing of the replacement may vary depending on the rules in the company's bylaws. Typically, directors can only be removed after their term expires, and these terms are often staggered so that only a third of directors are up for election at any year's annual meeting.[1]

The process of replacing directors, however, is not easy at large corporations. The biggest obstacle is the fact that individual shareholders do not have an incentive to become involved in the monitoring of the corporation. As directors typically have the support of management, the company will actively campaign amongst its shareholders to keep its directors. This means that it takes a committed group of shareholders who are willing to invest large amounts of time and money to win a voting contest against management-supported directors. If you are a small shareholder, do you really want to spend your own money to convince other shareholders to vote for different directors?

When there is a contested vote to elect directors, this is called a **proxy fight.** Each side of the contest (management vs. discontented shareholders) tries to persuade other shareholders to vote for their slate of candidates. As most shareholders do not actually attend the vote because of the costs of travel and the time requirement, they vote by filling out a proxy form that either specifies their vote or that designates an agent to vote their shares. Hence the phrase *proxy fight* describes a process where both sides lobby the list of shareholders seeking proxy votes in their favor.

Recent changes in SEC rules require firms to make it easier for shareholders to communicate with one another. This, along with the increasing ease of electronic communications, has made it easier for shareholders to communicate with one another and launch proxy fights. Large institutional investors such as the pension funds California Public Employees' Retirement System (CalPERS) and Teachers Insurance and Annuity Association-College Retirement Equities Fund (TIAA-CREF) have taken advantage of these changes to put pressure on corporate boards and management. Shareholder activism, including institutional shareholder activism, will be discussed in a later chapter.

EXAMPLE 4.1   Yahoo! Proxy Fight

An example of a proxy fight occurred following Microsoft's failed takeover of Yahoo! in 2008. After the Yahoo! board rejected Microsoft's offer, many Yahoo! shareholders were upset because this takeover would have paid Yahoo! shareholders a large premium. The concern was that the Yahoo! board rejected the takeover to protect their own positions as directors and the jobs of Yahoo! management, all at the expense of the owners of the company. In response, several class action lawsuits were filed suing the directors personally for destroying shareholder value. A proxy fight was also started by Carl Icahn, a billionaire and large Yahoo! investor, to replace all of the directors of Yahoo! at the annual meeting.

Even though proxy fights are expensive, Icahn was willing to spend large amounts of his personal funds to court shareholders. There were many upset shareholders willing to join his side. Interestingly, Yahoo! avoided the proxy fight at the last minute by agreeing to add two new directors who were chosen by Icahn. While this solution gave Icahn some personal control, it did not require any current directors to leave Yahoo!. Once the large shareholder gave up the fight, all of the directors nominated by Yahoo! management were elected at an uneventful shareholders' meeting, despite the large number of upset shareholders who wanted major changes at Yahoo!.

This example shows that even though the shareholders control the directors, it is very difficult in practice for shareholders to "fire" their board.

Source: http://www.techcrunch.com/2008/07/21/icahn-backs-down-from-yahoo-proxy-fight-in-return-for-three-yahoo-board-seats/

Board Committees

A great deal of important board work occurs at the subcommittee level and subsequently goes to the full board for approval. The reason for delegating responsibility to committees is that it is more efficient to allow for specialization of tasks on the board instead of bringing all actions to the full board. Many actions of committees then require a vote of the full board, while other committees are given the authority to act directly. Examples of committees include an **executive committee**, a **finance committee**, a **community relations committee**, and a **corporate governance committee**, among others. The most common board subcommittees are the following:[2]

- **audit committee**
- **compensation committee**
- **nomination committee**

The audit committee is charged with finding an independent auditor for the firm's accounting statements and the committee must ensure that the auditor does its job objectively. The compensation committee is responsible for setting and designing the executive compensation package. The nomination committee searches for and nominates candidates to run for vacancies among seats on the board of directors.

Board Structure Regulations Imposed by Exchanges and the Sarbanes-Oxley Act

The New York Stock Exchange (NYSE) and NASDAQ Stock Market—which as self-regulatory organizations (SROs) can impose their own set of regulations—require that their listed firms have an audit committee consisting primarily of independent directors. Since the scandals of 2001 and 2002, the exchanges have revised their regulations regarding the structure and function of a board of directors and the incentives provided to its members. Specifically, the NYSE mandates that companies have a majority of independent directors. A director is not independent if he (or immediate family) has worked for the company or its auditor within the past five years. Board members who are not also executives of the company must meet regularly without the presence of management.

The NYSE also requires specific functions of the board. For example, the nominating committee of the board must be composed entirely of independent directors and must perform certain duties. The same holds true of the compensation committee. Otherwise executives would have undue influence over their own compensation. The audit committee must also be independent; however, the members of this committee have an increased authority and responsibility to hire and fire the auditing firm. To handle this expanded responsibility, audit committee members must have the necessary experience and expertise in finance and accounting. To help maintain the independence of the audit committee, these board members may not receive compensation from the company, especially consulting fees, other than their regular director fees. Interestingly, the NYSE itself became a public company in 2006 and now trades on its own exchange as NYSE Euronext. Thus, they must abide by these rules too.

In the summer of 2002, the **Sarbanes-Oxley Act**, otherwise known as the **Public Company Accounting Reform and Investor Protection Act of 2002**, was passed. One section of the bill attempts to increase the monitoring ability and responsibilities of boards of directors and to improve their credibility. Specifically, the law makes the audit committee of the board of directors both more independent from management and more responsible for the hiring and oversight of auditing services and the accounting complaint process.

EXAMPLE 4.2 Historical Perspective—Is a Director Simply a Figurehead?

In 1934, William O. Douglas, a law professor who later served as an SEC chairman, and then as a U.S. Supreme Court justice for 36 years, claimed that directors do not direct. For the most part, his assertion has held true for some time. One director boasted in 1962, "If you have five directorships, it is total heaven, like having a permanent hot bath. No effort of any kind is called for. You go to a meeting once a month in a car supplied by the company, you look grave and sage, and on two occasions say, 'I agree.'"[3] For many years, a board of directors may have simply been something that corporations had for show rather than for a real purpose.

EXAMPLE 4.3 Who Are Directors?

Standard & Poor's 500 firms have about 11 directors each. How are these 5,500 or so board seats filled? The persons nominated by the firm's management or board's nominating committee often become directors. University deans or presidents and politicians are viewed as respectable figureheads but most directors are executives of other firms. For example, Korn/Ferry states that a person would have to possess 10 to 20 years of experience in a business leadership role, be a current COO (chief operations officer) or CFO of a large company, or be one of the top 15 executives at a very large corporation, to be considered a viable candidate for director. Sometimes a large individual shareholder submits a proposal to obtain a board seat. If the person is well-known or wealthy enough to launch an expensive campaign (i.e., a proxy fight), he or she might gather enough votes to be elected.

According to the 2007 Korn/ Ferry study, 96 percent of Fortune 1000 firms have a retired executive serving as a director, 78 percent have an executive from another firm, 52 percent have an academic, and 52 percent have a former government official. With regard to gender and race representation, board diversity seems to be improving. Eighty-five percent of boards have a woman as a director and 78 percent have a member of an ethnic minority, with African Americans sitting on 47 percent of our nation's boards. These are large increases from 1995, when 69 percent of the boards had a woman and 47 percent had an ethnic minority, with 34 percent being African American.

EXAMPLE 4.4   Is being a Director Worth It?

During the past 15 years or so, shareholders have become increasingly more demanding of directors and, as a result, directors have been working longer hours, taking more stock ownership in the firm to ensure a vested interest, challenging the CEO more often, and taking their duties more seriously. These demands are starting to take their toll on directors. According to recruiters Christian & Timbers, 60 percent of nominated directors are turning down appointments. Nonetheless, with director compensation averaging more than $150,000 per year—along with perks, travel, stocks, and stock options—all for working about 150 hours and attending eight meetings a year, directorship is lucrative.[4]

WHAT IS A "GOOD" BOARD?

Of course, boards that have members who have relevant experience and expertise are likely to be good boards. A board of a manufacturing firm probably should include someone who has worked in the same or similar industry for many years and has achieved some success in it. A board that consists of members who have different backgrounds may also be a good board. For example, the same manufacturing firm could benefit from someone who has marketing experience and from someone who has accounting experience. Each firm may need to decide for themselves what kind of background, experience, and expertise would serve the board and the firm optimally. But let us assume that all public firms have experienced and successful experts serving on their boards, currently a reasonable assumption. After all, if one looks at any board of a random large firm in the United States (and probably in any country), one will often find that the board consists of recognizable and successful business leaders and experts. If all boards consist of proven business leaders and business experts, then what might make one board better than another? We discussed earlier that there is increasing emphasis on having independent boards. In addition, perhaps small boards are better than large boards. We discuss each in turn next.

Independent Boards

There is a general consensus that when a board has a higher fraction of non-insiders (otherwise known as outside or independent directors), then it is presumed to be more effective at monitoring management. The logic is pretty straightforward. For example, one of the board's primary responsibilities is to evaluate, compensate, and possibly fire the CEO. What if the board consists of the following people: the firm's CFO, a friend of the CEO, a relative of the CEO, and a business collaborator of the CEO? This board is probably less likely to fire the CEO for poor performance. For this reason shareholders and regulators generally believe that outside directors are more objective at evaluating management. Research from academia confirms this intuition. When firms do poorly, the firms with a higher fraction of independent board members are more likely to fire the CEO.[5]

However, in today's business world, is it possible to find people who are entirely and unambiguously independent of the firm's management? For example, it may be unlikely to expect that two industry experts do not know each other personally. Also the definition of an independent versus inside director is not a black or white issue. A board member could be a cousin of the CEO or former employee of the CEO from another firm. These types of directors might be considered independent by the firm's management, but are they really? Because all directors may simply be a different shade of gray with regard to their independence stature, it makes it difficult for academic researchers to identify a relation between board independence and board effectiveness. This also makes it difficult for regulators to impose board independence regulations, as what is deemed independent is ambiguous.

Small Boards

A board with fewer members might be a better board. This view might be counterintuitive to some but not to others (think about how the American colloquialisms "more the merrier" and "too many cooks spoil the broth" both convey a supposed truism and yet represent opposite thinking). However, there is some research that has shown that smaller boards are more effective at enhancing a firm's value than larger boards.[6] The logic for why this might be deals with the "free-rider" problem. For a board with few directors, each board member may feel inclined to exert more effort than they would have otherwise, as they each realize that there are only a few others monitoring the firm. With larger boards, each member may simply assume that the many other members are monitoring. Further, with larger boards, it may be more difficult to reach consensus and thus to get anything meaningful done. Therefore, smaller boards may be more dynamic and more active.

Board Structure in the United States and Around the World

Figure 4.1 shows the average number of independent (outside) and inside directors for U.S. companies grouped by firm size and various industries.[7] While there appears to be some variation in the average board size, all industries show a large portion of independent directors. The average board size for all U.S. companies is 10, with 7 being independent.

Figure 4.2 shows the size and composition of boards in six countries as reported in the Korn/Ferry Annual Board of Directors Survey. Australia, France, and the United Kingdom have a majority of independent directors, while Germany and East Asia companies have a majority of insider directors. German boards have all insider directors. Boards in Australia, Non-Japan East Asia,[8] and the United Kingdom have smaller boards (nine members or less) on average. Obviously, not all countries share the United States's emphasis on independent directors. In addition, companies in different countries also seem to have differing views on board size.

Good for the Goose, Good for the Gander?

If independent boards are objective and if small boards are more active, then it would be tempting to conclude that all firms should have independent and small boards. What is good for one firm must be good for all firms. However, this may not be the case. Recall that we mentioned earlier that firms might have to decide what experience and expertise is optimal for their firm. This may hold true for board independence and board size. For example, a young

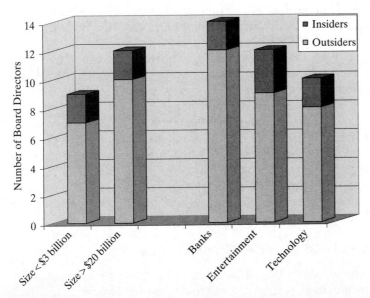

FIGURE 4.1 Average U.S. Board Size and Independence by Company Size and Industry

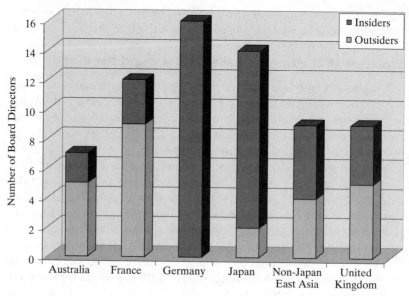

FIGURE 4.2   Average Board Size and Independence, 2004

growth-oriented firm may actually need more insiders, not outside-independent directors. If a firm's primary product is unique, then the firm's own employees might be the best people to serve on the board. Larger and more diversified firms may need more directors, not fewer directors, given the scale and diversified scope of its operations. From Figures 4.1 and 4.2, it even appears that some countries are inclined toward having more inside directors, and more directors overall, than other countries. May be for those countries, their board structures are best suited for their particular operating or legal environment.

Without specific regulations pertaining to board composition and size, each firm would be able to decide on its own what is the best board. However, who should make this decision? The firm's manager? He may be in the best position to pick a good board but his self-interest may get in the way. The firm's outside shareholders? Though they have the legal power to vote on board members, they may not have the power to appoint directors if they are unable to form a majority consensus. Also, while outsiders are more likely to be objective in appointing directors, they may choose less-suitable candidates for the nature of the corporation's business. Of course, there could be stricter regulations pertaining to board composition and size, but this would take away some of the firm's flexibility to form boards best suited for them.

Can Good Boards Lead to Better Firm Performance?

While independent boards and small boards might be better at monitoring the firm and the firm's managers, it is not clear that there is a positive correlation between board quality and firm performance. When one firm out-performs another, how can we tell if the board had anything to do with the performance difference? In professional sports, it is often difficult to single out who is to blame when a team does not have a winning season. Is it the players, the coaches, the executives, or the owners? While good boards may be good at fixing serious problems (in other words, they may be effectively reactive), they may not be good at creating value (in other words, they may not be effectively proactive).

Academic research echoes these dual sentiments. Most scholars agree that independent boards are more likely than inside directors to fire a CEO after a serious firm performance decline. However, academic researchers are almost equally divided on whether or not board quality and firm performance are positively related.

What might matter, when it comes to board compositions, is identifying which specific board committees are best served by independent directors and which may not be. For example, committees that determine CEO compensation and are responsible for the firm's audit may best be served by outsiders, but committees that make firm financing and long-term investment decisions may be served best by insiders.[9] Note from our previous discussion pertaining to recently adopted board structure regulations that regulators seem to agree with this viewpoint also.

POTENTIAL PROBLEMS WITH TODAY'S BOARDS

As already mentioned, one of the main functions of the board is to evaluate top management, especially the CEO. However, for most firms, the board's chair is also the firm's CEO. In 2007, only 41 percent of top firms had separated the positions of board chair and CEO. Further, only 11 percent reported that their chairman was actually an independent director.[10] Therefore the same person who manages the firm also calls the board meetings and sets the meeting agenda.[11] Also, directors typically receive all their information about the firm from management, so this information is controlled by the CEO/board chair as well. This being the case, is the board capable of seriously evaluating or challenging the CEO? We mentioned that it can happen but often only as a result of significant shareholder pressure. Even if the CEO is not the board chair, he is not necessarily under a more careful watch. While most boards have more outsiders than insiders, many of these so-called outside board members might have some sort of business or personal tie to the CEO.

The boards of firms that have been reeling from scandal (e.g., Tyco, Global Crossings, and Adelphia) were filled with former or current executives. Further, one of Tyco's outside directors was paid $10 million for helping to arrange the acquisition of CIT Group. Former Adelphia CEO John Rigas, along with his three sons, held four out of the nine board seats. Can this quartet be expected to be objective monitors?

Another problem with some boards is that directors do not have a significant vested interest in the firm. For example, for a period of time, most of Disney's outside directors owned little or no stock. In 1997, *Business Week* reported that the Occidental Petroleum board had approved a $95 million payout to its CEO, but two of its board members, George O. Nolley and Aziz D. Syriani, only owned 2,280 and 1,450 shares of the firm's stocks, respectively, despite the fact that they had sat on the board for 14 years.[12] The article also reported that Advanced Micro Devices director Charles M. Blalack and Microsoft director Richard Hackborn owned no shares of their firm. Will these board members act to increase shareholder value or to build a good relationship with the CEO?

EXAMPLE 4.5   Disney's Board During the 1990s

The Walt Disney Company CEO until 2005 was Michael Eisner. As CEO he was supposed to be monitored by Disney's board of directors. However, Disney's board was criticized by *Business Week* as one of the worst in corporate America as it consisted of numerous current Disney managers, such as the chief corporate officer (CCO) and heads of various Disney operations. Disney claimed, however, that 13 of the 16 board members were independent directors. These "outsiders" included: Reveta Bowers; headmaster of the school that Eisner's children attended; George Mitchell, a paid consultant to Disney and an attorney whose law firm represented Disney; Stanley Gold, president of Shamrock Holdings, which managed investments for the Disney family; Leo O'Donovan, president of Georgetown University, which one of the Eisner children attended and which received donations from Eisner; Irwin Russell, Eisner's personal attorney; and Robert Stern, architect for several Disney projects.

Would this board challenge Eisner? Not only did some of these directors work for Eisner but there were obviously others who also benefited from not angering him. In other words, this board had too many insiders and those with business or other vested interests with the CEO. A lucrative contract penned for Eisner netted him more than $700 million in the last years of the 1990s during a time where Disney's market value fell to less than half of what it was during the run-up of the 1990s.

However, the situation has been changing. For example, some firms, such as Ashland Inc., are setting stock ownership targets for their directors. To Eisner's credit, he asked his directors to own more stock. For GE, the outside directors are clearly aligned with shareholders, as they owned (at the beginning of the year 2000), an average of $6.6 million of GE stock each.[13] According to the 2007 Korn/Ferry study, 80 percent of the directors were required to own some of the board's company stock.

Are directors capable of providing the time and expertise required to fully understand the major operating and financial decisions of the firm? Some directors, especially those who are potentially good in that role, may be overextended. For example, many directors serve on multiple boards. According to a 1997 *Business Week* article, several people held directorships in 10 or more firms.[14] Coca-Cola has five directors (out of 13) who serve on at least five boards. In addition, most directors also have their own highly demanding full-time jobs. Often they are company executives themselves.

In addition, some directors simply do not have the expertise to be a board member. This means that independence, in and of itself, is not a sufficient quality for being an effective director. Some boards want to have a few figureheads, such as a celebrity (O. J. Simpson was once on the audit committee of Infinity Broadcasting) or a former army general, but other candidates probably could offer more help to the firm.

Finally, as mentioned before, some boards are simply too large, which makes it more unlikely that all directors will be actively involved and more difficult to accomplish needed work. Disney's board has 16 members and Enron's had 15. Is this too large and is this part of the problem? Some academic researchers believe so. As mentioned before, according to some studies, firms with fewer directors have higher market values, indicating their effectiveness.

In summary, many potential problems plague boards today. Many directors might not be truly independent, they might be too busy, and they might not have the expertise to carry out their obligations. These problems might explain why some corporate scandals occur.

EXAMPLE 4.6   Is Enron's Board Partially to Blame?

Enron's board, which consisted of 15 members, epitomized the notion of one that is "captive" to the firm's CEO. Board member John Wakeham was a British Conservative Party politician who had approved the building of an Enron power plant in Britain in 1990. Four years later Wakeham was on the Enron board. Director Herbert Winokur is chairman and CEO of Capricorn Holdings. He also sat on the board of National Tank Company, which sold equipment and services to Enron divisions for millions of dollars. Directors Charles LeMaistre and John Mendelsohn were former president and current president, respectively, of the M. D. Anderson Cancer Center, which received more than $500 million from Enron and its chairman, Ken Lay, during a five-year period. Director Wendy Gramm, a former chairwoman of the Commodity Futures Trading Commission, backed several policies that benefited Enron and other energy trading companies before she joined the Enron board. Her husband, Senator Phil Gramm, is a major recipient of Enron campaign donations. Board member Robert Belfer is founder and former chairman and CEO of Belco Oil and Gas Corporation. Belco and Enron had numerous financial arrangements. Director Charles Walker is a tax lobbyist. Firms partly owned by Walker were paid more than $70,000 by Enron for consulting services. In addition, Enron also made donations to a nonprofit corporation chaired by Walker. A Senate report argues that the board failed in their fiduciary duties to represent shareholders and that the Enron failure was partly due to the lack of the board's independence.

In 1999, auditors had already told Enron board members that the company was using accounting practices that "push[ed] limits" and were "at the edge" of what was acceptable. One director, Robert Jaedicke, had been an accounting professor at Stanford University. Also the board knowingly allowed Enron to move more than half of its assets off the balance sheet. Governance experts used by the Senate investigation stated that this activity was unheard of but only one Enron board member expressed any concern when it was occurring. The board even waived a code of conduct stipulation for CFO Andrew Fastow, allowing him to create private offshore partnerships that would conduct business with Enron. Under the Enron code of conduct, no employee is allowed to obtain financial gain from an entity that does business with Enron. Under Fastow's watch, these entities profited at Enron's expense, but the board idly sat by despite Fastow's obvious conflict of interest.

The Senate report concludes that the board missed a dozen red flags that should have warned them about possible shenanigans at the firm. For example, directors were told that in a six-month period, Fastow's partnerships had generated $2 billion in funds for Enron. While Enron's board apparently was not involved in the fraud, they should have put a stop to it.[15] After all, they were being paid more than $350,000 a year in salary, stocks, and stock options by Enron to be its directors. In the Senate report's conclusion, they state, "much that was wrong with Enron was known to the Board. . . . By failing to provide sufficient oversight and restraint to stop management excess, the Enron Board contributed to the company's collapse and bears a share of the responsibility for it."[16]

A class-action lawsuit was filed by Enron's shareholders and in January 7, 2005, Enron directors agreed to pay $168 million as part of Enron's overall settlement with its shareholders. $13 million comes directly from the directors' pockets. Shareholders claimed that Enron directors sold shares after false financial statements were filed. Enron directors claimed no wrongdoing. Only a few days earlier, WorldCom announced that its directors agreed to a $54 million settlement with its shareholders, with directors being personally responsible for $18 million of it. Traditionally, some have viewed the *business judgment rule* as being too lenient toward directors. That is, it is easy for directors to claim that they are doing the best that they can. Today, however, directors may be facing higher standards.

INTERNATIONAL PERSPECTIVE—BOARDS IN WESTERN EUROPE

Two-Tier Boards

Some European countries have firms with a two-tier board structure. For example, German firms have a management board that essentially runs the business and a supervisory board that appoints and supervises the management board. The supervisory board also controls the firm's compliance with the law and articles of the corporation and its business strategies. A person cannot belong to both boards. The Netherlands also has a two-tier board structure. Interestingly, in France, a firm can choose between having a one-tier or two-tier board structure but most choose the one-tier board. However, it could be argued that these two-tiered boards are similar to what the United States and the United Kingdom would deem as their top management and the board.

Board Regulations on Independence

As mentioned earlier, one of the primary issues pertaining to board quality and efficacy is board independence. Among Western European countries, the United Kingdom is probably most similar to the United States in its emphasis on independent directors. The U.K.'s *Combined Code on Corporate Governance*, released in July 2003, states that "Except for smaller companies, at least half the board, excluding the chairman, should comprise non-executive directors determined by the board to be independent." Before the passage of the Combined Code, the Cadbury Committee issued a *Code of Best Practice* recommending that each firm should have at least three independent directors. While it is too early to assess the 2003 Combined Code, there is some solid evidence that the Cadbury Committee's Code has been successful.[17]

However, the governance codes for the rest of the European countries do not explicitly require a specific number or fraction of independent directors. Instead they make "recommendations" or "suggestions" pertaining to independent directors. For example, the 1998 Cardon Report, commissioned by the Brussels Stock Exchange suggests that "The number of independent directors should be sufficient for their views to carry significant weight in the board's decisions." In Belgium's *Corporate Governance Act*, 2004, it states, "the composition of the board should be determined on the basis of the necessary diversity and complementarily." For France, the Viénot report of July 1999 recommends that at least a third of the directors be independent. Later, an October 2003 report, released by the French Association of Private Enterprise, "suggests" that for widelyheld firms, at least half of its directors be independent. Italy's *Corporate Governance Code* of 2002 states that "an adequate number of non-executive directors shall be independent." Spain's *Aldama Report* of 2003 suggests "a very significant number of independent directors, considering the company's ownership structure and the capital represented on the Board."

Clearly, the wide attention on director independence is a recent phenomenon. Further, the recommendations pertaining to director independence with regard to their number and/or fraction seem vague and do not seem to be explicit regulations. Is it enough to merely advocate board independence or do there have to be explicit regulations and backing? For example, the Cadbury Report makes explicit recommendations but they are not explicit regulations, but because the London Stock Exchange specifically asks listing firms whether or not they are compliant with the Cadbury recommendations, these recommendations seem to have "teeth" and have been found to be successful in improving governance for U.K. firms.[18]

Summary

A firm's board of directors plays an important role in reducing problems inherent in the separation of ownership and control. Indeed, the board is responsible for hiring, evaluating, and sometimes firing the firm's executives. In addition, the board oversees the firm's auditors and makes major strategic decisions for the firm. They are to conduct these activities in the best interests of the shareholders.

There are many potential problems with the organization of many corporate boards. For example, it seems that many directors lack the independence, the vested interest, the time, and sometimes the expertise to carry out their fiduciary obligations to shareholders. Enron's board is a telling example. However, the recent attention directed to boards has caused some changes to occur (especially regulatory changes) but it is too early to tell if these changes are taking hold.

WEB Info about Boards of Directors

Korn/Ferry International
www.kornferry.com

The Corporate Library
www.thecorporatelibrary.com

European Corporate Governance Institute
www.ecgi.de

International Corporate Governance Network
www.icgn.org

Review Questions

1. What regulations govern the functions and structure of boards of directors? What is legally required of directors? What are the primary roles of boards and board subcommittees?
2. Broadly speaking, what defines a good board? Do all firms benefit from this broad definition of a good board?
3. What is the relationship between board quality and firm monitoring, and between board quality and firm performance?
4. What are the main problems in modern boards? How might they be changed to fix those problems?
5. How are corporate boards of directors in Western Europe different from the United States?

Discussion Questions

1. How would you evaluate whether or not a board is doing a good job on a day-to-day basis? Also, how would you apply the *business judgment rule* standard on directors?
2. If you were the largest outside shareholder of General Motors (GM), who would you want on your board and why? If you are the largest outside shareholder of a firm that operates an Internet search engine that just recently went public, who would you want on your board and why?
3. Should there be regulations pertaining to board composition and structure? If you think so, then what kind of regulations?
4. As a potential investor in a stock, do you think it would be worthwhile to examine the firm's board before purchasing its stock? What would you look for?

Exercises

1. In the state you are in right now, find and describe the state laws pertaining to corporate boards.

2. Examine the 30 firms in the Dow Jones Industrial Average. Which firms have the same person holding the CEO and board chairman titles? Are certain types of firms more likely to have a CEO/Chairman?

3. Pick a company and identify all the board directors, their affiliations, and their compensation from the directorship. Much of this information can be obtained from proxy statements the firm files with the SEC.

4. Find three recent cases where the CEO of a firm was fired. What happened?

5. In the summer of 2002, WorldCom declared bankruptcy. It was the largest bankruptcy in history. A class-action lawsuit was filed by shareholders and subsequently settled. Investigate what happened to WorldCom and how its board of directors was complicit in WorldCom's problems.

6. In 2005, Walt Disney shareholders lost their long-running lawsuit against their board's hiring, firing, and compensating of Michael Ovitz, former President of Walt Disney. Describe the surrounding details and circumstances.

Exercises for Non-U.S. Students

1. Try to identify the board members of a public firm from your native country. In what way is the board composition and structure similar to and/or different from a comparable U.S. firm? Why do you think these similarities and/or differences exist?

2. What are the regulations pertaining to boards, if any, in your native country? Why do these regulations exist (or not exist)? In your opinion, do you think these regulations (or lack of regulations) are appropriate for your country?

Endnotes

1. The rules for the election, removal, and replacement of directors are found in the corporation's bylaws that are a set of internal rules adopted by the shareholders and directors.

2. Thirty-fourth Annual Board of Directors Study, Korn/Ferry International, (Los Angeles, CA, 2007).

3. Katrina Brooker, "Trouble in the Boardroom," *Fortune* (May 13, 2002): 113–116.

4. These statistics are based on averages reported in the 34th Annual Board of Directors Study, Korn/Ferry International, 2007.

5. Jerold B. Warner, Ross L. Watts, and Karen H. Wruck, "Stock Prices and Top Management Changes," *Journal of Financial Economics* 20 (1989): 461–492; Michael S. Weisback, "Outside Directors and CEO Turnover," *Journal of Financial Economics* 20 (1988): 431–460; Kenneth A. Borokhovich, Robert Parrino, and Teresa Trapani, "Outside Directors and CEO Selection," *Journal of Financial and Quantitative Analysis* 31, no. 3 (1996): 337–355;

Kathleen A. Farrell and David A. Whidbee, "The Consequences of Forced CEO Succession for Outside Directors," *The Journal of Business* 73, no. 4, (2000):597–627.

6. Jeff Huther, "An Empirical Test of the Effect of Board Size on Firm Efficiency," *Economics Letters* 54, no. 3, (1996): 259–264; David Yermack, "Higher Market Valuation of Companies with a Small Board of Directors," *Journal of Financial Economics* 40, no. 2 (1996):185–211.

7. Data is from the 34th Annual Board of Directors Study, Korn/Ferry International, (Los Angeles, CA, 2007).

8. Non-Japan East Asia firms are China (including Hong Kong), Malaysia, Singapore, and Thailand.

9. April Klein, "Firm Performance and Board Committee Structure," *Journal of Law and Economics* 41 (April 1998):275–303.

10. *www.cfo.com/article.cfm/8626959/c_8622258? f=TodayInFinance_Inside.* (January 31, 2007).

11. The ability to call a meeting and set an agenda can be extremely important in a corporation whose bylaws provide that only the chairman of the board can call a meeting and that the only topics of discussion at the meeting can be those on the agenda. When these limitations are in the bylaws, the CEO/board chair is especially powerful.

12. "Directors in the Hot Seat," *Business Week* (December 8, 1997): 100–104.

13. "The Best and Worst Corporate Boards," *Business Week* (January 24, 2000) from *www.businessweek.com*.

14. John A. Byrne, Leslie Brown, and Joyce Barnathan, "Directors in the Hot Seat," *Business Week* (December 8, 1997): 100–104.

15. John Byrne, "Commentary: No Excuses for Enron's Board," *Business Week* (July 29, 2002) from *www.businessweek.com*.

16. Source: "The Role of the Board of Directors in Enron's Collapse," U.S. Senate Report 107–170, July 8, 2002.

17. Jay Dahya, John J. McConnell, and Nickolaos G. Travlos, "The Cadbury Committee, Corporate Performance, and Top Management Turnover," *Journal of Finance* 57, no. 1 (2002): 461–483.

18. Jay Dahya, John J. McConnell, and Nickolaos G. Travlos, "The Cadbury Committee, Corporate Performance, and Top Management Turnover," *Journal of Finance* 57, no. 1 (2002): 461–483.

Investment Banks and Securities Analysts

This chapter deals with investment banks and securities analysts. Investment banks offer a variety of services but their most notable business is selling newly created securities. When a private firm wants to become a public firm, it does so by registering its stock with the Securities and Exchange Commission (SEC) and then selling stock to the investing public. To ease the process of becoming a public firm, investment banks have developed into specialists who help firms with all the necessary steps. Similarly, when an already public firm wants to raise additional capital to finance its ongoing activities or future growth, it might also obtain the services of an investment bank to sell new securities (i.e., stocks and bonds) to the public. Hence, one can think of investment banks as intermediaries who provide consulting services and who sell new securities on behalf of firms.

Related to investment banks are securities analysts. The primary job of securities analysts is to evaluate securities and then to make buy and/or sell recommendations to their clients based on their evaluations. In other words, these analysts review securities that are already issued, which is different from investment banks who are involved in issuing new securities. Analysts are also expected to make earnings forecasts for the firms that they follow in order to help investors make their own buy and/or sell decisions. Many securities analysts work for investment banks, while others work for other financial advisory firms such as brokers and financial advisors.

Most corporate governance texts might not consider investment banks and securities analysts as part of the corporate governance system. However, because investment banks evaluate their client firms' needs and bring investment opportunities to the market and because securities analysts frequently possess better information than most investors about a company, both investment banks and analysts are in a good position to monitor the firm and to identify problems for shareholders. We would expect investment bankers to sell "good" securities (i.e., they should not be selling securities of a poorly run firm) and for analysts to recommend "good" securities (i.e., they should not be recommending stocks that they think will go down in value). Therefore, they both do represent an important and integral part of the corporate governance system. This chapter first discusses investment banks and then it discusses securities analysts.

INVESTMENT BANKING ACTIVITIES

The basic investment banking service is to help companies issue new debt and equity securities. A firm can issue several different kinds of securities. The bank advises the company on the optimal security (stocks, bonds, etc.) for the amount of capital being raised, while taking into account the company's situation. The investment banks charge the company a fee for this service. The size of the fee depends on how much risk the investment bank takes to issue the securities. There are two methods that banks can use to issue stock and bonds: underwriting and using best efforts.

Think about the case of issuing stock. When **underwriting** an issue, the bank will guarantee that the company will receive a specific amount of capital. That is, the banker assures the company that a certain number of shares will sell at a target price. If too few shares sell at that price, the investment bank must buy those shares. For example, if a bank guarantees that it will be able to raise $100 million in capital for the issuing firm but is only able to sell $70 million worth of stock, then the bank would have to buy $30 million worth of stock. The fee for underwriting a $100 million issue is typically about $7 million for a new issue (i.e., for an initial public offering or IPO) and $5 million for issues raised by already existing public companies (i.e., for a seasoned equity offering or SEO).

If the investment bank did not want to assume the risk on a security issue, it could use the **best-efforts** method. The bank does its best to sell as much of the new security as possible for the company, but does not guarantee that the company will get its desired amount of capital. In effect, the company takes the risk of not receiving enough capital. Because the risk is low for the investment bank, the fee charged is much lower for the best-efforts method than for underwriting.

The process of selling securities to public investors first involves registering securities with the SEC (more about the SEC in Chapter 9). The document submitted to the SEC includes a preliminary prospectus containing information about the security issue and the company. For example, the prospectus details the company's financial condition, business activities, management experience, and how the funds raised will be used. The preliminary prospectus is updated based on SEC comments and market conditions. The bank distributes the final prospectus to investors interested in the securities issue. This information, which is publicly available on the SEC Web site, helps investors make decisions about the condition of the company and about buying the issue.[1] As one role of investment bankers is to help companies collect the information and put together the prospectus materials required by the SEC, investment bankers can be an important source of information and monitoring of a public company.

The prospectus and the banker's "road show" relay information about the company to investors. The road show is the marketing campaign done by investment bankers to generate interest and to market the issue. They travel the country visiting large institutional investors such as public pension funds and mutual funds. To sell to individual investors, investment banks use their brokerage operations. For a "hot" issue, investors call the brokers to order shares. In a less popular issue, the brokers call investors.

Information about the issuing firm is especially important to investors when the firm is new. When a firm offers stock to the public for the first time in an IPO, the firm is typically young, small, and mostly unknown to investors. The IPO firm's information that is filed with the SEC may be the only independent data available on the firm. Hence, investors rely heavily on this information. To the extent that investment banks are involved in gathering this information, investors are also relying on the investment bank because investors expect the bank to disclose all relevant information in order to make good investment decisions.

Investment banks experience greater risk when underwriting an IPO, as opposed to underwriting an SEO, because of the uncertainty involved with new firms. To mitigate some of the risk, banks tend to underprice IPO offerings. That is, banks offer the new shares of stock at a lower price than the demand for the stock would suggest. For example, on March 19, 2008, gigantic credit card company, Visa Inc., conducted the largest IPO in U.S. history, raising $18 billion. A syndicate of banks, with JP Morgan and Goldman Sachs as lead banks, conducted the underwriting services for this deal and those investors who purchased the stock from these investment banks bought it at $44 per share. Originally, the price range for the Visa IPO was in the $37 to $42 range, but there were not enough shares for all the investors who wanted them, so the price was ratcheted up to $44. Despite the price bump, the 406 million share IPO was still oversubscribed and many investors who were left out of the deal had to buy shares on the New York Stock Exchange (NYSE) later that day. On the first day that Visa stock traded on the NYSE, the stock price traded as high as over $60 per share and closed the day at $56.50. The first-day return for the stock was over 28 percent. The investment banks were probably well aware that the first-day trading price would be greater than $44 per share but they underpriced the stock offer anyway to ensure that they would sell all of the stock and reduce their liability to Visa Inc. Even though Visa is a well-known and established financial firm, investments banks still underpriced the IPO.

Underpricing IPOs lowers the risk to the underwriters and makes the new issues highly desirable to investors. After all, who would not want a 28 percent

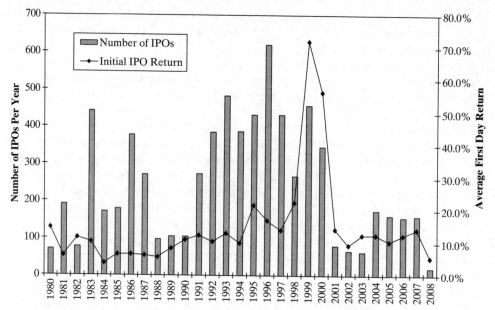

FIGURE 5.1 IPOs Issued and Their Average Initial Return from 1980 to 2008

return in one day? Figure 5.1 shows the number of IPOs offered in each year from 1980 to 2008.[2] The line represents the average first-day return for the offerings each year. Note that the average first-day return is positive in every year but that does not mean that every IPO experiences a price increase on the first day. Some IPOs are in high demand and earn a positive return—others are in low demand and decline in price the first day. The average initial return for IPOs in the late 1990s and 2000 was extraordinarily high. The average in 1999 was more than 70 percent! During the 1990s, the average underpricing in the United States was just over 20 percent. This compares to 16.5 percent in France, 40.2 percent in Germany, and 39.6 percent in the United Kingdom. In the recession of 2008, however, the initial return was only 5.3 percent, the lowest on the chart.[3]

CRITICISMS OF INVESTMENT BANKS

IPO Problems

Investment banks take small private firms public in IPOs. These small firms want to expand using the capital that the stock issue provides. Every small business owner would like to gain tens or hundreds of millions of dollars to spend, but few small businesses would make good public companies. That is, the business model of many small firms would not work effectively as large, national firms. In addition, small business owners may not be capable of running a large business.

Typically, only a small fraction (less than 1 percent) of firms that want to conduct an IPO actually do. Who decides which firms go public? While any firm can go public if they wish, it is difficult to sell your stock to the public if you do not have an investment bank involved. Accordingly, investment banks effectively make the decision about which firms will go public through the banks' decisions about taking the risk of underwriting an IPO or getting involved in a best-efforts IPO. If you run a small company and cannot find an investment bank to take your company public, you will have to find buyers on your own without help from a bank's customers and connections. It is also a bad signal to investors that market professionals did not want to touch your company's stock.

The banks thoroughly examine potential IPO firms. Traditionally, the policy of many banks has been to bring a firm public only if it has put together a good management team, developed a quality business plan, and perfected its business model enough so that it has earned profits in the past three quarters. The companies brought public from 1986 to 1995 experienced only a 1 percent failure rate.[4] This rate is defined as the firm's stock price falling to less than $1 (or delisted from the exchanges) within the first three years after the IPO. Investment banks did a good job of offering quality companies to investors during the late 1980s to the mid-1990s. As such they provided an important monitoring service to the investment community.

The situation began to change in the mid- to late 1990s. The stock prices of technology firms dramatically increased and were enormously popular with investors. The demand from investors for more technology stocks seemed insatiable. Hundreds of millions of dollars were to be made by taking tech firms public. The investment-banking industry raked in more than $2 billion in banking fees. There were not enough new firms that met the traditionally high-quality standards of the banks but investors did not seem to care. They seemed to want any new tech stock at any price. Notice how high the average first day returns of IPOs were in 1999 and 2000. The risk of underwriting these firms did not seem very high with such strong demand. To meet the high demand, banks began to bring inferior companies to the market.

EXAMPLE 5.1   PETS.COM Initial Public Offering

Consider the IPO of Pets.com. In 1999, the firm had only $5.8 million in revenue and reported an operating loss of $61.8 million. Yet Merrill Lynch launched the Pets.com IPO in February 2000. The firm raised $66 million in capital and Merrill received more than $4 million in fees.[5] Ten months later, Pets.com filed for bankruptcy and folded.

The firms that offered IPOs in the period 1998 to 2000 experienced a 12 percent failure rate, which is much higher than the historic 1 percent rate. Investment banks apparently lost their desire to be gatekeepers of quality firms and monitors for investors. Investors probably measure success differently; they measure it by their investment return. Of the 367 Internet firms that have gone public since 1997, only 15 percent have made money compared to their offer prices. More than 200 firms have lost more than 75 percent of their value.

What made this even worse for individual investors is that the average investor rarely can access good IPOs at the offer price. Instead such investors usually cannot buy the stock until it starts trading on the stock exchange. By then the stock has typically already increased in price. Consequently, poor returns are even worse for the average individual investor.

EXAMPLE 5.2   Investment Bank Tries to Unload its Own Risky Investment in IPO

Bear Stearns, a now defunct investment bank, proposed an unusual IPO in May 2007. A new company called Everquest Financial was formed primarily by two hedge funds run by Bear Stearns. Everquest Financial purchased $720 million in mortgage-backed securities from the Bear Stearns hedge funds and the proposed IPO would sell ownership of Everquest to public investors. Indirectly, this IPO would transfer the risk of these mortgage backed securities from the hedge funds to other investors.

As this IPO was proposed during the beginning of the real estate meltdown that ultimately led to the financial collapse of 2008, it was characterized in the financial press as an "unprecedented attempt by a Wall Street house to dump its mortgage bets."[6] The reason for the concern was that the value of $720 million was not an "arms length" valuation determined by the market. Instead, $720 million was what the Bear Stearns hedge funds decided the securities were worth. Could an investment bank use its IPO expertise to unload troubled assets without a real market valuation? This was a bold test of how powerful investment banks were in convincing customers to buy into any IPOs the bank brought to market. And the answer was apparently a resounding no, as the IPO proposal was pulled about six weeks after it was first proposed. It is not known exactly what killed the deal, but it is hard to imagine how Bear Stearns would find buyers for Everquest Financial.

A footnote to this example is that Bear Stearns did not survive the mortgage industry collapse of 2007 and financial crisis of 2008. In March 2008, Bear Stearns was forced by pending insolvency due to its investments in mortgage-backed securities into a government-assisted takeover by JP Morgan.

Structured Deals

When companies need more capital, they turn to investment banks. Raising capital can be difficult. As an extreme example, consider a firm facing bankruptcy. In bankruptcy, the equity of the firm is taken from the stockholders, who gain nothing, and given to some of the creditors. Therefore investors are not likely to buy additional shares of a financially troubled firm. The firm would also have trouble borrowing money from banks or from bond investors because these creditors typically do not recoup all their money in the bankrutpcy court. Investment banks may be able to help in this situation by arranging for non-traditional financing from a large investor or investment group.

Often a firm has trouble raising capital, even if it is not on the brink of bankruptcy. For example, the current creditors of the firm may have stipulated in their loans that the firm cannot borrow more money unless they are repaid first. An investment bank can help put together a restructuring of the current financing mix that pays off the current loans and replaces them with a new mix of debt and equity.

One criticism of investment banks is that they sometimes have been active participants in helping companies raise capital outside traditional avenues, thus manipulating earnings. Enron's strategy was to launch structured deals using special purpose entities (SPEs) created in tax havens such as the Cayman Islands. The SPEs were formed as partnerships that created the appearance of third-party companies doing business with Enron. The "business" actually turned out to be loans that were not recorded as debt but instead, recorded as revenue. For the structured deals to work, Enron needed complicated structures to fool auditors and regulators. To help create and fund the deals, Enron turned to investment banks. Large institutional investors frequently funded these partnerships.

EXAMPLE 5.3   Enron's Partnerships

Enron invested heavily in an Internet start-up called Rhythms NetConnections. Rhythms stock had jumped and the investment of $10 million grew to $300 million, a $290-million profit! Due to restrictions on selling ownership in the recent IPO, Enron could not sell this stock right away. Because of its mark-to-market method of accounting, Enron could book the gain. However, Enron worried that a big decline in price later would require booking a large loss.[7] Enron could not persuade investment banks to hedge the price risk because of Enron's huge position in the high-risk start-up Rhythms. Consequently, Enron created a partnership called LJM in the Cayman Islands that would guarantee the profit.[8] Enron CFO Andrew Fastow would run the partnership. The new partnership was funded by Enron stock. Therefore Enron was really insuring itself. The Rhythms profit would represent 30 percent of Enron's total profit for the year. The danger was that if both Rhythms stock and the Enron stock prices fell, LJM would not have enough capital to make the guaranteed payment. Enron would then have to reverse the profit and record a loss of $290 million. The large loss would further depress the Enron stock. Even with this risk, Enron created LJM and completed the deal. Enron considered LJM a large success and entered into similar arrangements to hedge other risky tech stock holdings. They called these arrangements Raptor partnerships.

The myriad of partnerships created was actually a sophisticated Ponzi scheme. Enron dealt with nearly 700 SPEs in all. Enron created fictitious profits to meet earnings expectations. Those profits would have to be offset in the future as losses. As the losses came due, Enron continued the process and created new structured deals to hide (or delay) the losses and generate additional profits. In this way the deals quickly mushroomed in number and in size. Eventually the scheme collapsed when Enron's stock price fell in 2001. Many of the partnerships funded with the stock were unable to complete their transactions. Enron was forced to disclose $1 billion in losses that it had previously booked as profits and was forced into bankruptcy.

Investment banks have denied any wrongdoing, saying they are not responsible for Enron (or any other firm) fraudulently booking loans as revenue. However, the banks probably suspected that Enron's financial statements were misleading—at the very least. Even if the banks did nothing illegal, they violated the trust of their clients and public investors by participating in a scheme designed to hide a firm's financial troubles. The institutions failed in their corporate governance role as a monitor. This failure is particularly concerning because JP Morgan and Citigroup (the two largest players in the Enron fiasco) were the nation's two largest financial institutions at the time.

While the Enron example details the role of investment banks in Enron's structured deals, evidence exists that banks have helped other firms create questionable SPEs. During the early 2000s, JP Morgan pitched these financing vehicles to other firms and entered into arrangements with seven companies. Citigroup discussed structured deals with 14 companies and developed them with three.[9] Deals have also been structured by the bankers of Credit Suisse Group, Barclays PLC, FleetBoston Financial Corporation, Royal Bank of Scotland Group PLC, and Toronto-Dominion Bank.

SECURITIES ANALYSTS

Analysts generally fall into two categories: buy-side and sell-side. Institutional investors, such as pension funds and mutual funds, hire analysts. Their purpose is to help decide which stocks the fund should buy; therefore they are referred to as **buy-side analysts**. The recommendations of these analysts are not public and they are only seen and used by the institutional investors. Fund managers are managing money on behalf of individual investors, such as retirement accounts, so they are an important part of the corporate monitoring system (more on institutional investors in Chapter 7). Alternatively, brokerage and investment banks also employ analysts. These analysts hope that their research will generate enough interest in a security that their firm will generate trading commissions or underwriting business. As such, brokerage and investment bank analysts are commonly known as **sell-side analysts** and they often appear to act like salespeople for the stocks that they cover. The recommendations of sell-side analysts are commonly made public. Many investors rely on these recommendations and therefore sell-side analysts are also part of the corporate monitoring system. Our focus here will be on sell-side analysts.

To do his job, a sell-side analyst will look at a firm's operating and financial conditions, the firm's immediate and long-term future prospects, the effectiveness of its management teams, and the general outlook of the industry in which the firm belongs. Most analysts follow a specific industry to gain expertise in a particular sector. Based on their evaluations, analysts will make earnings predictions. Usually they will try to predict the quarterly earnings per share (EPS) numbers. These predictions are useful to investors who rely on these estimates to determine the health of the companies in which they may or may not own stock. For example, many investors use P/E ratios (the market price of a share of stock divided by its annual earnings per share) as an important gauge of a stock's attractiveness as an investment. Some investors like to examine forward-looking P/E ratios. That is, they use a P/E ratio for next year's estimated earnings. Therefore these earnings estimates are important and useful to investors.

Perhaps more important, the analyst also makes trading recommendations to investors. For example, an analyst may suggest buying or selling a particular stock. These recommendations usually boil down to one-word or two-word recommendations such as "hold" or "buy." Further, some recommendations are ambiguous, such as "accumulate," "market perform," and "neutral." Is an "accumulate" recommendation as strong as a "buy" recommendation? Does a "neutral" rating mean "don't sell" and/or "don't buy?" Is a "market perform" rating good or bad? However, while we still see these kinds of recommendations today, there has been a trend toward making analysts' ratings simpler and less vague. Analysts at Goldman Sachs, Lehman Brothers, Merrill Lynch, Morgan Stanley, Prudential, and other places are now using a three-tier rating system (buy, hold, and sell) to eliminate the ambiguity between ratings.[10]

| **EXAMPLE 5.4** | **Analyst Recommendation Causes $369 Billion Decrease in Stock Market Value?** |

On November 1, 2007, Meredith Whitney, an analyst for CIBC, downgraded Citigroup and suggested the bank may have to cut its dividend. Citigroup had recently reported a 57 percent decrease in earnings due to the troubled mortgage industry, but almost every analyst thought Citigroup was large enough and healthy enough to weather the crisis. Her recommendation shocked the market because she was staking her reputation on her claim that Citigroup bank was short on regulatory capital. Citigroup shares fell by 8 percent in response to this report, falling from $41.90 to $38.51. The S&P 500 also tumbled 2.6 percent in trading, which corresponds to a $369 billion decrease in U.S. stock market value.[11]

While it is debatable whether the entire decrease in the S&P 500 was caused by the investment reported, the sharp reaction of both Citigroup stock and the market show the potential influence of analyst recommendations. From a corporate-governance perspective, an analyst such as Whitney can alert shareholders to problems that management has not yet revealed. But she did more than warn about a pending capital shortfall. In an interview she said of the Citigroup CEO, Charles Prince, "[t]here's no question he has to leave." Prince stepped down as CEO three days later. While it is not clear what role, if any, Whitman's downgrade and call for his removal played, the timing of events suggests that they had some impact.

In retrospect, not all analyst recommendations have such an impact. But the example of Whitman and Citigroup shows that analysts' opinions can be important and also that there is a role for analysts in corporate governance.

Analyst recommendations should be timely. For example, if on a particular day an interested investor finds that the analyst's recommendation for a given stock is a buy, then that recommendation should reflect the analyst's most recent opinion. This means the recommendation should be updated frequently. If a news item breaks that could potentially affect an analyst's recommendation, then a revised and updated recommendation should be disseminated immediately. For her or his largest customers, the analyst may even make a phone call. However, a recommendation revision may sometimes have to go through an approval process, which may take a couple of days. Lengthy research reports that are mailed out or personally presented to potential investors may be a bit less timely as well. Nonetheless, many investors rely on analysts for timely advice.

Quality of Analysts' Recommendations

The traditional roles of the analysts are to conduct thorough analyses of their assigned firms in order to make earnings estimates and to make trading recommendations. Further, they should also make timely stock recommendations. Are analysts good at these functions?

With regard to predicting earnings, analysts have consistently been slightly conservative. That is, analysts make earnings predictions that end up being slightly lower than the eventual actual earnings. This result may seem odd, especially given their known penchant for being overly optimistic. These "conservative" earnings predictions are well-known phenomena and involve two factors. First, companies like to meet or beat earnings expectations. Management will then be viewed as being good at their jobs and the company will be viewed as being as good as, or better than, expected.

Second, for analysts to do a good job at predicting earnings, they need information. If analysts have full access to the firms that they follow, such as personal meetings with the CEO or other top executives, then their task becomes easier. Will a CEO be 100 percent cooperative with an analyst who sets the estimate too high? Probably not. In fact, Bill Gates and sales chief Steve Ballmer of Microsoft once purposely criticized their own firm to analysts in order to depress their expectations. Later, on being told by one analyst that they had succeeded in painting a grim picture, Gates and Ballmer gave each other a high-five![12] This being the case, what is the general outcome of these two factors? Analysts make slightly conservative estimates because this is what management wants.[13] This result makes the CEO happy and willing to grant future access to the analyst. The analyst ends up being "off" on an estimate only by a very small margin and is still considered a good analyst. The company will either make or beat the estimate and it will be considered a good company. "Under promise, over deliver" is the name of this game.

The ability of analysts to predict earnings accurately may suffer in the future. Since October 2000, the SEC has prevented firms from divulging privileged information to any analyst. Information that the firm wishes to convey to an analyst must simultaneously be conveyed to the public. This new rule is known as **Regulation Fair Disclosure** or **Reg FD**. The SEC believes it unfair that some investors, through analysts, can gain private information that other investors cannot. The SEC policy creates a level playing field for all investors. For the analyst without privileged access to information, forecasting accuracy is likely to decline. However, forecasts now may possibly become more honest assessments of future earnings. The effect that this SEC regulation will have on analysts' forecasts cannot be predicted but one academic study finds that, since the SEC regulation was passed, forecasts have become less accurate.[14]

What about analysts' ability to recommend stocks? It is unclear whether analysts are good at picking stocks. Older academic studies from the 1970s contended that analysts did not have good stock-picking abilities. However, more recent studies suggest that analysts may have some marginal ability as stock pickers.[15] If you were to buy stocks recommended as a "strong buy" during 1985 to 1996 and hold them until the rating was downgraded, you would have outperformed the market by 4.3 percent per year, not considering transactions costs. Analysts did indeed pick good stocks. However, if transaction costs were considered, you would have underperformed the market by 3.6 percent. While the picks were good, they were not good enough to implement a successful trading strategy.

Perhaps even more revealing is the fact that during the early 2000s, only 2 percent of all stocks carried a sell recommendation,[16] despite the unambiguous bearishness of the markets at that time. Knowledgeable investors, however, know that a neutral or hold recommendation is really a sell signal. Nonetheless, the optimistic phrases used by analysts still promote a bullish attitude and not all investors are knowledgeable.

POTENTIAL CONFLICTS OF INTEREST

Analysts and the Firms They Analyze

Analysts want access to high-quality information. Analysts may be better than the rest of us at assessing the quality of a firm but they also want to be better than the next analyst. To do this analysts will try to obtain as much information as possible. Of course the best source of a firm's information is the firm itself and analysts want to be able to have frank discussions with the firm's management. This situation represents an obvious conflict of interest. How can an analyst who needs access to management turn around and give the firm a bad rating? Would the analyst be able to gain access again?[17] Therefore analysts may have their hands tied. They may want to be objective but their objectivity may prevent them from getting access in the future.

In addition, because analysts typically specialize in a particular industry or two, they get to know the managers in those industries. They may even develop friendships with them. Specializing in a particular industry or sector allows the analyst to become an expert in the different influences and nuances of the industry. However, human nature tends to be optimistic and the circumstance where analysts are friends with the firm's management makes being objective difficult.

Analysts Working at Investment Banks

Analysts can work for an independent research firm, for a brokerage firm, or for the brokerage operation of an investment bank. Most high-profile analysts work for investment banks.

Consider that investment banks have corporate clients that are also firms that their analysts follow. The fees for investment-banking services can easily run into tens of millions of dollars. Will these analysts feel free to make public honest assessments if it would jeopardize those banking fees? If an analyst came out with a negative rating for a stock that his colleagues at the bank had underwritten earlier, then would not the bankers be upset? In addition, if a non-client firm received a negative assessment from an analyst, that firm might not give the analyst's firm any investment-banking business. Analysts and investment bankers at the same bank are not supposed to collude or even influence each other when they are evaluating the same firm. This supposed separation between analysts and bankers within the bank is commonly referred to as a "Chinese Wall." However, analysts who work at investment banks may feel the need to compromise their integrity for the good of their employer.

Academic studies provide evidence consistent with this problem.[18] They find that stocks recommended by analysts who work at investment banks underperform stocks recommended by independent analysts. Also, according to a commentary in *Business Week*, the stock-picking performance of independent analyst firms, such as Callard Asset Management and Alpha Equity Research, outperformed the stock-picking performance of powerhouse investment banks, such as Goldman Sachs, Solomon Smith Barney, Morgan Stanley, and Merrill Lynch.[19] This evidence suggests that conflicts of interest faced by analysts at investment banks may compromise some of their recommendations.

In the late 1990s, analysts more commonly became a part of the investment banking team. When bankers were pitching their services to a firm who wanted to issue securities, an analyst would be there. After the bankers were hired to underwrite the security, they took the analyst on the road show to help market the issue to institutional investors. In this capacity, analysts become salespeople and promoters of the firm instead of objective analyzers of financial performance. As a result, a part of analysts' compensation has increasingly been dependent on the investment-banking business that they can bring to the institution. For example, some star analysts have been receiving 75 percent of their compensation from the investment-banking side of the firm. As such, equity research departments were starting to seem like a support function for investment banking. This trend bucks the traditional view of what analysts do for a living. This partnership between traditionally separate arms of an investing banking firm leads to a serious conflict of interest problem.

| **EXAMPLE 5.5** | **Merrill Lynch: Analysts Versus Investment Banking** |

Merrill Lynch has been criticized for two apparent conflicts between analysts and investment banking in which the firm took the side of the bankers. The charge was that an analyst with a bearish recommendation on a firm was replaced with another analyst who was bullish to obtain investment-banking business from the firm. Specifically, a more optimistic analyst replaced the previous analyst covering Enron in order to gain favor with Enron executives. Early in 1998, analyst John Olson recommended Enron stock with a "neutral" rating. Olson's negative rating and his personal style rubbed Enron executives Jeffrey Skilling and Ken Lay the wrong way. Merrill Lynch bankers complained to their CEO about not gaining any investment-banking business with Enron while Olson rated the firm so poorly. The investment banking business kept going to banks where the analysts rated Enron as a "buy" or better. In August 1998, Olson left Merrill for another company. Merrill then hired Donato Eassey to be the analyst covering Enron. Eassey quickly upgraded Enron to "accumulate." By the end of 1998, Merrill was providing investment-banking services to Enron that would generate $45 million in fees.[20]

In another situation in 1999, Merrill replaced analyst Jeanne Terrile, who covered Tyco International, after Tyco CEO Dennis Kozlowski complained to Merrill CEO David Komansky.[21] The new analyst, Phua Young, promptly upgraded Tyco to a "buy" rating. The next year, Merrill underwrote Tyco's $3 billion stock issue. Both examples illustrate the strong power that public companies have over analysts who work at investment banks and the motivation of banks to be optimistic in order to gain underwriting business.

NEW REGULATIONS   The days of analysts aspiring for a piece of the investment-banking action may be over. Under the impetus of the Sarbanes-Oxley Act, the National Association of Securities Dealers (NASD rule 2711) and the NYSE (rule 472) both put forth new or amended rules that would address the conflict of interest problem in analyst research and opinion. The SEC approved these new regulations in the summer of 2002. Under the new rules, sell-side research analysts cannot

1. be subject to supervision from investment-banking operations;
2. have their compensation tied to investment-banking deals; and
3. promise favorable ratings to lure investment-banking deals.

In addition, when an analyst provides research opinion, she must disclose whether

1. she received compensation based on investment-banking revenue;

2. she holds a position as officer or director in the subject company; or

3. the subject company is a client of the firm.

To resolve SEC allegations of analyst misconduct, Merrill Lynch and nine other investment banking firms[22] settled with the SEC in 2003 and paid a combined $1.4 billion in fines and penalties. They also agreed to new analyst recommendation procedures (including following the new NASD and NYSE rules).[23] This settlement is known as the "Global Analyst Research Settlement." The Settlement between the Wall Street firms, the SEC, NASD, and the NYSE closely mirrors the NASD and NYSE new rules. However, it also mandates some additional rules, such as requiring banking and research departments to be physically separated and that the research department have a dedicated legal department. Also when giving analyst opinion on security issues, the investment bank must also offer at least one independent research "buy," "sell," or "hold" rating alongside their own analysts' ratings.

Have these new rules changed the analyst rating's bias? A recent study investigates this question. The authors examine the number of buy, hold, and sell ratings given by analysts during the approximately two years before and two years after the Settlement.[24] Notice from Panel A of Figure 5.2 that before the new rules, analysts rated 60.7 percent of the firms a "buy." Only 4.2 percent were rated a "sell." After the new regulations, analysts recommended 42.9 percent of rated firms a "buy" and 11.7 percent a "sell." It appears that the new rules have reduced the rating's bias. However, there still appears to be some over optimism.

Panels B and C focus on just those firms that are issuing equity (IPO or SEO). Some of the worst analyst bias appeared in investment-banking firm affiliated analysts touting firms in which the bank was seeking as a client. Panel B shows that nearly 70 percent of these firms were given "buy" ratings and only 2.1 percent were given "sell" ratings. This optimism has weakened somewhat since the new regulations. After the new rules, 49 percent of issuing firms were given a "buy" rating by affiliated analysts and 6.5 percent were given "sell" ratings. Compare these rating's percentages with those given by analysts not affiliated with an investment bank reported in Panel C. Unaffiliated analysts were also optimistic before the rule change, giving a buy rating to 63.9 percent of the firms issuing capital. This changed to 48.0 percent after the rule change.

In addition to this evidence from academic studies, there were reports and cases from industry. After a detailed review of the effect of the research analyst conflict rules, the NASD and NYSE jointly authored a report in 2005.[25] The report concluded that it appeared the rules were helpful in minimizing conflicts and benefitting investors through more "balanced and accurate research." They also made recommendations for amending the rules in a few places where the effectiveness could be improved and the burden on the analyst's firms decreased. Based on this report, the NASD and NYSE published proposed amendments to the rules in January 2007.[26] On the enforcement

PANEL A   ALL RATINGS

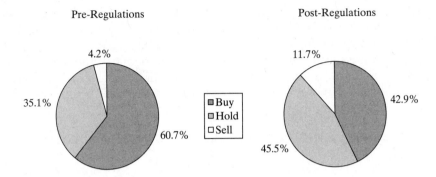

PANEL B   RATINGS ON FIRMS ISSUING EQUITY BY BANKING AFFILIATED ANALYSTS

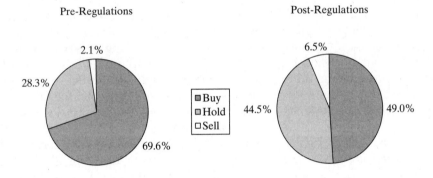

PANEL C   RATINGS ON FIRMS ISSUING EQUITY BY UNAFFILIATED ANALYSTS

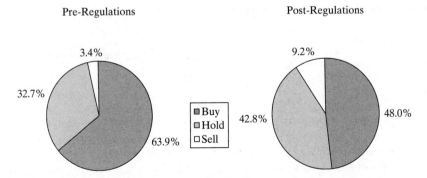

FIGURE 5.2   Distribution of Analyst Recommendations Before and After the Rule Changes

front, the NASD fined the firm Sanford C. Bernstein & Co. and research analyst Brad Hintz a total of $550,000 for violations of the conflict rules. Specifically, Hintz sold shares in Morgan Stanley and Lehman Brothers while he had favorable ratings in place for both firms.[27] Overall it appears that the NASD and NYSE rule changes along with the Settlement have reduced the analyst ratings bias. This is the conclusion of academic studies and an internal review by the NASD and NYSE. Further, the Hintz case shows the exchanges are willing to impose large penalties to enforce the rules, the threat of which should increase compliance.

Summary

Investment banks play a vital role in the American corporate system: They help firms acquire the capital they need to expand business operations. In order to underwrite the securities that firms' issue, the banks become intimately familiar with the operations of those firms. This situation gives them a unique ability to be corporate governance monitors. Capital is a scarce commodity and investment banks should act responsible and bring only high-quality firms and security issues to the public. During the Internet craze, the banks failed in this role.

Analysts evaluate a firm's performance and future prospects and then make trading recommendations. For the most part, they generally seem good at it. However, two conflicts of interests in the system may compromise their objectivity at times. First, analysts want to gather good information through access to the management team of the firm, which requires a good relationship. This might be difficult to do when the analyst thinks the firm's prospects are poor. Second, analysts at investment banks have been rewarded for luring investment-banking business to their employer. Consequently they were encouraged to be bullish on the firms they follow to keep both potential and current investment-banking clients happy. Rules aimed at limiting these conflicts of interest have been passed. The SEC has also mandated that analysts certify that the opinions they express reflect their personal views. Some of these rules already seem to be working.

WEB Info about Investment Banks and Analysts

CFA Institute
www.cfainstitute.org

SEC Securities Analysts page
www.sec.gov/divisions/marketreg/securitiesanalysts.htm.com

Review Questions

1. What are the main ways an investment bank offers a security for sale?
2. Discuss why and how investment banks can be considered potentially effective monitors of corporations.
3. Why does it seem like IPOs are underpriced in the offering?
4. Describe how investment banks contributed to the investor confidence crisis in the early 2000s.
5. What is the financial analyst's function? How might analysts be important participants in the monitoring of the firm?
6. Are analysts good at evaluating firms? Elaborate.
7. Name and describe the conflicts of interest analysts face.

Discussion Questions

1. Provide some ideas on how investment banks can be made more conservative with regard to taking firms public.
2. When investment banks take firms public, they have in effect two clients: the going-public firm and the investors who buy the new shares. Which client do you think the bank is mostly concerned with? Why might they be equally concerned with both?
3. How would you standardize analysts recommendations?
4. Some people think that fewer recommendations, such as simply recommending buy, hold, or sell, is the best system. What do you think is the rationale behind this view? Do you agree?
5. What is your overall view of the sell-side analyst's profession? Given that the accuracy of their recommendations does not directly lead profits for the analyst's firm, how do you think sell-side analysts should be compensated?

Exercises

1. Find a firm that recently conducted an IPO. What are the details of the offering? Which investment bank(s) underwrote the offering? How successful was the offering from the perspectives of the firm, the banks, and investors? Do you think the firm was ready to conduct an IPO? Explain.
2. Find a firm that is scheduled to conduct an IPO in the near future. What types of information are provided to the interested investor? Describe how the information is useful in making a buy versus no-buy decision.
3. Provide a status report on the current state of investment banking. Are they underwriting fewer IPOs and SEOs? If so, then are they in danger of getting into financial trouble?
4. Go to the AIMR Web site (*www.aimr.org*). Identify and describe the ideas that AIMR proposes to improve investor confidence in analyst recommendations. Evaluate the potential of these ideas for resolving the problems.
5. Describe the actions of Jack Grubman, former analyst for Salomon Smith Barney, Mary Meeker, the Internet analyst at Morgan Stanley, and Henry Blodgett, former analyst at Merrill Lynch, that has led many to criticize analysts.
6. Pick a company and report its analysts' recommendations for trading and their predictions of future earnings. Pick another company in the same industry and do the same. Does one company have a wider dispersion of analysts' recommendations and predictions? Why do you think this is?

Exercises for Non-U.S. Students

1. Describe the investment-banking business in your country. Do you think it does a good job of bringing only good firms public? Explain your opinion.
2. Describe the nature of analysts in your country. Are securities analysts important in your country? How are they compensated?
3. To what extent are the problems outlined in this chapter pertinent to your country? Explain.

Endnotes

1. All filings by public companies since about 1996 are available publicly through the EDGAR search retrieval system on the SEC Web site (*www.sec.gov*).

2. Jay Ritter and Ivo Welch, "A Review of IPO Activity, Pricing, and Allocations," *Journal of Finance* 57, no. 4 (2002):1795–1828, and updated data available on Jay Ritter's Web site (*http://bear.cba.ufl.edu/ritter/*).

3. Alexander Ljungqvist and William Wilhelm, "IPO Allocations: Discriminatory or Discretionary?" *Journal of Financial Economics* 65, no. 2 (2002): 167–201.

4. Andrew Ross Sorkin, "Just Who Brought Those Duds to Market?" *New York Times*, April 15, 2001, 3.1.

5. Peter Elstrom, "The Great Internet Money Game," *Business Week* (April 26, 2001):16.

6. Matthew Goldstein, "Bear Stearns' Subprime IPO," *Business Week* (May 11, 2007).

7. Peter Fusaro and Ross Miller, *What Went Wrong at Enron* (Hoboken, NJ: John Wiley and Sons, 2002).

8. Peter Behr and April Witt, "Visionary's Dream Led to Risky Business," *Washington Post*, July 28, 2002, A1.

9. Jathon Sapsford and Paul Beckett, "Citigroup, J.P. Morgan Marketed Enron-Type Deals to Other Firms," *Wall Street Journal*, July 23, 2002, C13.

10. Stephanie Smith, "How are Analysts Changing?" *Money* (September 2002):89.

11. Nick Baker and Michael Patterson, "CIBC's Whitney Spurred Market Swoon on Citigroup Call," *Bloomberg.com*, November 2, 2007.

12. Justin Fox, "Learn to Manage Your Earnings and Wall Street Will Love You," *Fortune* (March 31, 1997): 77–80.

13. Many academic articles have cited this phenomenon. For example, see Francois Degeorge, Jayendu Patel, and Richard J. Zeckhauser, "Earnings Management to Exceed Thresholds," *Journal of Business* 72 (1999).

14. Anup Agrawal, Sahiba Chadha, and Mark Chen, "Who Is Afraid of Reg FD? The Behavior and Performance of Sell-Side Analysts Following the SEC's Fair Disclosure Rules," *Journal of Business* 79 (2006).

15. Brad Barber, Reuven Lehavey, Maureen McNichols, and Brett Trueman, "Can Investors Profit from the Prophets? Security Analyst Recommendations and Stock Returns," *Journal of Finance* 56 (2001):531–563.

16. Marcia Vickers and Mike France, "How Corrupt Is Wall Street?" *Business Week* (May 13, 2002): 37–42.

17. One analyst said that without access, it becomes difficult to make quality stock assessments, akin to playing basketball with one hand tied behind your back (Marcia Vickers and Mike France, "How Corrupt Is Wall Street?" *Business Week* (May 13, 2002):37–42).

18. Roni Michaely and Kent L. Womack, "Conflict of Interest and the Credibility of Underwriter Analyst Recommendations," *Review of Financial Studies* 12 (1999):653–686. Brad Barber, Reuven Lehavy, and Brett Trueman, "Comparing the Stock Recommendation Performance of Investment Banks and Independent Research Firms," unpublished working paper at the University of Michigan.

19. Emily Thornton, "Research Should Pay Its Own Way," *Business Week* (June 3, 2002): 72.

20. Olson, Eassey, and Merrill Lynch all deny that anything inappropriate occurred. Indeed, Eassey was one of the few analysts to downgrade Enron when its troubles began to become public. See Richard Oppel, "Merrill Replaced Research Analyst Who Upset Enron," *New York Times*, July 30, 2002, 1.1.

21. Charles Gasparino, "Merrill Replaced Its Tyco Analyst After Meeting," *Wall Street Journal*, September 17, 2002, C1.

22. The firms were Citigroup Inc.; Credit Suisse First Boston Corp.; Morgan Stanley; Goldman Sachs Group Inc.; Lehman Brothers Holdings Inc.; Bear Stearns Cos.; U.S. Bancorp Piper Jaffray, a unit of U.S. Bancorp; JP Morgan Chase & Co.; UBS AG and Merrill Lynch & Co. Former Merrill analyst Henry Blodget and former Citigroup analyst Jack Grubman also reached settlements with the SEC.

23. Colleen DeBaise, "Analyst Research Settlement with SEC Gets Final Approval," *Wall Street Journal*, (November 3, 2003): C.12.

24. The data is from Ohad Kadan, Leonardo Madureira, Rong Wang, and Tzachi Zach, "Conflicts of Interest and Stock Recommendations: The Effects of the Global Settlement and Recent Regulations," Washington University working paper (July 2005).

25. Joint Report by NASD and the NYSE On the Operations and Effectiveness of the Research Analyst Conflict of Interest Rules, December 2005.

26. *www.sec.gov/rules/sro/nyse/2007/34-55072.pdf.*

27. FINRA News Release, "Sanford C. Bernstein & Co., Research Analyst Brad Hintz Fined $550,000 for Violations of Research Analyst Conflict of Interest Rules," February 8, 2006.

Creditors and Credit Rating Agencies

So far we have discussed corporate governance as if only stockholders should care about it. However, those who lend money to the firm (i.e., creditors) are also important investors in the firm. Therefore, lenders also care about corporate governance because a well run firm is more likely to have the cash to pay off its loans. In general, there are two kinds of lenders, institutional lenders such as a commercial bank, pension or insurance company and individual investors. While both kinds of lenders have the same corporate governance concerns, the institutional lender typically makes a larger loan and, hence, has more incentive to monitor the actions of the firm.

Creditors can trade their claims just as stockholders can. For example, bondholders can sell their bonds to other investors (and banks can sell their loans too, but primarily to other institutions). If firms suffer from poor corporate governance, then the value of their bonds might decline just like the value of the stock. If a firm collapses from poor corporate governance then lenders may get back only pennies on the dollar of their loan.

While a bank may find it worthwhile to monitor the firm that they lend to (because millions, even billions, could be at stake), individual bondholders may not have the resources to do so. Fortunately debt, in and of itself, could be a governance mechanism (we will explain this in more detail soon). Further, there are also credit rating agencies that rate the safety level of corporate debt. As such, they can provide important information to potential bond investors. Therefore the existence of corporate debt creates three important corporate system monitors or devices:

1. monitoring by institutional lenders;
2. debt, in and of itself, can be a disciplinary mechanism; and
3. monitoring and debt ratings by credit agencies.

DEBT AS A DISCIPLINARY MECHANISM

When a firm has debt, it usually has to make promised interest payments. If the firm misses an interest payment, the lender can use the court system to obtain a legal judgment that the company must pay or face bankruptcy. On the other hand, the firm's stockholders are not promised anything. Even though a firm can pay a dividend to its stockholders at the discretion of its board of directors, it is not legally obligated to do so. Because interest payments represent fixed obligations of the firm, debt actually imposes discipline on to the firm's management. That is, the firm's management has to generate enough revenue to cover the firm's interest expense. If the managers fail to do this, then they will end up in bankruptcy court where they could lose control of the firm to a creditor.

While interest expense represents an important revenue hurdle that managers have to overcome and is thus a potentially effective motivator for management, it also discourages superfluous spending by management. That is, it limits managerial discretion. Of course, having to make large interest payments can also restrict a manager's flexibility to make value-enhancing capital expenditures when opportunities "suddenly" arise. Therefore, the use of debt to discipline firms may be limited primarily to mature firms.

Finally, in addition to a promised interest payment, other explicit **covenants** (these are rules, promises, and/or restrictions that the borrower agrees to legally adhere to) can be written into the debt contracts, such as guarantees by the borrower to protect its collateral value. The breaking of any covenant usually triggers a requirement that the firm repay the loan principal immediately. As most firms that violate covenants are in bad financial shape, there is not enough cash to repay the loan and the firm ends up in bankruptcy court where a judge can transfer control of the firm from management to creditors. Accordingly, because creditor rights are usually more explicit and comprehensive than shareholder rights, debt potentially provides better protection to investors than equity.[1]

EXAMPLE 6.1   Do Firms Have Enough Debt?

Some firms have significantly more annual earnings than annual interest expense. A times-interest-earned (TIE) ratio is usually measured as earnings before interest and taxes (EBIT) divided by total interest expense. For example, the TIE ratio for IBM is over 80. That is, IBM can pay its annual interest expense more than 80 times over. On the one hand, a high TIE ratio seems great but on the other hand, it could signal that the firm has low capital investment expenses for future growth opportunities. This latter scenario is not necessarily bad because firms eventually enter a maturity stage in their lifecycle. But if the firm is not paying dividends (or enough dividends) then the firm could be retaining and holding on to too much cash. Cash is not the most productive asset and sometimes cash can be spent on bad projects such as extra perks for management, which is not good for shareholders.

One remedy for this problem would be to use excess cash to repurchase stock or raise dividends and then to borrow funds to finance its projects. The increase in interest expense may lead to a reduction in net income but with fewer shares outstanding the net income per share could be higher as a result of this capital structure change. In addition, because debt has a tax advantage as interest is paid before taxes, increases in debt, in and of itself, should increase the value of the firm. IBM has a TIE ratio of over 80 but less than 15 percent of its total assets are financed with long-term debt and meanwhile, it holds billions in cash and cash equivalents and it pays billions in taxes. After much criticism from investors and shareholders, at the end of 2004, Microsoft, a firm also sitting on billions in excess cash, paid a special dividend of $3 per share, reducing its cash position by $32 billion.

INSTITUTIONAL LENDERS AS CORPORATE MONITORS

Banks will of course monitor firms that they lend to. Sometimes a firm will develop a long-term relationship with a bank. Relationship banking might be beneficial to the borrowing firm on at least two counts. First, the firm might be able to get a favorable interest rate from its bank. Second, the firm may feel it will be easier to renegotiate debt contracts (if necessary) with a single lender (i.e., the bank) than with disperse lenders (i.e., bondholders).

However, getting favorable interest rates from banks often entails the firm having to expose private information to the bank. For example, a firm may wish to borrow billions of dollars to embark on a new project. The firm could issue *public* debt (i.e., bonds) but may find that the interest rate (i.e., coupon rate) is too high for one reason or another (e.g., the firm could already have a lot of debt, the firm could have little collateral assets, etc.). This firm could opt to borrow from a bank or insurance company, but to get a favorable rate it may have to reveal intimate details of its project to prove that it is worthy of a low interest rate. Further, the firm may have to agree to numerous covenants to get the favorable bank rate. As a single lender, it is easy for a bank to enforce covenants. Therefore the bank may end up having too much power over its borrowers.[2]

Why Didn't Lenders Raise a Red Flag during the Recent Corporate Scandals?

A firm's creditors and stock holders are often *both* viewed as investors but in reality creditors are literally lending to stockholders, thus putting these two investors on opposite sides of the credit claim. Therefore, these two investors do not necessarily share the same objectives for the firm.

Stockholders, as owners of the firm, are entitled to the firm's net income *after* all expenses are paid. As the interest owed creditors is a business expense, stockholders can only claim the income of the firm after the creditors are paid. In other words, creditors' claims have seniority over equity holders' claims. This by itself can cause divergent incentives between the two claimants. Say, for example, the firm has to choose between a risky project with an uncertain high payoff and a safe project with a more certain marginal payoff. The return on the safe project may barely leave anything left over to stockholders once creditors are paid. Therefore stockholders may favor the risky project over the safe one. Creditors, on the other hand, might be equally indifferent to both projects if both of them can cover the firm's interest expense. Because creditors get their returns first, they may have less incentive to monitor managerial behavior than stockholders.

Of course there is the possibility that managerial risk-taking may be so excessive that interest payments and principle repayment cannot be made. If such a case occurs, creditors can legally force the firm into bankruptcy where the firm may be forced to liquidate its assets to recover at least some of their investment.

In the recent scandals, creditors may not have become involved in monitoring management because the creditors hold a senior claim on the assets and income of the firm, as compared to stockholders. If management is wasting cash and making bad decisions, this does not affect the creditors so long as the firm remains healthy enough to pay its interest and principal as they become due. Hence, creditors may be less active in monitoring than stockholders.

Do Creditors Influence Corporate Governance in Bankruptcy?

If the creditors are not paid, they usually rely on the legal system to force payment. If a firm has more liabilities than assets, it is insolvent and there is not enough for all creditors to collect what is owed. At this point, the firm enters the bankruptcy system where a court decides who is paid, how much and whether the firm survives. Most firms voluntarily declare bankruptcy when it becomes clear that bankruptcy is inevitable. An involuntary bankruptcy occurs when creditors petition a bankruptcy court and the court agrees the firm is insolvent.

Bankruptcy is a complicated process, but the goal is to fairly settle the claims of all of the creditors depending on the priority of their loans and the security interests they hold. There are two general types: Chapter 7 and Chapter 11. In Chapter 7, the firm is liquidated which means all assets are sold and the proceeds divided among the creditors. More common, however, is Chapter 11, where the firm is allowed to restructure its liabilities and perhaps emerge from bankruptcy as a viable firm. Chapter 11 is more common because there are many stakeholders, such as employees, who prefer that firms stay in business. Accordingly, there is pressure on lawmakers to set up bankruptcy rules to give companies a chance to restructure their liabilities and start fresh.

The usual result when a company successfully emerges from Chapter 11 bankruptcy is that stockholders of the old firm completely lose their investment and control. Some former creditors emerge as the new stockholders.[3] This occurs because there is not enough value in the company to pay all the creditors, so as part of the negotiations in bankruptcy court, creditors who are not paid in full agree to take equity in the reorganized firm. As the former stockholders receive value only after the creditors are paid, there is nothing left for them and their stock becomes worthless. Hence, when a company emerges from bankruptcy and starts trading in the stock market, the shares being traded are not the same shares as the pre-bankruptcy shares. Instead, they are new shares that were initially issued to pre-bankruptcy creditors as part of the bankruptcy settlement.

A key feature of the bankruptcy process is that all decisions are presided over by a bankruptcy judge who has a lot of discretion. Creditors often ask the judge to take actions such as replacing management of the firm, but this will only happen if the judge agrees with the reasoning. Accordingly, although creditors have a strong position in bankruptcy because they are owed money and have the right to approve any settlement, they do not have the power to unilaterally dictate terms to the judge. Instead, the whims of the judge and the vagaries of a complicated set of bankruptcy laws may restrict the ability of creditors to make changes in corporate governance. For example, the bankruptcy rules include an "exclusivity" rule that allows the bankrupt company the sole right to propose a restructuring for the first 18 months of the bankruptcy. This rule prevents creditors from presenting competing proposals that may make more economic sense. Why allow management of a company that was driven to bankruptcy to be the only party proposing how the company could restructure? Large investors have suggested this rule limits the power of creditors to quickly make changes and shorten the bankruptcy process.[4]

CREDIT RATING AGENCIES

Just as analysts help rate stocks for potential stock investors, credit rating agencies rate bonds for potential bond investors. With these ratings, credit rating agencies provide information to investors on the likelihood of a company making its required payments of interest and principal. As bonds are essentially long-term loans, bond investors want to know whether the firm will be around for the ten or more years the bonds are outstanding.

The safety level of a bond is very important to those who choose fixed-income investments. The best return a bondholder can receive is both interest payments during the term of the bond and the principal upon maturity of the bond. Therefore bondholders focus on safety. How do you know if a firm's debt is safe or risky? Most corporate bonds are given a safety rating by at least one of the credit rating agencies. The rating process involves the company conducting a credit analysis and giving the bond a grade which informs investors about the risk of a bond.

A Brief Historical Perspective

A brief history will help the understanding of how the credit industry works and of its importance. John Moody invented credit ratings in 1909 when he published a manual of ratings on 200 railroads and their securities.[5] He made his money by charging investors for the manual. By 1916, The Standard Company, the predecessor to Standard & Poor's, started rating bonds and Fitch started rating bonds in 1920. By the 1970s, photocopy equipment was so prevalent that many investors obtained ratings without paying for the published books. As there was a demand for bond ratings due to requirements of the banking system (discussed in the next paragraph) and it was no longer profitable to charge potential bond investors, rating companies changed their business model to charging bond issuers fees to rate their bonds. As a bond rating is required to sell to many investors, firms were forced to pay this fee if they wanted to reach a large portion of potential bond investors. Accordingly, bond ratings are now freely distributed to investors once they are determined by the rating company.

After the stock market crash of 1929 and the Great Depression, the government looked for ways to restore confidence in the banking system. The securities acts of 1933 and 1934 went a long way toward increasing regulation of the banking and securities industries. However, in 1936, the government expanded the role of credit ratings by requiring that commercial banks only hold high-quality debt. Specifically, the Comptroller of the Currency decreed that banks could only own "investment-grade" bonds (this and other categories of ratings are illustrated in the next section). Because one large and influential type of investor (commercial banks) needed credit ratings on debt instruments in order to buy them, all bond issuers wanted to be rated. And the bond issuer is the one who pays for the rating. This applies to commercial firms, state and local governments, and even foreign governments.

While the credit rating helps investors understand the riskiness of a bond issue, the system has a built-in conflict because the company pays the bill for its own rating. A company planning a bond issue could discuss it with several credit agencies and see which one would give them the highest grade. This potential for "shopping" for ratings can lead to an issuer receiving too high a rating. Why would this matter? A high quality rating for a company means that they can offer bonds at a low interest rate and still easily sell them all. A lower quality rating would require offering the bonds at a higher interest rate and it would cost the firm millions of dollars more in interest payments. So there is a concern that unscrupulous rating companies might sell high ratings to firms willing to pay higher fees for them.

After a scandal in 1975 where ratings companies did not foresee the huge default of Penn Central Corporation on its bonds, the SEC designated three ratings agencies as the only ones satisfying rating regulations. The three anointed agencies, called **Nationally Recognized Statistical Rating Organizations (NRSROs),** were Moody's, Standard & Poor's, and Fitch. In response to demands from other rating companies to achieve NRSRO status, the SEC ruled on requests on an individual basis, which resulted in new companies added to the list. In 2006, the "Rating Reform Act of 2006" standardized the process for granting NRSRO recognition.[6] Additional NRSRO companies were added to the list since then, with the total reaching 10 approved NRSROs by the end of 2008. Nevertheless, Moody's and Standard & Poor's remain by far the biggest players in this industry.

There is some debate whether the additional firms will increase competition and make the ratings agencies more responsive to changes in the risk of the companies they monitor. The situation of a small number of firms in an industry is called an oligopoly. Limiting the number of ratings companies under SEC rules protect the listed firms from further competition by preventing any other firms from joining the industry. This potentially has the effect of keeping fees high and keeping small credit agencies out of the market. Small credit agencies that are not NRSROs exist but they cannot tap into the fees companies are willing to pay for NRSRO designation. Instead, they must survive on the fees investors will pay for the evaluations. Finding substantial subscribers is difficult when the NRSROs provide free ratings. Under the regulations issued to implement the new law, the SEC is charged with applying the rules consistently so that small companies can meet the designation.[7] The result is that some small ratings companies have achieved NRSRO status and are now competing directly with Standard & Poor's and Moody's. Whether this results in a decrease in the 30–50 percent estimated profit margin earned by the big players Moody's and Standard & Poor's is an unresolved question. One effect that is already noticeable is that the "issuer pays" rule is challenged by Egan-Jones, a new NRSRO. Egan-Jones does not charge issuers a fee to rate companies but instead charges its customers (primarily institutional investors) to access its rankings.[8]

The Ratings

To assess the credit worthiness of companies, the credit agencies employ financial analysts who examine the firms' financial positions, business plans, and strategies. This means that the analysts carefully review public financial statements issued by the companies. To assist in their investigations, the SEC has granted the agencies an exemption from disclosure rules so that companies can reveal nonpublic or sensitive information to the agencies in confidence. Companies have no obligation to reveal special information but they often do so to convince the agencies that their debt issues should be rated highly. Credit analysts for the NRSRO can often question CEOs and other top executives directly when conducting reviews because of the importance of credit ratings.

The rating systems of Moody's and Standard & Poor's are shown in Example 6.2. Notice that the two ratings agencies have similar systems.[9] Also, both agencies can partition the ratings further. Moody's includes 1, 2, or 3 after the rating to show that the firm falls near the bottom, middle, or top of the scale within the category. Standard & Poor's uses a minus (–) or plus (+) sign. Consider two companies that want to borrow $1 billion by issuing bonds. The rating company rates the first company in the "high quality" category. This firm will have to pay 6.9 percent (or $69 million) in interest every year. The second firm is rated "non-investment grade" and would have to pay $99 million annually. These amounts differ substantially. Riskier companies pay higher interest.

If a company becomes financially stronger over time, then the bond rating will also improve. Therefore, the interest rate demanded by investors will fall, as illustrated in Example 6.2. When interest rates fall, bond prices rise. Consequently, if a firm becomes safer, then the price of its bonds will increase, which is what bondholders want. Alternatively, if the firm becomes riskier, then bond prices fall. The worst-case scenario for a bondholder is for the issuing company to default on the bonds and file for bankruptcy protection. Bondholders typically receive only a small portion of their principal back if a firm defaults.

The ratings that credit agencies issue have historically been good predictors of the default potential of a debt issuer. Only 0.79 percent of firms rated at the highest level (best quality) default.[10] This percentage increases to only 1.14 percent for issuers rated as high quality. However, the increase in the default rate substantially increases to 26.43 percent in the non-investment-grade bonds and 52.50 percent in the CCC category.

EXAMPLE 6.2   Ratings of Bond Safety and Example Bond Yields

	Moody's Rating	Standard & Poor's Rating	Example Bond Yield, %
Best Quality	Aaa	AAA	6.4
High Quality	Aa	AA	6.9
Upper-Medium Grade	A	A	7.1
Medium Grade	Baa	BBB	7.8
Non-Investment Grade	Ba	BB	9.9
Highly Speculative	B	B	10.5
Defaulted or Close to It	Caa to C	CCC to D	20 to 90

When a firm begins to struggle financially, credit agencies downgrade the ratings on its securities. A bond issue rated AAA– might be downgraded to AA+ or even AA. If the business operations or cash position of the firm continues to decline, the rating could fall further. Each downgrade signals to investors that the bonds are becoming riskier. In response, the price of the bonds declines and investors experience a capital loss. The term "investment grade" in the regulations is interpreted as ratings of BBB– or higher. If a bond slips to BB+ or lower, it is not considered investment grade. In fact, the popular term for non-investment-grade bonds is "junk bonds." For additional protection of a bondholder's principal, many modern debt offerings include a rule (or covenant) that requires the company to increase the interest payment made on the bonds if the rating slips to junk status. Some bond covenants require the company to pay back the principal if the rating slips to junk. While this sounds like a good idea for bond investors, in practice it often triggers the very bankruptcy filing that bondholders try to avoid. A firm's debt is downgraded to junk-bond status because the company is having some financial difficulty. But this downgrade triggers higher interest payments or even an immediate demand for payment on hundreds of millions of dollars in principal. Hence, the very covenant rules that try to protect the interest of bondholders can actually drive a company toward insolvency.

Recent Research

Are credit rating agencies the best sources of information as to the probability of financial distress? Recent research examines the role of securities analysts at large brokerages in reviewing outstanding debt issues and making recommendations to investors as to credit quality. Professors Johnston, Markov, and Ramnath find that there is an active market in producing brokerage reports that are similar to those produced by credit rating agencies. The authors collect a sample of 5,920 debt reports issued by 15 brokerages over the years 1999 to 2004. These reports were written to convey information to the brokerage firms' customers who are investors in bonds. Many brokerage reports offer opinions as to the credit rating and expected changes to the credit rating. Given that these reports appear duplicative of the credit rating agency reports, the authors test whether there is additional information conveyed to investors from brokerage reports to justify the expense of producing them.

Their results show that analysts are more likely to follow the debt of firms with a higher probability of financial distress, larger outstanding debt and higher debt-to-equity ratios. In other words, it is less likely a brokerage firm will spend resources to produce an analysis of a small amount of debt issued by a stable company. Instead, the real question that seems to be of value to investors is the risk of bonds issued by a firm with higher probability of default.

In comparing analyst reports with those of credit rating agencies for the same bonds, the authors find that the brokerage reports appear more timely with respect to downgrades in credit quality. When the brokerage analyst publishes a report less than 30 days before the credit rating agency downgrades a bond, the authors find a statistically significant decrease in firm value in response to the brokerage report. This suggests there is real information conveyed in the brokerage report and that the brokerage report is more timely than the credit agency report. In contrast, for brokerage reports issued less than 30 days after a credit agency downgrade, there was no significant effect on stock price. So once the credit agency has acted, the brokerage report did not provide additional information to the market.

Rick Johnston, Stanmir Markov, and Sundaresh Ramnath, "Sell-Side Debt Analysts," *Journal of Accounting and Economics*, Vol. 47 no. 1-2 (2009): 91–107.

Criticisms

The biggest criticisms of credit rating agencies is that they improperly set the initial rating and are then slow to downgrade the rating once a company gets in financial trouble. While the total record of credit agencies is fairly accurate, they have made some dramatic mistakes. A questionable call by the credit agencies occurred with the issuance of WorldCom bonds in May 2001. WorldCom issued an American record $11.9 billion of bonds, of which $10.1 billion was new financing. Standard & Poor's rated WorldCom and the massive debt issue investment grade, with a BBB+; Moody's rated it A3.[11] The massive offering by WorldCom should have come with a robust analysis by the investment banks as the underwriters and by the credit rating agencies.

One year later, in May 2002, the credit agencies downgraded WorldCom debt to junk-bond status. The rationale behind the downgrade was that WorldCom's total debt of $30 billion was too high.[12] Why were the agencies unconcerned with the debt level the previous year when WorldCom increased its debt by 50 percent with the massive bond issue? The agencies' initial seal of approval on the giant bond issue and the company downgrade one year later that was based on an issue that was known all along seems hard to believe. The high rating by the agencies allowed WorldCom to borrow that much money in the first place. The next month, on June 25, 2002, WorldCom disclosed that it had improperly booked $3.8 billion as capital investments instead of operating expenses over the previous five quarters. It found several more billion in accounting fraud over the next couple of months.

A more recent scandal involving the credit rating agencies involves the artificially high ratings given to pools of mortgage debt that were packaged into bonds. Called "securitization," the repacking of individual bonds into large pools allows mortgage lenders to sell the mortgages they funded to third-party investors. With the proceeds of this sale, the mortgage lender can then make additional mortgage loans, which may again be repackaged into pools, and so on. The problem arose in when lenders increased the volume of mortgages they issued throughout the mid-2000s to the point where, in 2006, more than $2.5 trillion was loaned to buy houses.[13] Where did the lenders find a record number of borrowers? Only by relaxing lending standards such as the required down payment, credit history, and income requirements. In 2006, "NINJA" loans or "no income, no job, no assets" loans were common where the lender allowed borrowers to simply state their income and assets without requiring verification. Borrowers with bad credit were also welcomed with "subprime" mortgages that had higher interest rates. Of course, the effect of this imprudent lending is that, once housing prices started falling, mortgage defaults skyrocketed in 2007, triggering the financial collapse of 2007–2008.

What was the role of the credit rating agencies in this financial meltdown? Each of the pools of mortgages was rated by a credit rating agency before it was sold to investors. Many mortgage backed pools were rated as AAA, the highest rating even if the mortgages that comprised this pool were subprime mortgages. The reason for this high rating was the there was a diversification effect from pooling mortgages so that some defaults on individual mortgages did not affect the whole pool significantly. Using historical patterns and simulation analysis, credit rating agencies consistently found ways to rate mortgage backed securities as AAA even though they paid more interest than other AAA obligations. The high yields on AAA rated mortgage backed securities attracted investors and created a demand for more mortgage-backed products. Through what is called "financial engineering," derivative mortgage instruments called collateralized debt obligations (CDOs) were created that invested not in mortgages, but in mortgage backed bonds. The CDO issuer would buy up lower rated mortgage-backed securities and pool them together in a CDO that the credit rating agency would bless with an AAA rating.

Overall, events have shown that the credit rating agencies severely understated the risk of mortgage backed bonds and CDOs. Beginning in mid-2007, the agencies downgraded tens of billions in debt, with some ratings falling from AAA to B.[14] How can a bond fall from "Best quality" to "Highly speculative" overnight? Similar to the Enron example below, the credit rating agencies did not do a very good job of predicting credit risk on a timely basis.

EXAMPLE 6.3   Enron's Credit Rating

The price of a share of Enron stock was $90 in August 2000 but by April 2001 the stock price had fallen to $60 per share. In the late summer, the price continued to fall and reached less than $40 per share. Even in November 2001, just before Enron declared bankruptcy, the stock had declined to less than $5 per share. This decline in Enron's stock price should have been a huge warning that something was drastically amiss. As it turned out, the credit agencies might have been more enablers than watchdogs.

The investment banks had raised capital for Enron's offshore partnerships, which Enron used to falsify loans as profits. The banks had invested hundreds of millions of dollars of their own money in Enron and its associated partnerships. The banks knew that if Enron filed for bankruptcy protection, their losses would be enormous. The banks also knew that if the credit rating agencies were to downgrade Enron to non-investment grade status, at least $3.9 billion in debt repayment would immediately be required. Enron would be forced to declare itself insolvent.

On November 8, 2001, the news about the partnerships and the massive losses became public. The stock price went down to less than $10 per share. The banks needed to act quickly or take massive losses; they wanted the credit agencies to hold off on their downgrade while they looked for new capital with which to save Enron.

Apparently the credit agencies delayed in downgrading Enron to non-investment grade. At first they merely downgraded the firm to the lowest levels of investment-grade ratings. Because companies seek a rating on debt they issue and investment banks help them issue the debt securities, banks and credit agencies frequently work together. The bankers may have used this relationship to convince the credit agencies to give them some time to save Enron.

To locate a buyer, investment banks Merrill Lynch and JP Morgan looked across town from the headquarters of Enron and found Dynegy. Enron and Dynegy executives began merger negotiations in November 2001. If they could agree, Dynegy would infuse Enron with $1.5 billion of cash to tide them over until the final merger could take place. The credit rating agencies knew that if the merger did not take place, Enron would be in deep financial trouble. Yet instead of communicating this enormous risk to bondholders via a downgrade to junk-bond status, the agencies waited. Given what the agencies knew, this situation was a large gamble for bondholders, like flipping a coin. Heads the merger goes through and the financial situation improves, tails it does not and Enron probably goes into bankruptcy. Investors might take this risk in speculative stocks but not in investment-grade bonds. The stock price had fallen to less than $5 per share. The credit rating agencies failed to warn investors how risky the situation had become.

On November 26, the Enron merger with Dynegy was dead. Enron was still discovering how vast the partnership problems were becoming. The designated credit rating agencies downgraded Enron to junk-bond status on November 28. Enron's stock price fell to $0.61 per share. On December 2, 2001, Enron filed for bankruptcy protection. Bondholders waited in line at bankruptcy court with other creditors and hoped to regain some of their principal.

Credit agencies are not blameless in the corporate scandals of 2001 and 2002 or the financial crisis of 2007–2008. Indeed, their special relationships with companies allowed them to obtain private information that other monitors, such as independent analysts, might not receive. Of the outside monitors, credit rating agencies might have been in the best position to detect corporate fraud and warn investors. Yet in some cases these groups were one of the last to respond. And they may have given improperly high ratings to begin with. When NRSRO-designated agencies do make mistakes, they often claim the company executives lied to them. However, the agency's job is to validate the information they receive and then make conclusions based on its own analysis. What purpose do agencies serve as independent monitors if they simply follow the lead of the company executives?

As noted above, another criticism of credit agencies is that their basic revenue has a built-in conflict because companies pay to have their own bonds rated. This creates a situation where the company may tell an agency they will take their business to a competitor unless they receive the rating they want. A related criticism is that credit agencies have started to enter the consulting business. An example is the CDOs above, where the issuer works closely with the credit agency to ensure the CDO bonds have the desired ratings. If the credit agency is earning lucrative consulting fees, then it might not be able to provide unbiased analysis of the firm's financial position. To show the extent of this conflict of interest, over the period from 2002–2007, the revenues of the top three credit rating agencies more than doubled, primarily due to the growth in mortgage-backed bonds and CDOs.[15]

A second criticism is that courts have ruled that the ratings produced by credit rating agencies are opinions that are protected speech covered by the First Amendment. In other words, if you buy a bond based on a faulty rating, you will not be able to successfully sue the credit rating agency because they will claim the rating was only their opinion.[16] And we are all entitled to our opinions, no matter how wrong they might be. Accordingly, when disgruntled companies or investors have sued the credit agencies, the agencies have been successful in using the free speech protection as a defense. Even in the Enron case discussed above, the lawsuits against the agencies were dismissed.

The combination of protection from new competitors and protection in court against claims due to bad ratings, make credit agencies nearly invincible. Even though they did so poorly in rating mortgage based bonds from 2002 to 2006, there may be no consequences. That is, market forces (such as competition) and the court system may have difficulty disciplining them. On the other hand, the fact that the ratings agencies were heavily involved in the creation of CDOs as consultants, a court may look beyond the "opinion" defense. Also, the role of credit rating agencies in the financial crisis of 2007–2008 was the subject of a Congressional hearing in October 2008, which may lead to changes in the law that currently protects them to a great degree.[17]

INTERNATIONAL PERSPECTIVE

Japan's Main Bank System

In most countries, bank debt is the primary form of corporate borrowing and even the primary source of new financing. Japan is an interesting case (and Germany is similar to the Japanese case in many respects). Most developing markets rely on bank debt due to the lack of a sophisticated public debt market, but Japan and German are developed markets whose firms rely heavily on bank debt. Firms in Japan have built long-term relationships with banks, usually with each firm having a "main bank." These main banks usually own equity and place its own personnel into important management positions (including directorships) of the borrowing firms.

During the 1980s, the Japanese main bank system was viewed as an ideal corporate governance model. Such bank-reliant firms had few conflicts among creditors, large stockholders, and management, as they were all linked by a single entity, the main bank. Because the bank had dual stakes as both a creditor and equity holder, they were well known as active monitors of the Japanese firm. As a result, these firms were able to maintain high debt levels and had little need to maintain liquid financial slack. That is, firms did not have to keep cash reserves because they were able to get cash quickly from their main bank whenever they needed it. Further, when these bank-reliant firms experienced financial difficulties, the main banks were able to bail them out before the problem became serious. Thus, banks were viewed as effective monitors of firms.

However, in 1990, the Japanese market crashed and Japan has been in a bear market ever since, thus raising some doubts as to the efficacy of the main bank system. What might be the flaws of having influential bank monitors? First, banks might encourage client firms to pursue profit stabilization rather than profit maximization, in order to protect their claims as the firms' largest creditors. That is, banks might have too much power over their client firms, where they influence the firm in the best interests of a creditor rather than as a stockholder. Second, and perhaps most importantly, when banks experience financial difficulties, as Japanese banks did during the 1990s, then their client firms will also suffer.[18]

Creditor Rights around the World

Creditors may also be protected by the legal system. For example, do a country's laws make it easy or difficult for a creditor to seize the collateral of a loan when the firm goes into bankruptcy reorganization? Do firms need the permission of the creditors to reorganize? Example 6.4 shows the strength of creditors' rights in countries throughout the world.[19] The index can vary from 0 to 4 and was formed by determining whether the laws in the country have any of the following four creditor rights:

1. no automatic stay on the assets in reorganization;
2. secured creditors get paid first;
3. restrictions for going into reorganization; and
4. management is replaced in reorganization.

A Creditor Rights index value of 4 means the country strongly protects creditors.

The companies are categorized by the legal origin from which the laws have evolved. The English legal system is based on **common law**. French, German, and Scandinavian legal systems are based on **civil law**. Common law is formed by precedents and judges that resolve specific disputes. Civil law uses statutes, comprehensive codes, and legal scholars to organize and formulate rules. Example 6.4 shows there is considerable variation of creditor rights within each legal origin. But on average, countries that have an English-origin legal system have stronger protections for creditors. This empowers creditors to monitor the firm.

EXAMPLE 6.4   **Creditor Rights Around the World**

A higher number indicates stronger creditor rights.

Country	Creditor Rights	Country	Creditor Rights
Australia	1	Argentina	1
Canada	1	Belgium	2
Hong Kong	4	Brazil	1
India	4	Chile	2
Ireland	1	Colombia	0
Israel	4	Ecuador	4
Kenya	4	Egypt	4
Malaysia	4	France	0
New Zealand	3	Greece	1
Nigeria	4	Indonesia	4
Pakistan	4	Italy	2
Singapore	4	Mexico	0
South Africa	3	The Netherlands	2
Sri Lanka	3	Peru	0
Thailand	3	Philippines	0
United Kingdom	4	Portugal	1
United States	1	Spain	2
Zimbabwe	4	Turkey	2
English-origin average	**3.11**	Uruguay	2
		French-origin average	**1.58**
Austria	3		
Germany	3	Denmark	3
Japan	2	Finland	1
South Korea	3	Norway	2
Switzerland	1	Sweden	2
Taiwan	2	**Scandinavian-origin average**	**2.00**
German-origin average	**2.33**		

Summary

When a company obtains capital through bor-rowing money, it also obtains another gover-nance mechanism. The need to pay interest and principle payments disciplines executives to manage the cash flow of the firm carefully and discourages superfluous spending. Those insti-tutions and investors who lend the firm money become another monitor of the firm. Large creditors, such as banks, insurance companies, mutual funds, and pension funds, often devel-op close relationships with firms and can be ef-fective monitors. Individual investors tend to rely on the recommendations of credit rating agencies.

The credit agency's purpose is monitoring debt issuers to protect public investors. However, the industry's structure creates a situation in which the agencies interact only a little with the investors they are protecting. Instead debt issuers pay agencies to give a rating. Agencies work with the issuers and the investment bankers to obtain information about the debt issue. Most of their business relies on the interactions with corporate participants, not with investors. In this process they gain access to private information about the firm. Overall, the NRSRO-designated agencies have done a good job of showing bond investors the level of risk they take in various bond issues, but there have been many high-profile situations where the agencies do a poor job.

Most of the agencies' interactions and the fees they earn are with the firms they rate, not the investors who use the ratings. This circum-stance can create misaligned incentives. In addi-tion, the U.S. government has made credit rating a closed and low-competition industry that seems to have unusual immunity under the First Amendment from being sued for poor ratings. This immunity prevents investors from seeking damages when the agencies make mistakes. The misaligned incentives, lack of disciplinary market and legal forces can make the agencies lax in their watchdog duties.

WEB Info about Credit Rating Agencies

SEC Division of Market Regulation: Credit Agencies
www.sec.gov/divisions/marketreg/ratingagency.htm

Standard & Poor's
www2.standardandpoors.com

Moody's
www.moodys.com

Review Questions

1. Describe how debt, in and of itself, might keep management in check?
2. Describe the efficacy of financial institutions to be corporate monitors.
3. How are credit rating agencies important for firms, investors, and investment banks?
4. Why is the distinction between investment-grade and non-investment grade ratings so important?
5. The SEC awards the Nationally Recognized Statistical Rating Organization designation. What criteria do they use to give the designation?
6. How did the rating agencies fail Enron bondhold-ers and creditors?
7. Name and describe the conflicts of interest that credit agencies face.

Discussion Questions

1. Debt financing has a tax advantage that equity financing does not have. Given this fact, do you think large U.S. firms have enough debt? In your opinion, what kinds of firms might be able to handle more debt?
2. If you were a CEO of a small high-tech firm and you wanted to borrow money for your firm, would you borrow from an institution such as a bank or would you issue bonds? Why? What if you were the CEO of General Electric?
3. In the United States it is difficult for a bank to be a lender and a stockholder for legal reasons (refer to the Glass-Steagall Act). What do you think are the costs and benefits of preventing bank lenders from being stockholders?
4. There are only 10 NRSRO-designated rating firms. What might be done to increase the number of rating firms?

Exercises

1. This chapter mentioned IBM as a possible candidate to have more debt in its capital structure. Identify another firm and describe why it is an ideal candidate to have more debt.
2. Find two firms from the same industry, but with different debt ratios. Work out why the two firms have different debt ratios. Find another pair of firms that have different debt ratios, but for a reason other than the ones that you cited for the first pair.
3. Identify a firm that has more bank debt than public debt and vice versa. Work out why each firm prefers its debt type.
4. Obtain the ratings from at least four credit rating firms for one company's debt. Compare the ratings.
5. Obtain the credit ratings for a firm's debt over the past five years. How and why has the rating changed?

Exercises for Non-U.S. Students

1. What is the primary source of financing for the firms in your country? Do you think this is best for the future financial development of your country? Explain.
2. Do you think banks have too much or too little power in your country's corporate landscape? Explain.
3. Compared to the firms in the United States, do the firms in your country have more or less debt in their capital structure? Why do you suppose this is? Do you think this is good or bad for your country's firms?
4. Does your country have credit rating agencies? If so, describe the system and compare them to the U.S. credit rating agency system.

Endnotes

1. There is large literature on how debt, in and of itself, can restrict managerial discretion and is thus a corporate governance device. Michael C. Jensen, "The Agency Costs of Free Cash Flow: Corporate Finance and Takeovers," *American Economic Review,* Vol. 76, no. 2 (May, 1986) is a representative and well-known academic paper on this topic.
2. Perhaps the best academic papers that discuss monitoring by lenders are Diamond, Douglas W., "Monitoring and Reputation: The Choice between Bank Loans and Directly Placed Debt," *Journal of Political Economy* 99, no. 4 (1991): 689–721; Rajan, R., "Insiders and Outsiders: The Choice Between Relationship and Arm's Length Debt," *Journal of Finance,* 47 (1992): 1367–1400;

and Sharpe, S., "Asymmetric Information, Bank Lending and Implicit Contracts: A Stylized Model of Customer Relationships," *Journal of Finance*, 45 (1990): 1069–1087.

3. *http://en.wikipedia.org/wiki/Chapter_11,_Title_11,_ United_States_Code.*

4. See, for example, Carl C. Icahn, "Bankruptcy Rules Thwart the Recovery," *Wall Street Journal Online*, January 9, 2009.

5. Amy Borrus, Mike McNamee, and Heather Timmons, "The Credit-Raters: How They Work and How They Might Work Better," *Business Week* (April 8, 2002): 38.

6. *http://en.wikipedia.org/wiki/Nationally_Recognized_ Statistical_Rating_Organizations.*

7. *www.sec.gov/rules/final/2007/34-55857.pdf.*

8. *www.egan-jones.com/nrsro.aspx.*

9. Ratings categories are from *www.moodys.com* and *www.standardandpoors.com.*

10. Standard & Poor's estimates use data from 1981–2007.

11. "WorldCom Smashes Records with $11.9 bn Blowout Bond," *Euroweek*, May 11, 2001, 4.

12. Gregory Zuckerman and Shawn Young, "Leading the News: WorldCom Debt Is Slashed to 'Junk'," *Wall Street Journal* (May 10, 2002): A3.

13. Roger Lowenstein, "Triple-A Failure," *The New York Times* Magazine (April 27, 2008).

14. See, for example, Alistair Barr, "S&P May Downgrade $12 Bln of Subprime Securities:

Rival Rating Agency Moody's Cuts 399 Mortgage-Backed Securities," *MarketWatch.com*, July 10, 2007.

15. The figures were obtained from *http://oversight. house.gov/documents/20081022112135.pdf.*

16. Frank Partnoy, "How and Why Credit Rating Agencies Are Not Like Other Gatekeepers," in *Financial Gatekeepers: Can They Protect Investors?* Fuchita & Litan, eds., 2006.

17. Transcripts from the hearing are at *http://oversight. house.gov/story.asp?ID=2250.*

18. Good academic articles about Japan's main bank system are: Takeo Hoshi, Anil Kashyap, and David Scharfstein, "The Role of Banks in Reducing the Costs of Financial Distress in Japan, *Journal of Financial Economics* 27 (1990): 67–88; Michael S. Gibson, "Can Bank Health Affect Investment? Evidence from Japan," *Journal of Business* 68 (July 1995): 281–308; and David E. Weinstein and Yishay Yafeh, "On the Cost of a Bank Centered Financial System: Evidence from the Changing Main Bank Relations in Japan," *Journal of Finance* 53 (1998): 635–672.

19. The creditor rights index values are obtained from Table 4 of Rafael LaPorta, Florencio Lopex-de-Silanes, Andrei Shleifer, and Robert W. Vishny, "Law and Finance," *Journal of Political Economy* 106 (1998): 1113–1155.

Shareholders and Shareholder Activism

If a company is poorly governed, the effect is felt by shareholders through a loss in value of the shares they own. What can shareholders do to improve corporate governance or change the actions of managers? Unfortunately, in terms of direct action, not much. However, shareholders are not entirely powerless. There are a number of indirect actions that can affect corporate governance. At the company's annual meeting, shareholders can vote to replace ineffective directors and shareholders can make proposals to change the way the firm is governed. And, of course, shareholders also have legal rights they can pursue if management or the board is looting the company for personal advantage. Shareholders can bring a lawsuit against directors and/or officers to recover damages or force them to comply with the law.

When shareholders try to change the way the corporation is run, the actions are referred to as "shareholder activism." While the list of corporate governance control actions by shareholders seems impressive at first, in practice, shareholders rarely have much success influencing corporate governance. One reason is that it is costly to be a monitor. If you own a small amount of stock in a company, the benefit to your personal wealth from improving this stock's performance is much smaller than the cost of forcing a change. Hence, only large shareholders typically find it worthwhile to be a shareholder activist. The other reason shareholder activism is not successful is that the rules allowing such activism are stacked in favor of management and the board. As we will discuss in the following text, winning a proxy fight to change directors or getting a shareholder proposal passed at the annual meeting are both low probability events. Nonetheless, there are always poorly performing or incompetent managers, which means there are always disgruntled shareholders who decide to become activists. And if enough shareholders try to change corporate governance, some will have an effect. Hence, shareholder activism remains an important part of corporate governance.

A high profile example of shareholder activism is found in the recent fallout after Microsoft failed in its bid to acquire Yahoo! After spurning a merger proposed by Microsoft at a price of $31 per share in February 2008, Yahoo!'s stock price slid throughout the year until it dropped below $10 at one point. This extreme decrease in price was a serious loss in value for Yahoo! shareholders who would have been much wealthier if the Yahoo! board accepted Microsoft's offer. The actions of disgruntled shareholders included all the responses discussed in the preceding text: one large shareholder, Carl Icahn, nominated replacement directors for the entire Yahoo! board and started a campaign to build support among shareholders; another shareholder proposed at the shareholder meeting that management bonuses be more tightly tied to performance to give management an incentive to pull Yahoo! out of its slump; and numerous lawsuits were filed by other shareholders against officers and directors seeking to punish those whose decisions destroyed shareholder value.

In the following text, we discuss the incentives of small and large shareholders to become activists, and the types of activism: shareholder proposals, director election contests, and lawsuits. The details of the Microsoft-Yahoo! failed merger are presented throughout to show a high-profile example of shareholder activism in action.

WHAT IS SHAREHOLDER ACTIVISM?

There is no formal definition of shareholder activism. Loosely speaking, any time shareholders express their opinions to try to affect or to influence a firm they are being activist shareholders. Shareholders who submit proposals to be voted on at annual shareholder meetings could certainly be considered an activist. Even writing a letter to management regarding some aspect of the firm's operations or social policies could be considered investor activism. We discuss the activism by three kinds of shareholders: individual shareholders, large shareholders (defined as the owner of a large portion of a firm's shares), and institutional shareholders. Note that these shareholder types are not mutually exclusive. Either an individual or institutional investor can be a large shareholder.

Activism by Individual Shareholders

An individual investor with only a modest number of shares is able to attend shareholder meetings, submit proposals to be voted by at those meetings and vote at those meetings. Lewis Gilbert is generally credited with being the first individual shareholder activist.[1] In 1932, as the owner of 10 shares of New York's Consolidated Gas Company, he attended its annual meeting. While at the meeting, he was surprised and appalled that he was not given a chance to ask questions. After all, he was a part-owner (albeit a small one) of the firm. Subsequently,

Gilbert and his brother pushed for reform and, in 1942, the SEC created a rule to allow shareholders to submit proposals that could be put to a vote.

Lee Greenwood is an activist shareholder well-known to General Mills management. Greenwood once simply suggested that Wheaties® should appear on airlines and in hotels.[2] Among individual shareholder activists, Evelyn Y. Davis is perhaps the most well-known and has been featured in *People* magazine.[3] As the modest shareholder of about 120 firms, Davis attends about 40 shareholder meetings each year. What does she do at these meetings? As everyone from journalists to executives seems to put it, she "raises hell." Davis has berated executives for everything from questionable merger decisions to the enormous size of their pay. Most individual shareholder activists use less dramatic methods. However, enough people like Evelyn Y. Davis vigorously and frequently make themselves heard to have been deemed "corporate gadflies."

EXAMPLE 7.1   Individual Investors in Action

During 2000, the stock price of Computer Associates (CA) had dropped from a $70 high in January to about $30 in September. In the following year, Sam Wyly sponsored a proposal to unseat four CA board members.[4] After a highly publicized and expensive campaign, Wyly's proposal was defeated, primarily because it also sought to unseat the firm's cofounder and board chairman, Charles Wang. This example does not mean, however, that proposals, and even defeats, are fruitless or that shareholders should give up. Robert A. G. Monks spent $250,000 to run for a board seat at Sears in 1991. His effort resulted in defeat but the publicity eventually caused Sears to make massive changes on its own.[5]

Proposals do sometimes gain majority support. John Chevedden sponsored a proposal in 2001 to change the way board members are elected at Airborne Freight and he gained the support of 71 percent of the voting shareholders.[6] During that same year, Guy Adams beat tremendous odds with his bid for a board seat. As the owner of 1,100 shares of Lone Star restaurant stock, or 0.005 percent of the company, he was disgruntled because his stock had plummeted in value while the CEO's income rose. Consequently Adams ran for a board seat, one held by the restaurant CEO Jamie B. Coulter. Despite the fact that Adams had never before served on a corporate board and had no restaurant experience, Adams actually won. What does he plan to do with his newfound authority and power? He says he will be a watchdog for other Lone Star investors.[7]

Monitoring by Large Shareholders

Is it good for firms to have a large shareholder? Anecdotally, the answer seems to be "yes" for shareholders but "maybe not" for managers. For example, for many years Kirk Kerkorian was the largest shareholder of Chrysler and because of his large vested interest in that company he battled with former Chrysler chairman Robert Eaton for years over how the firm should be run.[8] Eaton probably felt he had to listen to Kerkorian as Kerkorian could have probably influenced Eaton's salary and even job security. For example, in 1996, Kerkorian was able to force Chrysler to disburse much of its cash holdings to shareholders in the form of stock repurchases or dividends. Chrysler's minority shareholders benefited from having a fellow shareholder who was active and influential. However, Kerkorian was both active and influential probably because he was a large shareholder.

Some managers of firms can also be one of its large shareholders. For example, Bill Gates owns over 8 percent of Microsoft Corporation, which probably explains why he seems to have such a strong vested interest in Microsoft's growth and financial success. Microsoft's minority shareholders directly benefit from Gates's shared interest to enhance the value of Microsoft shares. Note that a key difference between Gates being a large owner and Kerkorian being a large owner is that Gates is actually both a manager and an owner of Microsoft, while Kerkorian is simply an owner. So in the case of Microsoft, a person whose wealth is significantly tied to a firm is also directly responsible for running the firm. This duality minimizes conflict of interest problems between owners and managers (note also that as a top manager, Gates can also monitor his fellow managers). In the case of Chrysler and Kerkorian, the existence of a large outside shareholder seemed to exacerbate the conflicts between management and owners. However, in both cases, minority shareholders seem to come out as clear beneficiaries.

In the academic literature, large shareholders (both manager-owners and just plain owners) are in fact found to be active monitors of the firm.[9] This should not be surprising as they have the incentive *and* the power to be effective monitors. Think of it this way: if two firms are identical in every way but one firm has one or two large shareholders who own 10 percent of the firm each, while the other firm has dispersed shareholders where no single shareholder owns more than 0.1 percent of the firm, then which firm might be better monitored by its shareholders? Probably the firm with the large shareholders. It is also worth pointing out that the latter hypothetical firm probably resembles many real public firms for at least two reasons. Some public firms can be so large that it would take a lot of wealth to own a significant fraction of it. Further, most investors may not wish to forgo the benefits of portfolio diversification by investing so heavily in any one particular firm. So, while large shareholders are useful monitors, there may not be a lot of investors who have the capital or the desire to be a large shareholder.

Institutional Shareholders: An Overview

Institutional shareholders have the potential to exert effective influence. One academic study finds that proposals sponsored by institutional shareholders have a much greater chance of success than ones sponsored by individuals.[10] Fortunately, institutional shareholders, especially public pension funds, have become more active in their oversight of companies. One reason for their increased activity is their increasing ownership stakes. That is, institutional investors are large shareholders. The pie charts in Figures 7.1 and 7.2 show the percentage of U.S. equities held by different shareholder types for the years 1970 and 2002.[11]

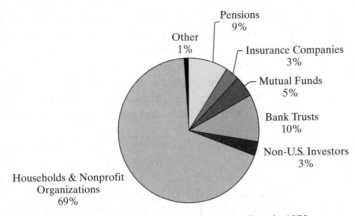

FIGURE 7.1   Shareholders of Stocks by Investor Type in 1970

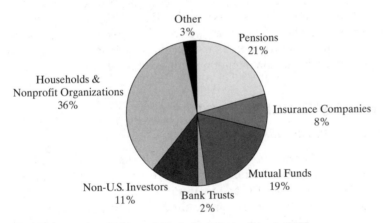

FIGURE 7.2   Shareholders of Stocks by Investor Type in 2002

From these charts, it can be seen that institutions now own a larger percentage of shares than they did in 1970. The most dramatic increases are with pension funds and mutual funds. In fact, according to anecdotal evidence, we might expect fewer than 100 funds to hold about half of the U.S. stock market in any given year during the 2000s.[12] As such, these funds do have the economic incentive to be more active, and some actually have been.

Further, note that both pension funds and mutual funds actually manage money on behalf of many smaller investors. In fact, under the Employee Retirement Income Security Act (ERISA), pension funds have a fiduciary responsibility to their plan participants and beneficiaries. Hence, pension funds in particular are in a position to be active shareholders. They also have fewer restrictions compared to mutual funds on how much of a firm they can own. Pensions can take on a relatively large ownership stake and subsequently engage in a long-term active ownership role in the firm. In contrast, mutual funds have to diversify their holdings into at least 20 separate companies or the mutual fund may face additional taxation.[13] Therefore, not surprisingly, public pension funds often lead the way with regard to institutional shareholder activism.

Since the early 1990s, a few public pension funds have taken on a relational investor role with a long-run mindset. These funds have tried to influence the firms they own, mainly through direct communication with management and other shareholders, by identifying poor corporate performers and through pushing for reforms.[14] For example, the public pension fund CalPERS, which has $190 billion in assets and serves 1.4 million members, has targeted Sears and Westinghouse in the past and has pushed for them to divest laggard divisions. Also, during July 2002, the chairmen of 1,754 major U.S. firms all received a letter from the TIAA-CREF, the country's largest pension fund, asking them to account for stock options as an expense.[15] Activism by TIAA-CREF is quite common; they constantly monitor firms and make numerous recommendations for reform.

To help increase their influence, many pension funds belong to a coalition called the Council of Institutional Investors (CII), whose primary objective is to help members take an active role in protecting their assets. Given that pension funds control more than $3 trillion worth of assets, they certainly do have an incentive to come together and exert influence.

TYPES OF SHAREHOLDER ACTIVISM

Shareholder Proposals

The first type of shareholder activism is shareholder proposals. SEC rules permit anyone owning more than $2,000 or 1 percent of a firm's stock on a continuous basis for at least one year to submit a proposal to be considered and voted on at a meeting of the shareholders. With Rule 14a-8, the SEC gives shareholders a method to suggest changes in corporate governance. The shareholder proposal rules require all publicly traded companies to solicit proposals prior to their shareholder meetings. If these proposals meet the requirements of the company's bylaws and are sufficiently related to the company's business, then the company is required to include a summary of the proposal in the proxy statement issued to all shareholders at the annual meeting.[16] At the annual meeting, the shareholder proposal will then be voted on by all shareholders. If it passes, the proposal can be either binding or advisory on management, depending on the nature of the proposal and the rules for each type of proposal.

One prohibition in shareholder proposals is that nominations for the election of directors are not allowed. Instead, directors are nominated under the company's internal bylaws or through an independent campaign seeking the votes of shareholders called a contested election of directors or **proxy fight**. This form of activism is covered in the next section.

More than a thousand shareholder proposals are submitted each year. Many shareholder proposals are governance-oriented, primarily attempting to forge an alignment between shareholder views and managerial actions. For example, proposals may address issues related to antitakeover amendments, shareholder voting rules, or board composition.[17] For example, following the failed Microsoft-Yahoo! merger in 2008, many shareholders of Yahoo! were not happy about how poorly management had run the company. One shareholder, the United Brotherhood of Carpenters Pension Fund, offered a shareholder proposal at the annual meeting that proposed that executives be paid bonuses only for superior performance and not for average performance or simply for serving as executives long enough.[18] If this proposal passed, it would have the effect of tying the incentive of management more closely to successful results for Yahoo!. At the 2008 annual meeting, the proposal, identified as Proposal No. 3, was rejected by voters by a 2-1 margin. Why didn't more shareholders vote for something that would apparently be helpful to the company? As will be discussed in more detail in the following text, management usually resists shareholder amendments quite strongly and the mechanics of collecting votes are stacked against shareholder activists.

EXAMPLE 7.2 **Fictitious Excerpt of Notice of Pretend Company Shareholder Meeting**

Item No. 4

Ms. Gwen Smith, 1234 Main St., South Park, MI 48199, owner of approximately 101 shares of common stock, has given notice that she intends to present for action at the annual meeting the following resolution:

> To be resolved: "That the Board of Directors no longer issue executive stock options, nor allow any current stock options to be repriced or renewed.
>
> REASON: 'The firm appears to be issuing too many stock options. Instead, executives should be compensated with actual stock instead of options. Actual stock may better align management and shareholders. If you AGREE please mark your proxy FOR this resolution.'"

The Board of Directors recommends a vote AGAINST the adoption of this proposal for the following reasons:

Pretend Company has granted stock options for many years and believes it to be a useful incentive compensation tool.

Management endorses the granting of stock options as an incentive to generate long-term stock price appreciation. Eliminating executive options may impair the firm's ability to retain high quality executives and to achieve sustained future growth.

The Board of Directors recommends a vote AGAINST this stockholder proposal, Item No. 4. Proxies solicited by the Board of Directors will be so voted unless stockholders specify a different choice.

Other shareholder proposals are related to social goals such as not dealing with countries that abuse human rights. While it may appear that these proposals are not business related, there is a link in the sense that boycotts are a reality of the business world and there is potentially a large loss in sales if a powerful political group is offended by a company's action. Accordingly, there are frequently shareholder proposals to limit a company's involvement with countries or businesses with offensive policies. Continuing with the Yahoo! example, at the 2008 annual meeting, there were two proposals related to Yahoo!'s involvement with the issue of human rights: Proposal No. 4 requested a corporate policy against cooperating with other countries" requests to censor the Internet; and Proposal No. 5 establishing a Board Committee on Human Rights.[19]

Although shareholder proposals appear to be a useful way to change corporate governance, in practice, most shareholder proposals do not pass, especially those that go against management desires. Typically, management and the board resist shareholder proposals forcefully and the proposals cannot muster enough votes. In the case of Yahoo!'s 2008 shareholder meeting, the Board of Yahoo! recommended voting against all three proposals. Proposal No. 3 earned only 33 percent of votes cast, which was far more than Proposals No. 4 and 5, which earned 5.8 percent and 3.1 percent, respectively.[20] These results are typical of the votes on shareholder proposals, as shareholder activists are usually unsuccessful.

One reason shareholder proposals fail is that it is difficult and expensive for one shareholder to communicate with all other shareholders. This creates an uneven playing field because expense is not a concern for management and the board who can freely spend the company's money in lobbying against shareholder proposals. As an individual shareholder, how much of your own money are you willing to spend in an uphill battle to change governance? Most spend little and hope that the description in the company's proxy statement is enough to convince shareholders to vote in favor of the proposal. Another reason it is hard to win approval of a shareholder proposal is that management collects proxy cards before the meeting that show how shareholders want to vote. These proxy cards give management the authority to act on behalf of the shareholder in voting. If no vote is registered for a proposal, then management can choose how to vote those shares on that proposal. In other words, management controls the votes of the uncommitted shareholders who return their voting proxy but do not take a position on the shareholder proposals.

For both reasons, it is difficult to change governance through submission of shareholder proposals. To successfully win a vote on a proposal, you have to overcome the board's money advantage in lobbying against proposals and you have to collect enough votes to counter management's control of the proxy votes of disinterested shareholders. Nonetheless, proposals are one of the only ways small shareholders can express concern with management actions. So they remain a common feature of a company's annual meeting. Further, if a large shareholder supports a shareholder amendment, it is more likely that money will be spent on lobbying other shareholders and the prospects of passing improve. Later in this chapter, we consider how large shareholders such as institutional investors may be more active monitors of management using shareholder proposals and other techniques.

Contested Election of Directors (Proxy Fights)

Another action shareholder activists can take is to try to replace directors serving on the board. After all, the directors are the shareholders' representatives at the firm, so the directors should be accountable to shareholders and subject to replacement if the company is performing poorly. While it seems like it would be easy for shareholders to replace an ineffective board, the rules of the game are structured to make it quite difficult. As an example, consider again the Microsoft-Yahoo! failed merger. One of the first things disgruntled Yahoo! shareholders tried to do in April 2008 was to replace the board that had rejected the Microsoft offer. One large shareholder, Carl Icahn, took the lead in nominating nine new directors to entirely replace the existing directors. However, after a contentious fight for the votes of shareholders, Icahn gave up the battle and agreed to a compromise solution. The deal added Icahn and two of his nominated directors to an expanded Yahoo! board, while leaving in place eight of the nine directors who rejected Microsoft.[21] In other words, only one director lost his position following a high-profile proxy fight.

The Yahoo! case shocked many because, if ever there was a situation where directors would be replaced, this seemed to be it. Icahn was willing to spend significant resources to campaign for his slate of directors, neutralizing the company's financial advantage. And there were many disgruntled shareholders who wanted a change. However, these forces still had to counter the advantages held by Yahoo! management and the board under the rules for nominating directors.

The first difficulty shareholders have in replacing board members is that the nomination of board members is typically handled by a committee of the current board. This means the current board has the power to pick the candidates who will be voted on by shareholders. If shareholders believe the current board is incompetent, shareholders will probably not like the new director nominees chosen by a committee made up of incompetent board members. Further limiting shareholder choice, there is usually only one nominee for each seat, so the only power an unsatisfied shareholder has is to vote "no" for a director nominee and hope the board picks a better candidate next time.

To counter the board's control of director nominees, two avenues are available to shareholders. First, shareholders can make suggestions to the board as to who to nominate. The rules for making these suggestions differ depending on company bylaws. But there is no guarantee that the nominating committee will agree with the suggestions and the board will probably propose its own directors anyway. The second approach is to go around the board's nominating process and present your choice for director directly to the shareholders. This is called a proxy solicitation, which is governed by a complicated set of SEC rules under Rule 14A.[22] If you start a proxy solicitation, this creates a contested election of directors or, more commonly, a proxy fight. The proxy fight is fairly uncommon action by shareholder activists because of the expense required. The SEC requires a shareholder contesting a director election to make numerous mailings to all shareholders, to file many detailed documents with the SEC and to potentially make payments to the Company for their costs in providing shareholder information and conducting mailings.

In addition to cost, the proxy fight also has an uncertain outcome because management and the board have several advantages. As mentioned in the preceding text in discussing shareholder proposals, the voting rules favor management. Many shareholders return proxies to management that do not check a box for votes or that vote as management requests. This allows management to control the votes of disinterested shareholders who do not invest any time in determining who to vote for. Another issue that benefits management is that institutional investors like pension fund managers will often stick with management because they do not want to gain a reputation of opposing corporate management. In other words, to the extent pension funds primary business is administering the retirement plan of large companies, the pension funds might be afraid that corporate activism would cause managers to choose other pension funds for their employees. This issue is discussed further in the following section on the effectiveness of institutional activism.

In the Yahoo! proxy fight, it appeared several large institutional shareholders were going to side with management. This institutional support, combined with management and board ownership of 10 percent and management's control of the proxy votes from disinterested shareholders, may have been enough to win the fight.[23] Presumably, this is why Icahn agreed to settle for only 3 seats on an 11-seat board, instead of pushing for 9 seats on a 9-seat board. Overall, it was a disappointment to many Yahoo! shareholders that this was the best they could do to unseat a poorly performing board.

Given the difficulty and expense of replacing directors in a proxy fight, the SEC has proposed a rule that may help shareholders increase control. The proposed rule allows large shareholders to use the shareholder proposal rules to change the way directors are nominated in the company by laws.[24] For example, this would allow for shareholders to propose for vote a bylaw provision that required the board to nominate several candidates for each board seat and let shareholders have a real choice. In this way, shareholders could gain more control over the choice of directors without requiring an expensive proxy fight. While this proposed rule would probably help with corporate governance, its status is uncertain because, as of this writing, the rule has not been adopted as a final rule by the SEC more than a year after the required comment period ended. Also, the proposed rule limits the shareholders who can make a proposal to change the bylaws to large shareholders with more than 5 percent of the outstanding shares. So, small shareholders could not benefit directly under this rule. Only after a large shareholder opened up the nominating process would small shareholders potentially increase their control over nominations to the board.

Shareholders Lawsuits

Shareholders who are unhappy with the action of managers or the board can also turn to the legal system seeking relief. Because officers and directors have a fiduciary duty to act in the best interest of the shareholders, misconduct by officers and directors gives shareholders legal grounds to bring a lawsuit. The goal of the lawsuit could be to force the executives to follow company bylaws in the actions they take, or the goal could be to force the offending party to pay the shareholders for the lost value of their stock. The difference between these goals is that one has a direct impact on corporate governance and the other an indirect impact. If you sue only seeking a money judgment, this will not directly affect the governance of the company. Nonetheless, there is some corporate governance effect because it is a real wakeup call for an executive or director when a court orders you to pay shareholders because your misconduct has lowered the value of the stock.

There are two types of lawsuits that shareholders bring. The first is known as a derivative lawsuit, which is a special lawsuit brought in the company's name against the executives and/or directors. The idea behind the derivative lawsuit is that, even though the board is appointed as the agents of shareholders, the shareholders retain the right to step in and enforce the rules of the company if the directors are ignoring them.[25] In other words, if the board is ignoring its responsibility to monitor and punish executives who are involved in misconduct, the shareholders can bring an action on behalf of the company to force the directors and officers to comply with the rules. The shareholders can also force the directors and officers to repay money to the corporation. This lawsuit is called a "derivative" lawsuit because the shareholders are not actually the parties suing. The effect of this distinction is that, any money paid in a settlement of a derivative lawsuit goes to the company only and not to shareholders.

The other type of lawsuit is a direct suit where shareholders themselves file a lawsuit against officers and directors of a company. In a direct suit, the legal argument is that the officers and directors are agents of the shareholders who owe a duty to the shareholders to act in the shareholders best interest. A direct lawsuit typically alleges the officers or directors intentionally took actions that harmed the shareholders. If any amounts are paid under a direct suit, they go into the shareholders' pockets, not the company coffers.

Recent Research

How do derivative lawsuits improve corporate governance? Other than forcing a company to follow its own internal rules, are there any other effects on corporate governance? Recent research has shown that derivative lawsuits can be an effective corporate governance mechanism because they lead to changes in the composition of the board. Professors Ferris, Jandik, Lawless, and Makhija identified 215 derivative lawsuits filed against 174 companies over the period 1982–1999. For each company, they compared the following key variables related to corporate governance at the time the lawsuit was filed and three years after the lawsuit date: board size, percentage of inside directors, percentage of

outside directors, chair of board/CEO same person, and board departure rate. To control for changes in the overall economy during the same period, the authors constructed a control sample with one comparable non-sued company chosen for each company that was sued.

The strongest result of the study was a statistically significant decrease in the percentage of inside directors on the board of sued companies three years after the lawsuit (and a corresponding increase in outside directors). As discussed in the board chapter, it typically improves corporate governance to have outsider directors more involved. Hence, the derivative lawsuits appear to improve corporate governance. Another interesting result was that there was

Continued

a statistically significant decrease in the percentage of CEOs who were also board chair. Again, this is typically seen as an improvement in corporate governance because someone other than the CEO controls the board meetings. Overall, these results demonstrate that there were real effects on corporate governance in the firms that were sued three years after the derivative lawsuits were filed.

A different question is why an individual shareholder would pay the costs of bringing a shareholder lawsuit. If you had $10,000 invested in Yahoo! in early 2008, the decrease in value from the Yahoo! board turning down the Microsoft deal was about 20 percent depending on the date used for the calculation. This translates into a loss of $2,000 on your investment, which is not enough to support the high cost of bringing either a derivative or direct lawsuit. Nonetheless, there were at least 10 lawsuits brought against the Yahoo! board and some of its officers. Why would so many shareholders sue? One reason is that they are large shareholders who have a lot of money at stake. If your investment in Yahoo! was $100 million, then the potential to recover $20 million may be enough to support a lawsuit. A more important reason for a direct lawsuit is that there is a provision in federal law that allows for a **class action lawsuit,** which is a type of lawsuit where all shareholders join together in a single lawsuit. Most direct securities lawsuits are of the class action type and even if they are not initially class action, as in the Yahoo! case, a court will frequently combine them into a class action to save on court time of litigating the same suit over and over. At the time of this writing, the Yahoo! lawsuits have been consolidated into a class action (which also allows others to easily join). The effect of the class action lawsuit is that shareholders share the cost of prosecuting the lawsuit.

For both types of lawsuits, however, the biggest reason why shareholders might be willing to bring a costly suit is that, if the shareholders win the lawsuit, the company is required to pay the legal fees of the shareholders. The prospect of recovering attorneys'

fees has led to a situation where there are large law offices that actively look for opportunities to file class action lawsuits or derivative lawsuits. In many cases, the attorneys pay for the case and the shareholders reimburse them only if the case wins. In other words, the shareholders do not pay for the costs of the suit if it loses. This system where attorneys profit from successful shareholder lawsuits has led to changes in securities laws. The Private Securities Litigation Reform Act of 1995 was passed to reduce the number of frivolous lawsuits.[26] But according to the Securities Class Action Clearinghouse at Stanford Law School, there have been a steady stream of class action lawsuits since the new law in 1995.[27] As demonstrated by the examples of poor corporate governance throughout this book, there are apparently always some executives taking actions against shareholder interests—which means that there will always be nonfrivolous issues to sue over.

While it is still open for debate how many lawsuits filed by shareholders are merely attempts by attorneys to earn big fees, there is no question that lawsuits also play a role in corporate governance. If officers and directors are potentially liable to pay shareholders for their losses, this is a real disincentive to take actions that harm shareholders. Hence, there is a role for shareholder lawsuits in deterring opportunistic behavior by managers. One limitation on this power of deterrence should be noted, however. Directors and officers are typically covered by Directors and Officers (D&O) insurance policies and the company also agrees to indemnify officers and directors for payments made to settle lawsuits. This means that most shareholders actually collect from insurance company money and not from the pockets of the offending parties.[28]

Stephen P. Ferris, Tomas Jandik, Robert M. Lawless, and Anil Makhija, "Derivative Lawsuits as a Corporate Governance Mechanism: Empirical Evidence on Board Changes Surrounding Filings," *Journal of Financial and Quantitative Analysis*, 42 (2007): 143–166.

If you are a disgruntled shareholder, how do you decide which type of lawsuit to bring? It depends on whether you are more concerned with fixing the situation at the company or with getting back the lost value of the stock you own. The derivative lawsuit does not benefit shareholders directly, but can be useful to force compliance with company policies. On the other hand, the direct lawsuit is all about collecting money damages to cover the loss in stock value caused by the actions of officers and directors.

DOES INSTITUTIONAL SHAREHOLDER ACTIVISM WORK?

All of the types of shareholder activism described earlier were more likely to be undertaken by large shareholders because they have a greater incentive to take action. This raises the question of whether large shareholders like institutions regularly take advantage of the available actions. Determining whether activism bears positive results is difficult because, more often than not, good subsequent firm performance cannot be directly linked to increased activism. According to one study commissioned by CalPERS, Steven Nesbitt of Wilshire Associates conducted a before and after analysis of 42 firms targeted for reform by CalPERS. After being targeted, the aggregate stock returns of these 42 firms over a five-year period were 52.5 percent higher than the returns of the S&P (Standard & Poor's) 500 Index. Prior to being targeted, these same firms had under-performed the S&P 500 by 66 percent over a five-year period.[29] Michael P. Smith of the Economic Analysis Corporation conducted an independent study of CalPERS' activism and found that the combined gain to CalPERS for their activities related to 34 targeted firms was $19 million during the 1987–1993 period, while the total cost to their monitoring was only $3.5 million.[30] His evidence also suggests that CalPERS' activism works.

However, counter evidence also exists. In one academic study, the authors found that shareholder proposal submission did not lead to any obvious improvements in firm performance, even for those firms where the proposals passed.[31] In a study that examined the effects of targeting by CII, the authors found no subsequent improvement for the targeted firms and little evidence of the efficacy of shareholder activism.[32] Due to the inconsistent evidence, whether activism really changes firms for the better is unknown. Perhaps one of the main problems is that activism has its own set of shortcomings, which we discuss next.

POTENTIAL ROADBLOCKS TO EFFECTIVE SHAREHOLDER ACTIVISM

Mutual funds and pension funds try to earn a high return on their portfolios. However, many active investors have a speculative or short-run view of the stock markets and they make trading and investment decisions based on short-term trends. The short-term view of these investors limits their desire to be activists.

Institutional investors might be interested in good performance for the short term and then subsequently sell the stock to move on to something else. John Bogle makes the same contention; he has been calling on mutual fund managers to engage in more activism but instead he witnesses mutual funds engaging in speculative investing. According to anecdotal evidence, it is not uncommon for equity funds to turn their portfolio over at an annual rate of more than 100 percent.[33] If the equity funds do not like the future prospects of a firm, they simply sell the stock instead of working to change the firm.

Other than the activism of public pension funds, what about private (or corporate) pension funds? Are these groups active? Private pension funds are extremely quiet on the activism front. Jamie Heard, CEO of Institutional Shareholder Services, is not aware of a single corporate pension fund that has become a governance activist.[34] In total, private pension funds own almost 50 percent more assets than public pension funds. As a group they could be a strong monitoring force and exert influence to protect shareholders. However, private fund advisors face a huge conflict of interest problem: Corporate executives hire them to manage pension assets. If these advisors take an aggressive approach with the firm's management, then they will not be retained to manage the assets for very long. Executives probably do not want to see activism by shareholders because it interferes with their activities. Therefore, they would not hire pension fund advisors who are activists. This being the case, private funds usually just go along with the firm's management, even though their fiduciary duty is supposed to be with their beneficiaries, the employees, and retirees. A recent study confirms this. The authors find that mutual funds that manage a firm's 401(k) plans often voted with management.[35] In other words, mutual funds will not bite the hand that feeds them.

The regulatory and political environment may also hinder large institutional shareholders from engaging in activism. Under the Investment Company Act, mutual funds that own more than 10 percent of any one company must face additional regulatory and tax burdens. Half of the mutual fund assets must be vested in at least 20 firms (that is, a firm cannot constitute more than 5 percent of half the fund's portfolio). These ownership restrictions apply to pension funds as well. Specifically, ERISA imposes a rather strict diversification standard. As stated by Bernard S. Black, a Columbia law professor and well-known advocate of shareholder activism, "pension funds are encouraged by law to take diversification to ridiculous extremes."[36]

Why do these restrictions exist? Bernard S. Black and another law professor, Mark J. Roe, have adamantly argued that legal restrictions stand in the way of large investors engaging in the beneficial oversight of corporations.[37] The pair contends that the legal and regulatory environment prohibits or discourages institutional investors from becoming too large, from acting together, and from becoming significant owners. At the same time these investors face tremendous SEC paperwork if they do wish to accumulate a significant stake in a firm, while also facing unfavorable tax ramifications in the process. Meanwhile, only a few laws actually encourage or make it easier for institutions to be effective owners.

To see what shareholder activism by institutions could look like if there were no legal restrictions, consider the case of hedge funds, which are large investment funds that operate outside of most regulations. In a recent study, hedge fund activism over the period 2001–2006 was examined and the authors found that the hedge funds had success or partial success two-thirds of the time when they proposed strategic, operational, and financial remedies for companies in which they were large shareholders.[38]

INTERNATIONAL PERSPECTIVE

The public firms in the United States and in the United Kingdom have the most dispersed ownership structures in the world. This should not be surprising. For an individual investor, it costs a lot of money to own even 1 percent of these large, publicly traded firms. Institutional investors might have enough capital to be significant owners but they have regulatory restrictions preventing them from owning a significant fraction of any one firm.

In many other countries, however, there is greater ownership concentration where large shareholders are more prevalent. The two most common types of large shareholders are family-owners and state-owners. These large shareholders, especially family-owners, actively participate in management. For example, the Li Ka-Shing family owns and controls some of the largest firms in Hong Kong. The Wallenberg family owns and controls some of the largest firms in Sweden (such as ABB).

To own and to control the firm might seem like an optimal governance arrangement, as owner-controllers are unlikely to behave suboptimally and consequently minority (i.e., small) shareholders reap the benefits as well. However, because these owners have to be active in management and give up having diversified portfolios, there is a cost of this ownership structure to the large owners. Further, there is a chance that these family-owners may enjoy some private benefits of control (e.g., perks, large salaries, etc.) at the expense of their other smaller shareholders. That is, someone might have to monitor the family-owners.

In recent years, shareholder activist groups have begun to pop up in countries where family-ownership is prevalent. For example, the specific focus of the People's Solidarity of Participatory Democracy (PSPD), a leading shareholder activist organization that began its activism activities in the late 1990s in Korea, is to target family-owned firms (known as *chaebols*) for reform. Whether or not these shareholder activist groups will be successful remains to be seen.

Finally, it should be mentioned that a poor corporate governance infrastructure might have led to the prevalence of family-ownership and control to begin with. Some countries might not offer shareholders strong shareholder rights. With a poor governance environment, investors may have felt that they had to look out for themselves so they concentrated their wealth and maintained control. Therefore, significant governance reforms, ones that would protect minority shareholder rights, may probably have to be put in place before family-owners are willing to delegate control and diversify their wealth.

Summary

Shareholders have several actions they can take when managers are opportunistic and destroy shareholder value. One option, of course, is to sell their shares and walk away. But if the shareholders want to remain as shareholders and improve the corporate governance of their company their choices are shareholder proposals, proxy fights, and lawsuits. While each of these choices can be useful, they often have low probabilities of success and, even if they are successful, most small investors will not receive enough of a benefit to justify the cost of activism. Institutional investors, on the other hand, are large shareholders, so they may be able to monitor effectively through shareholder activism. In fact, institutional investors, such as pension funds, actually invest on behalf of their plan participants. Therefore, it could be argued that these investors should be activist shareholders.

There are some institutional investors that do earnestly try to engage in shareholder activism.

However, for the most part, most institutions are not active shareholders. This situation may exist because institutional investors face incentive problems, conflict of interest dilemmas, and regulatory constraints. Should we give institutional shareholders more power? Or is there a downside to them having too much ownership and power over U.S. public firms?

Web Info about Shareholder Activism

CalPERS Shareholder Forum
www.calpers-governance.org/forumhome.asp

Council of Institutional Investors (CII)
www.cii.org

Teachers Insurance and Annuity Association College Retirement Equities Fund (TIAA-CREF)
http://www.tiaa-cref.org/about/governance/index.html

Review Questions

1. Compare and contrast the ability of different types of investors to engage in shareholder activism.
2. What can investors do to monitor and influence a company?
3. How successful is investor activism?
4. Describe the roadblocks to effective shareholder activism.

Discussion Questions

1. The text states that perhaps there are some firms that require large shareholders and some that do not. What kinds of firms might belong in each category? Might this contention apply to other monitors? How?
2. Do you think institutional shareholders should be allowed to be larger shareholders of individual firms? Why or why not?
3. Which approach to shareholder activism (shareholder proposals, proxy fights, lawsuits) do you think is more effective in monitoring managers and improving corporate governance? Can you think of any changes you would make to any of these forms of corporate activism that would make them more effective?
4. In your opinion, do you think shareholder activism works? Why or why not?

Exercises

1. Do some research and describe what is involved in submitting a shareholder proposal.
2. Describe the corporate governance objectives of institutional investor activist CalPERS (or TIAA-CREF).
3. Go to the Council of Institutional Investors Web page (*www.cii.org*). What shareholder initiatives are they following?

4. Pick two firms in the same industry and identify their largest shareholders. If their ownership structure is similar or different, try to identify why this might be. Pick two firms in different industries and identify their largest shareholders. If their ownership structure is similar or different, try to identify why this might be.
5. Do some research and find both types of shareholder lawsuits. Who is suing in each type of lawsuit? What are the allegations against officers and directors and what are the shareholders seeking?
6. Do some research and identify and describe the current regulations that mutual funds and pension funds must adhere to. In particular, discuss regulations that might hinder their ability to be more active shareholders.

Exercises for Non-U.S. Students

1. Who are the largest shareholders in your country? How do they control the firms that they own? Do you think having these large shareholder types (e.g., the family or state) is good or bad for minority shareholders? Explain.
2. Do small individual investors have any significant power in your country? Why or why not? If not, then do you foresee improvements in this regard in the near future? Why or why not?
3. Are pension funds and mutual funds significant shareholders in your country? Why or why not?
4. Is it easy for shareholders to change the directors of companies in your country? Can individual shareholders nominate director candidates to be voted on by all shareholders?

Endnotes

1. See, for example, "Ending the Wall Street Walk," a commentary on the Corporate Governance Web site *www.corpgov.net.*
2. Lee Clifford, "Bring Me the Head of Your Board Chairman!" *Fortune*, October 2, 2000, 252.
3. Richard Jerome, "Evelyn Y. Davis for America's Most Dreaded Corporate Gadfly," *People*, May 20, 1996, 69.
4. David Shook, "Rebel Stockholders are on the Move," *BusinessWeek*, September 6, 2001, *www.businessweek.com/investor/content/sep2001/pi2001096_073.htm.*
5. Robert A.G. Monks and Nell Minow, "Sears Case Study," *www.thecorporatelibrary.com.*
6. David Shook, "Rebel Stockholders are on the Move," *BusinessWeek*, September 6, 2001, *www.businessweek.com/investor/content/sep2001/pi2001096_073.htm.*
7. David Grainger, "Driving a Stake into Lone Star" *Fortune*, August 13, 2001, 32–34.
8. Daneil Mcginn, "Don't Cry for Krik," *NewsWeek*, Feburary 19, 1996, *www.newsweek.com/id/101518/output/print.*
9. Perhaps the most well-known academic studies that discuss the benefits of having large shareholders include Harold Demsetz and Kenneth Lehn, "The Structure of Corporate Ownership: Causes and Consequences," *Journal of Political Economy* 93 (1985): 1155–1177; Andrei Shleifer and Robert Vishny, "Large Shareholders and Corporate Control," *Journal of Political Economy* 94 (1986): 461–488; and Randall Morck, Andrei Shleifer, and Robert Vishny, "Management Ownership and Market Valuation: An Empirical Analysis," *Journal of Financial Economics* 20 (1988): 293–315.
10. Stu Gillan and Laura Starks, "Corporate Governance Proposals and Shareholder Activism: The Role of Institutional Investors," *Journal of Financial Economics* 57 (2000): 275–305.
11. Source: NYSE Fact Book Online, */www.nyxdata.com/factbook.*
12. Marc Gunther, "Investors of the World, Unite!" *Fortune*, June 24, 2002, 78–86.
13. See Internal Revenue Code Section 851(b)(3).
14. "Ending the Wall Street Walk," Corporate Governance Web site, *www.corpgov.net*: Stu Gillan

and Laura Starks, "A Survey of Shareholder Activism," *Contemporary Finance Digest* 2 (1998): 10–34.

15. The letter is available for viewing on the TIAA-CREF Web site, *www.tiaa-cref.org*.

16. The rules for shareholder proposals are found at 17 C.F.R. 240.14a-8.

17. Stu Gillan and Laura Starks, "Corporate Governance Proposals and Shareholder Activism: The Role of Institutional Investors," *Journal of Financial Economics* 57 (2000): 275–305.

18. See Proposal No. 3, Yahoo! Notice of Annual Meeting of Stockholders, Proxy Statement, June 9, 2008.

19. Yahoo! Notice of Annual Meeting of Stockholders, Proxy Statement, June 9, 2008.

20. Yahoo! Announces Results of 2008 Annual Stockholder Meeting, press release, August 1, 2008.

21. Yahoo! Revised Definitive Proxy Statement, July 28, 2008.

22. The rules for proxy solicitation are found at 17 C.F.R. 240.14a.

23. Market Watch, Yahoo Proxy May Come Down to Battle of Big Funds, July 18, 2008.

24. Securities and Exchange Commission, Shareholder Proposals, Proposed Rule, Release No. 34-56160, July 27, 2007.

25. Depending on the applicable state corporation law, there is usually a requirement of showing that the board has failed to act before a derivative lawsuit can be brought. For more information on the details of derivative lawsuits, see *http://en.wikipedia.org/wiki/Derivative_suit*.

26. *http://en.wikipedia.org/wiki/Private_Securities_Litigation_Reform_Act*

27. *http://securities.stanford.edu/index.html*

28. Intentional fraud is typically not covered by either insurance or indemnification by the company, so executives in cases like Enron were required to pay their own funds to shareholders in settlement of lawsuits.

29. Source: "Ending the Wall Street Walk," Corporate Governance Web site, *www.corpgov.net*.

30. Michael P. Smith, "Shareholder Activism by Institutional Investors: Evidence from CalPERS," *Journal of Finance* 51 (1996): 227–252.

31. Jonathan M. Karpoff, Paul H. Malatesta, and Ralph A. Walkling, "Corporate Governance and Shareholder Initiatives: Empirical Evidence," *Journal of Financial Economics* 42 (1996): 365–395.

32. Wei-Ling Song, Samuel H. Szewczyk, and Assem Safieddine, "Does Coordinated Institutional Investor Activism Reverse the Fortunes of Underperforming Firms?" *Journal of Financial and Quantitative Analysis* 38 (2003): 317–336.

33. Remarks by John C. Bogle before the New York Society of Security Analysts on February 14, 2002. For the text of the speech, go to *www.vanguard.com*.

34. "Ending the Wall Street Walk," Corporate Governance Web site, *www.corpgov.net*, Stu Gillan and Laura Starks, "A Survey of Shareholder Activism," *Contemporary Finance Digest* 2 (1998): 10–34.

35. Gerald Davis and E. Han Kim, "Business Ties and Proxy Voting by Mutual Funds," *Journal of Financial Economics* 85 (2007): 552–570.

36. Bernard S. Black, "Institutional Investors and Corporate Governance: The Case for Institutional Voice," in *The Revolution in Corporate Finance*, 3rd Edition (Oxford: Blackwell Publishers, 1998).

37. Mark J. Roe, "Political and Legal Restraints on Ownership and Control of Public Companies," *Journal of Financial Economics* 27 (1990): 7–41.

38. Alon Brav, Wei Jang, Frank Partnoy, and Randall Thomas, "Hedge Fund Activism, Corporate Governance, and Firm Performance," *Journal of Finance*, 63 (2008): 1729–1775.

Corporate Takeovers:
A Governance Mechanism?

Mergers and acquisitions (M&A) are significant and dramatic events. Yet they are relatively commonplace in corporate America when compared to the rest of the world. In recent years, the United States has experienced some of the largest M&A ever. For example, Pfizer agreed to acquire Wyeth in 2009, America Online (AOL) acquired Time Warner in 2001, Exxon and Mobil merged in 1999, and SBC Communications merged with Ameritech, also in 1999. These mergers, among others, created some of the largest firms within their industries. During the 1990s and 2000s, the United Kingdom seemed to ride its own merger wave. Some of these recent large mergers have been cross-border mergers, such as Vodafone's (United Kingdom) acquisition of AirTouch (United States). Less than one year later, Vodafone Air Touch acquired Mannesmann (Germany). Other European firms such as Netherland's InBev are frequent acquirers of other firms. In a high-profile transaction in 2008, InBev acquired Anheuser-Busch, the largest brewer in the United States, creating the world's largest beer company.

The number and value of U.S. M&A transactions, for each year from 1980 to 2008, is presented in Figure 8.1. The number of acquisitions spiked in the mid-1980s; the wide availability of junk debt to finance corporate acquisitions is a common explanation for the spike. The figure also highlights the dramatic rise in M&A activity that took place during the 1990s, with a decrease in activity around the recessionary early-2000s. Since then, M&A activity has increased to the highest levels on the chart in terms of number of deals and dollar value.

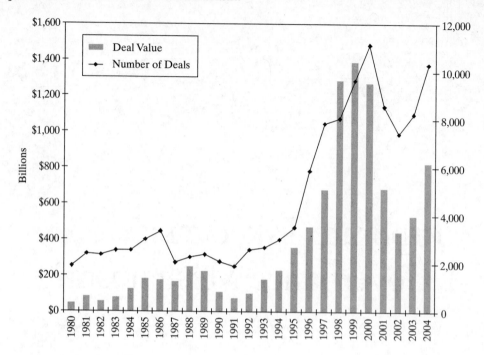

FIGURE 8.1 United States and U.S. Cross-Border M&A Transactions

Data Source: Mergerstat

There are many characteristics associated with M&A. Mergers can be characterized by:

- the type;
- the valuation of the firms involved;
- the payment;
- the new corporate structure; and
- the legal issues.

The legal effect of a merger is that two firms combine their operations into a single firm. The merger type could be between firms in the same industry or different industries, or they could even be vertical mergers where a firm might acquire one of its suppliers. The firm that is buying is called the **acquirer** and the firm that is being sold is called the **target**. Mergers where both the acquirer and the target firm's management and board agree to the deal are known as **friendly** mergers. If the target firm management and board does not want to be acquired, the attempt to take over control of the target is called a **hostile takeover.**

In friendly mergers, management and the boards of both firms negotiate over what is a "fair" price and the deal is not finalized until shareholders of both firms approve the deal. In a hostile takeover, the acquirer attempts to buy all the stock of the firm by making a temptingly high offer to the shareholders to buy their stock. Once a controlling block of stock is acquired, the acquiring firm then uses the voting power of this stock to approve a merger. Many takeovers start hostile and end friendly. If the target company resists negotiation, the acquirer may make an offer to shareholders as a way of putting pressure on target management to approve the deal. In either type of acquisition, payment can be made with a combination of cash, borrowed money (often known as leveraged buyouts [LBOs]), and newly issued stock of the acquiring firm.

What will the new corporate structure look like? Who will be in charge and, which managers or business lines will be retained? Government agencies try to determine if a merger significantly reduces competition, in which case it may be deemed illegal, and therefore challenged, by the federal government. There is also the general issue of costs and benefits of conducting M&A, to both the firms and to society. Many business schools have separate courses that treat M&A as a stand-alone topic.

At this point a question that business students might ask is, "Why is a book on corporate governance discussing M&A?" During the 1980s, there were occasions where "bad" firms were acquired by other corporations and even (famously) by individual investors, who then subsequently imposed dramatic changes (such as firing the target firm's top managers) to improve the acquired firm's profitability. These kinds of corporate acquisitions were often resisted by the target firm's management because they were afraid of losing their jobs after their firms were acquired. These kinds of hostile takeovers are sometimes known as "disciplinary takeovers" because they represent one process in which "bad" managers and/or "bad" operating procedures can be eliminated once their firms are taken over. In other words, if a firm is poorly managed, one way to force management and the board to make changes is to buy all of the shares of stock in the company and then use the voting power of this stock to replace the board and management.

We first provide a brief overview of M&A. However, this chapter is not about M&A *per se*; students are highly encouraged to read other corporate finance books if they wish to learn more about this exciting topic. After the brief introduction, we then discuss hostile takeovers in more detail and also characterize the nature of the disciplinary takeover. Perhaps most importantly, we then discuss how firms and their managers are able to defend against unwanted takeovers. We believe that these takeover defenses (both at the firm-level and at the U.S. state-level) may have severely hindered the disciplinary takeover market during the last two decades. We then offer some international perspective on takeovers.

BRIEF OVERVIEW OF MERGERS AND ACQUISITIONS

Mergers and acquisitions can occur for a variety of reasons. Firms can merge for strategic reasons to improve operational or financial synergies. In 1999, the merger between Exxon and Mobil led to reduced oil exploration costs. Firms can merge to diversify by expanding into new businesses. The AOL and Time Warner merger brought together new and old media (i.e., AOL's Internet service and Time Warner's cable [CNN, HBO] and print media [*Time, People, Sports Illustrated*]).

Mergers can be both synergistic and diversifying. The Morgan Stanley and Dean Witter merger brought together an investment bank that underwrote securities and a retail brokerage firm that sold securities. A diversifying merger can also be extreme in the sense that two very different businesses are joined together. General Electric's acquisition of the television company, NBC, during the 1980s, is a classic example of an extreme diversifying merger. Corporate diversification can make the combined firm's profits more stable but there is some debate about whether or not diversifying mergers are good for shareholders.[1]

Most of the recent mergers have occurred for growth and for increased market power. Mergers between Oracle and PeopleSoft, between Hewlett-Packard (HP) and Compaq, and between NationsBank and BankAmerica, can be viewed as market-power enhancing mergers. In recent years, these kinds of mergers seem to be popular with banks, pharmaceuticals, oil companies, and telecommunication firms. In a broad sense, we could classify all of these merger types into one category: they are *synergistic* in nature through the cutting of costs and risks and through economies of scale.

While we generally view mergers and acquisitions as being somewhat different (a merger is often viewed as a combination of two firms, whereas an acquisition is viewed as one firm buying another), almost all mergers are essentially acquisitions, as there is often an explicit buyer and seller when two firms are joined together. ExxonMobil is often thought of as a merger between equals but in reality Exxon acquired Mobil. Or put another way, Exxon "took over" Mobil. AOL purchased Time Warner. Daimler purchased Chrysler.[2]

Are corporate takeovers good for shareholders? In the first chapter, we mentioned that Hewlett-Packard's takeover of Compaq was not viewed positively by some HP shareholders nor was it viewed positively by the stock market. When HP announced its plans to acquire Compaq, HP share price immediately declined. There is a popular view that smaller firms are more nimble and more *focused* than larger firms in their ability to generate profits. In addition, some believe that managers want to take over companies simply to increase their "empire." This kind of acquisition is often referred to as "empire building." If both of these beliefs are true (and they are both widely popular beliefs), then takeovers may not be good for the acquiring firms' shareholders. Today there are people who believe that the HP-Compaq merger was bad for both of these reasons—which may be why CEO Carly Fiorina lost her job.

THE TARGET FIRM

Most of the time the target firm (i.e., the firm being acquired or taken over) will enjoy a share price *increase* when its acquisition is announced to the public. Why might this be? A firm, or even an individual investor, may be interested in taking over a target firm because they believe that that firm is not performing up to its full potential or that it could become an even better performer under someone else's control. The acquirer's goal under these circumstances would be to take over the firm and then to turn it around (i.e., to make it profitable) by cutting its fixed or variable costs (either by getting rid of unnecessary expenses or through financial synergy with the acquiring firm), improving its operational efficiency, or by getting rid of its "bad" managers.

Sometimes students new to finance might think it is odd that a successful firm would want to acquire an unsuccessful firm but the rationale is pretty simple. If a firm or an individual were to acquire a successful firm then they would have to pay a large sum for it and the subsequent net gains after the takeover may be limited. However, if a firm or an individual were to acquire an unsuccessful firm then they would only have to pay a relatively small sum for it. The subsequent net gains may be significant if they are able to convert the unsuccessful firm into a successful one. Unfortunately for the acquirer, because the stock market anticipates these subsequent improvements in target firms once they are taken over, the target firms' share price will *immediately* increase when its acquisition is announced. Acquirers almost always end up paying a significant premium for target firms. As the gains go to the target shareholders in most acquisitions, firms making offers typically offer a premium when making a bid for the target shares. An extreme example of this is the $60 per share bid News Corporation (News Corp.) offered in May 2007 to acquire Dow Jones, whose stock was trading at $37.12 per share.[3] An interesting debate among academics and among financial experts in general is whether or not the premium paid for target firms is ever fully recovered. That is, does the acquisition end up being a positive NPV (net present value) project for the acquirer?

Because the acquirer often pays a premium for the target firm, the target firms' shareholders might like it when their firms are taken over. However, the target firms' management team and board of directors may oppose being acquired. Once firms are acquired, many of the target firms' managers are then subsequently fired so that the acquirer can install their own management team into the newly acquired firm. Board members are also frequently replaced. As you can easily imagine, corporate CEOs and presidents generally do not like being fired. When management and the board balks at a takeover bid from an interested acquirer, the acquirer may then try to take their takeover bid directly to the target firm's shareholders in a hostile takeover. However, it can be argued that whether or not a takeover is "hostile" is in the eye of the beholder. Many initial hostile acquisitions are eventually approved by the target firm. Also some firms, fearing a hostile takeover, may try to work out a "friendly" deal with a potential acquirer. In both of these cases, the firms involved may publicly state that their merger was a friendly one.

EXAMPLE 8.1 **Microsoft Fails in Hostile Takeover Attempt of Yahoo!, But Who Is the Real Loser?**

Throughout 2007, Yahoo! was losing ground to Google in their competition for Internet search advertising. To try and revive a stagnant stock price, Yahoo! replaced its CEO in June 2007 with company founder Jerry Yang. However, changes in strategy under the new CEO did not improve Yahoo!'s success and Microsoft initiated discussions of a proposed acquisition of Yahoo!. The benefits of this acquisition would be access to Microsoft's ample resources, as well as a restructuring of Yahoo!'s operations to make Yahoo! more profitable. In other words, this merger would be part strategic and part disciplinary takeover. The Yahoo! board, led by Jerry Yang, rejected Microsoft's proposal. In January 2008, Yahoo!'s performance had fallen even further and the company was forced to lay off 1,000 employees. Its stock price fell below $20 per share, which was the lowest price in years.[4]

In February 2008, Microsoft decided to again try to takeover Yahoo!, but this time it went around the board and offered $31 per share directly to the shareholders. This represented a 62 percent premium above the previous day closing price of $19.18 per share.[5] With this offer, Microsoft was trying to create pressure on the board and management of Yahoo! to negotiate a deal. The Yahoo! board, however, rejected the Microsoft offer, claiming it substantially undervalued Yahoo![6] In follow-up negotiations, Microsoft raised its offer to $33, but the Yahoo! board's minimum price was $37. Further complicating the deal, Yahoo! enacted a "poison pill" severance plan that would require more than a billion dollars be paid to employees who lost their jobs or were adversely affected by a takeover. This effectively raised the cost of a takeover beyond the price per share offered.

The combination of the board resisting the proposed takeover and the poison pill caused Microsoft to walk away from the deal. While the Yahoo! board claimed they were driving a better bargain on behalf of shareholders and were protecting employees who would be hurt by the takeover, the numerous lawsuits filed claim the board and management were protecting their own jobs at the expense of the shareholders. In fact, the aftermath of the failed Microsoft-Yahoo! takeover suggests the shareholders of Yahoo! were the big losers. On the day Microsoft announced it was walking away, the stock price fell to $23 and then in the next few months fell below $20. Compared to a price over $30 per share in a takeover, Yahoo! shareholders lost at least a third of the value of their investment. Following a high-profile proxy fight led by Carl Icahn to oust all the directors on the board because they rejected the Microsoft bid, Yahoo! was forced to make changes. The company added additional outside board members and eventually replaced its CEO in January 2009.[7] However, as of March of 2009, the value of Yahoo! stock remained below $15 per share, less than half of Microsoft's offer.

The Notion of the Disciplinary Takeover

Most of the time, when a firm takes over another firm, we generally do not think of it as a "disciplinary takeover." Profitable firms can also be taken over. Time Warner was making about $27 billion in revenue when it was taken over by AOL, which was making less than $5 billion in revenue (though the merged firm has struggled since the 2001 merger, suffering a $99 billion write-off of the value of AOL in 2002[8]). Even hostile takeovers are not always viewed as disciplinary takeovers. PeopleSoft was a profitable firm in the process of trying to take over J. D. Edwards (combined, they were expected to make about $3 billion in annual revenue) when Oracle made a hostile takeover bid for PeopleSoft during the summer of 2003.[9]

However, because some (if not most) firms that get taken over are poorly performing firms, there are many people (such as academics) who view takeovers as an important governance mechanism. If a manager is not doing a good job, either because he is bad at managing or because he is abusing his managerial discretion (i.e., he is using his power for self-serving ends), then his firm might get taken over and he will subsequently be fired. In this sense, the fear of a potential takeover might represent a powerful disciplinary mechanism to make sure that managers perform to the best of their abilities and to make sure that managerial discretion is controlled.[10] In a study of over 250 takeovers during 1958–1984, the study's authors found that over half of the target firm's top manager (usually the CEO but sometimes the president) was fired within two years of the takeover. These statistics are probably representative of today's takeover landscape. Even though Oracle's takeover of PeopleSoft might not have started off as a disciplinary takeover, many of PeopleSoft's top management team eventually got fired after Oracle's takeover. PeopleSoft's CEO, Craig Conway, was even fired just before the takeover was consummated because PeopleSoft's board felt that Conway was responsible for losing $2 billion in shareholder value.[11] While Conway's ability as a CEO can be debated, a takeover (or the fear of a takeover) represents a potentially powerful way to dismiss managers (or to motivate managers) that might not be looking out for their shareholders' best interest otherwise.

Therefore, in addition to the synergy motive for mergers mentioned previously, we could classify a second broad merger category as the disciplinary takeover. It is important to note that mergers can be for both reasons. It could easily be argued that Daimler's acquisition of Chrysler was both a synergistic merger (the two automakers produce different types of cars and primarily serve different geographic markets) and a disciplinary takeover (Chrysler was struggling to maintain sales growth and Daimler felt that Chrysler could make a turnaround if it had Daimler-style management). Similarly, the takeover of Dow Jones by News Corp. was both a synergistic merger because it added to one of the world's largest media empires, as well as a disciplinary takeover because one goal was making changes in a company with lackluster performance.

However, while takeovers may be viewed as a governance mechanism, it is not clear that they are an *effective* one. That is, we might *not* be able to rely on them as being an efficient contributor to the corporate governance system. First, as mentioned above, an acquirer may have to pay too much for a target. Second, takeovers could occur for the wrong reasons (e.g., empire building, corporate diversification). Third, even if the acquirer is able to pay a "fair" price for a target, the amount usually is still significant.

While the idea of disciplinary takeovers as a governance device might be new to some, it may be a more familiar idea to those of us who remember the "corporate raiders" of the 1980s. Corporate raiders, such as Carl

Icahn and T. Boone Pickens were well known to identify firms that could not control their spending. For example, Carl Icahn took over TWA (Trans World Airlines) in 1985 and then dramatically cut TWA's costs. Corporate raiders are obviously *not* seeking a synergistic-type takeover; their takeovers are clearly of the disciplinary type. These disciplinary takeovers benefited target firms' shareholders. They got rid of "bad" managers and in the process they themselves also enjoyed a profit. *However*, we would be remiss if we did not mention an alternative viewpoint. These corporate raiders were also seen as villains. Because raiders often cut jobs to control costs, many people viewed raiders as heartless cost-cutters who only cared about making profits.

Once raiders obtain enough shares of a firm, they can force management to make changes. Kirk Kerkorian, a large shareholder of Chrysler for many years has always been an activist shareholder. For example, in 1996, he forced Chrysler to disburse their large cash holdings to repurchase stock. Kerkorian's large purchase of General Motors (GM) stock, in the spring of 2005, had many analysts predicting future improvements at GM. By the end of 2006, however, Kerkorian had sold all of his GM stock and GM shareholders lost a potentially important monitor of management and shareholder activist. GM shares have fallen steadily since from about $30 per share to worthless in GM's 2009 bankruptcy. Another example of a corporate raider forcing change was discussed in Chapter 7 where Carl Icahn bought a large block of shares in Yahoo! and forced his way on the board through a proxy fight.

If a disciplinary takeover is profitable, in and of itself (even in the absence of a synergy motive) and if it is an effective governance mechanism, then the question that begs asking is why did we not see more of them during the 1990s and 2000s, as we did in the 1980s? Even when bad firms were taken over in recent years, a synergy-oriented reason rather than a pure investment-oriented reason was usually cited. There are several possible reasons. First, management opportunism and questionable actions such as "cooking the books" can lead to a temporary, but artificially, high stock price. No one would want to pay an artificially high price to take over a firm and fix things so that the true lower price was revealed. Second and mentioned previously, it costs a lot of money to buy a firm. In the 1980s, junk debt was a popular financing vehicle for takeovers but this form of capital is no longer widely available. A third reason, and perhaps the most important, is that today there are too many defenses against takeovers. That is, firms can install takeover defenses, which may have effectively disabled this governance device from playing an active role in our corporate governance system. These takeover defenses are discussed next.

TAKEOVER DEFENSES

For the United States, we can place takeover defenses into two categories: those at the firm-level and those at the U.S. state-level. Firm-level defenses can be broken down further into pre-emptive defenses that try to prevent takeovers and reactionary defenses that are enacted after a takeover attempt has begun. State-level defenses are state laws that regulate and limit takeovers. Firms lobby the state to enact such laws. We discuss firm-level takeover defenses first.

Firm-Level Pre-Emptive Takeover Defenses

The term **poison pill** represents any strategy that makes a target firm less attractive immediately after it is taken over. Most poison pills are simply favorable rights given to its shareholders. One popularly used poison pill gives target firm shareholders the right to buy the acquirer's stock for a deep discount if its firm is acquired. For example, in November 2004, News Corp. adopted a plan that, in the event a shareholder obtained a 15 percent stake in the company, offered all the other shareholders the chance to buy one share of News Corp. at half price.[12] The effect of this policy was to dilute the ownership percentage of a potential acquirer, making acquisition more difficult. Of course this makes the firm much less attractive to takeover from the acquirer's standpoint.

A related poison pill is to create **blank-check preferred** which means the company gives the board the right to issue preferred stock at any time with any voting rights the board determines. This allows the board to resist a takeover because they can put super-voting preferred stock in friendly hands. Other types of poison pills involve a firm's debt becoming immediately due once it is taken over or an immediate deep-discount selling of fixed assets once it is taken over. Well over half of the S&P 500 firms have a poison pill.[13]

A **golden parachute** is an automatic payment made to managers if their firm gets taken over. Because the acquirer ultimately bears the costs of these parachutes, their existence make those firms less attractive to take over. An example of a golden parachute was adopted by Yahoo! in February 2008 after Microsoft made an offer to buy the shares from Yahoo! shareholders. Yahoo!'s golden parachute plan is triggered by a takeover attempt and allows any employee who resigns after an "adverse change" in his or her duties to receive immediate vesting of options and a severance payment of 18–24 months' salary.[14] According to Carl Icahn, the cost of this plan was about $2.4 billion, which was a real disincentive to a firm such as Microsoft considering a takeover of Yahoo!

Other takeover defenses are **supermajority rules** where two-thirds, or even 90 percent, of the shareholders have to approve a hand-over in control. Firms can also have **staggered boards**, where only a fraction of the board can get elected each year to multiple-year terms, thereby making it difficult to gain control of the board in any one particular year.

Firm-Level Reactionary Takeover Defenses

Greenmail is like a bribe that prevents someone from pursuing a takeover. For example, David Murdoch owned 5 percent of Occidental Petroleum in 1984 and because Occidental's management feared a hostile takeover bid by Murdoch, they bought his shares at a significant premium.[15]

Other reactionary defenses to unwanted takeover bids include the firm's management trying to convince its shareholders that the offer price is too low (from Example 8.1, note that Polaroid management did this in their defense against Shamrock's hostile takeover), raising antitrust issues, finding another acquirer (also known as a *white knight*) who might not fire management after the takeover, or finding an investor to buy enough shares (also known as a *white squire*) so that he can have sufficient power to block the acquisition.

State-Level Antitakeover Laws

In general there are five common state-level antitakeover laws. **Freeze-out** laws stipulate a length of time (usually about three years) that a bidder that gains control has to wait to merge the target with its own assets. **Fair price** laws make sure that shareholders who sell their shares during a later stage of an acquisition get the same price as any other shareholder who sold their shares to the acquirer earlier. Individual firms can also adopt this type of provision. **Poison pill endorsement laws** protect the firm's rights to adopt poison pills. A **control share acquisition** law requires shareholder approval before a bidder can vote his shares. A **constituency** statute allows managers to include non-shareholders' (such as employees or creditors) interests in defending against takeovers.

Three states have rather extreme antitakeover statutes. Pennsylvania and Ohio allow target firms to claim the short-term profits made by acquirers and Massachusetts mandates staggered boards.

There are also federal acts (e.g., Sherman Act, Clayton Act) that prevent mergers that would significantly reduce competition but these acts are designed to ensure a competitive environment rather than to protect firms from unwanted takeovers. This task falls to the Bureau of Competition of the Federal Trade Commission (FTC) and the Antitrust Division of the Department of Justice (DOJ). These two government agencies uphold antitrust policy. Their main focus is on anti-competitive business practices and on ensuring a competitive industry environment in the face of mergers between companies.

EXAMPLE 8.2   States that have at Least Four of the Mentioned Antitakeover Laws[16]:

Arizona	Florida	Georgia	Idaho
Illinois	Indiana	Kentucky	Massachusetts
Maryland	Minnesota	Missouri	New Jersey
Nevada	New York	Ohio	Oregon
Pennsylvania	Rhode Island	South Dakota	Tennessee
Virginia	Wisconsin		

EXAMPLE 8.3 **Oracle's Hostile Takeover of PeopleSoft**

On June 2, 2003, PeopleSoft announced that it would be acquiring rival J. D. Edwards, which would make the combined firm the second largest enterprise application software vendor behind SAP.[17] Four days later, Oracle, also an enterprise application software vendor, made an unsolicited offer to acquire PeopleSoft for $16 per share. PeopleSoft management issued a negative response to the bid. Twelve days later, Oracle upped the bid to $19.50 per share. Over the course of the next year and a half, numerous dramatic events played out. For one, DOJ filed a lawsuit against Oracle citing antitrust issues, as the merger would dramatically reduce competition in the industry. In addition to challenging the DOJ suit, Oracle was lobbying its own battles against PeopleSoft. In particular it tried to put its own slate of nominated candidates up for election to PeopleSoft's board and they challenged PeopleSoft's poison pills, one of which would have flooded the market with millions of PeopleSoft shares if it were acquired and another that would have automatically refunded PeopleSoft's customers two to five times their license fees if the firm were acquired. It was also speculated that a white knight, possibly IBM, would come to PeopleSoft's rescue. Meanwhile PeopleSoft's stock price was crumbling, prompting its board to fire its CEO, Craig Conway. At the end of 2004, PeopleSoft's board approved a takeover deal with Oracle for $26.50 per share.

ASSESSMENTS OF TAKEOVER DEFENSES

Are Takeover Defenses Bad for the Governance System?

It is hard to say whether or not these takeover defenses are the only cause of the demise of the disciplinary takeover. Most of these takeover devices (both firm-level defenses and state-level antitakeover laws) were invented and implemented during the mid-to-late 1980s, in direct response to the high level of hostile takeovers that were taking place at the time. We may surmise, therefore, that takeover defenses at least contributed to the end of disciplinary takeovers.

If takeover defenses prevent disciplinary takeovers then their existence causes us to be left with one less governance mechanism. In this sense, takeover defenses are bad for the governance system. Studies have shown that when a firm adopts an antitakeover mechanism, their firm's stock price declines on the news.[18] However, this is not to say that we staunchly advocate eliminating antitakeover mechanisms. The matter is simply not clear-cut. Corporate raiders are often looking for quick profits. We generally encourage managers and investors to have a long-run focus. Further, we can certainly sympathize with those who viewed the corporate raiders of the 1980s as heartless villains.

In the least, however, we should continue to evaluate the pros and cons of antitakeover defenses in light of the reevaluation of corporate governance that is taking place today. Perhaps there is a middle ground that can be achieved. Some antitakeover devices appear only to benefit managers. For example, golden parachutes directly benefit outgoing managers, but who else? Also there is a lot of evidence that the extreme antitakeover laws in Pennsylvania, Ohio, and Massachusetts have harmed firm value and thus shareholders.[19]

On the other hand, many firms with takeover defenses do eventually agree to be acquired. When they do the acquisition price tends to be much higher than the original offer. Therefore fighting against the merger for a while may cause the bid price to increase, thereby increasing wealth to the target firm's shareholders. For example, in the failed Microsoft-Yahoo! takeover, Microsoft raised its offer from $31 per share to $33 per share, but was still rejected by management and the board of Yahoo![20] In their defense to the various lawsuits filed by shareholders, management and the board of Yahoo! argue they were acting in shareholders' best interest in rejecting the offers because they were driving a harder bargain.

INTERNATIONAL PERSPECTIVE

The United Kingdom seems to be experiencing its own merger wave since the early 1990s. In fact, Vodafone's (United Kingdom) recent takeover of Mannesmann (Germany) is the largest ever hostile takeover. The United States and the United Kingdom probably have the most antitakeover laws, yet they also have the most M&A activity in the world. Figure 8.2 shows the fraction of

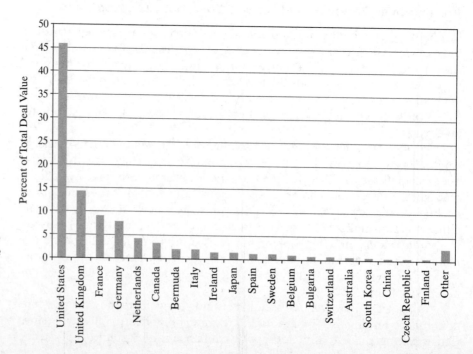

FIGURE 8.2 Percentage of Acquisition Deal Value by Country (Identified by Location of Target Firm), 2004

Data Source: ZEPHYR: published by Bureau van Dijk Electronic Publishing

M&A activity (out of all M&A activity worldwide) that was conducted in each country in 2004. The United States and the United Kingdom comprise 60 percent of all the M&A that took place.

In bank-centered financial systems, unlike the U.S. capital markets system, banks seem to play a significant role in determining which firms merge. For example, a study finds that banks are influential in German mergers.[21] Japan is also a bank-based system and, in general, it is a country that has believed in protecting its firms from hostile takeovers, especially from foreigners.[22] However, Japan has been suffering a protracted bear market since its market crash in 1990, so it is hard to argue that its opposition to hostile takeovers has been good for shareholders (but, of course, this is not to say that M&A are the cure for Japan's economy either).

After the Asian financial crisis of 1997–1998, many Asian governments relaxed the foreign ownership restrictions of their firms. This action will attract foreign capital and at the same time a larger presence of outside investors may lead to an improvement in firm-level governance. However, whether or not the presence of outside investors (or an acquirer of an entire firm) will lead to better governance remains to be seen.

Within Asian countries and in many other countries around the world, they also have their own unique set of circumstances that make M&A difficult. For example, in Japan multiple corporations cross-own one another and in Korea, families are powerful controlling shareholders of many firms. Both of these arrangements make it difficult for an acquirer from outside these tight networks to take over a firm. The strength of Japan's cross-ownership has been weakening in recent years. And there is a lot of pressure on family-run businesses in Korea, from both within and outside that country, to break up their multiple business conglomerates. In the future, we may see more hostile takeovers in other parts of the world, but whether or not they will be viewed as an important corporate governance mechanism also remains to be seen.

EXAMPLE 8.4   **The Largest Hostile Takeover Did Not Occur in the United States**

In late October 1999, German telecommunication and engineering giant, Mannesmann, made a bid for Orange, a telecommunication firm in the United Kingdom.[23] Vodafone, the largest telecommunication firm in Britain, perhaps fearing a new competitor in its own backyard, responded with its own takeover bid of Mannesmann. Vodafone's Chris Gent sought out Mannesmann's Klaus Esser to make a friendly merger offer but Esser refused it. Gent then made his offer directly to Mannesmann shareholders. In the following months, a very public battle took place, where each firm took out full-page ads with each side trying to convince Mannesmann shareholders that they were in the right. In February 2000, the two firms finally agreed to merger terms and consummated the largest hostile takeover in the world valued at $173 billion.

Summary

In the United States, mergers and acquisitions have been on the rise since the 1980s. In the beginning many of these acquisitions could have been characterized as hostile takeovers, as acquiring firms were looking to take over target firms whose management and boards did not want their firm to be bought. Many of these acquirers believed they could take over a poorly performing firm and then convert them into profitable firms. In this way M&A can be viewed as a corporate governance device, and thus these hostile takeovers were viewed as "disciplinary takeovers." However, the recent mergers we have seen seem to be more focused on simply increasing market power. What happened to the disciplinary takeover? In response to the hostile takeover activity of the 1980s, many firms and states adopted antitakeover devices, thereby weakening a potentially powerful corporate governance device. Besides the United States, takeover activity is only common in the United Kingdom. However, given collapses in corporate governance around the world, there is a good chance that we may see a new increased worldwide M&A activity in the near future.

WEB Info about Mergers and Acquisitions

Mergerstat
www.mergerstat.com

Zephyr
www.bvdep.com/ZEPHYR.html

Bureau of Competition, Federal Trade Commission
www.ftc.gov/bc/index.shtml

Antitrust Division, Department of Justice
www.usdoj.gov/atr/

Review Questions

1. What are the two broad rationales for takeovers? What are some of the specific rationales?
2. Discuss how takeovers can be viewed as a governance mechanism.
3. List and describe various takeover defenses.
4. Discuss why takeover defenses might be bad for shareholders.

Discussion Questions

1. In your opinion, who benefits when firms have takeover defenses? Who is hurt when firms have takeover defenses? In sum, which is greater the benefits or the costs?
2. Do you believe that takeovers can effectively contribute to the corporate governance system? Why or why not?

Exercises

1. Daimler Benz was adamant that its takeover of Chrysler was really a "merger between equals." From Daimler's viewpoint, why was it important that Chrysler shareholders believed this? Do some background research.
2. Find a recent hostile takeover attempt not mentioned in this chapter. Was it successful? How did it eventually get resolved? Regardless of the outcome, do you think the target firm is now better off? Explain your answer.

3. Conduct some research and discuss the costs and benefits of state antitakeover laws. In particular, what benefit is it to the states to have these laws?

4. Find a firm with a poison pill and describe it. Find another firm from the same industry that does not have a poison pill and identify why one firm has a poison pill and the other does not.

5. This chapter suggests that hostile takeovers might be good for corporate America. Do some research and argue that hostile takeovers are bad for corporate America.

Exercises for Non-U.S. Students

1. Compare and contrast the M&A market in your country to the United States. Also, do some research to work out what led to the differences between the two countries (e.g., if you find that M&A activity is low in your country, then what might be the cause; is it historical, economic, social, political, ownership related, etc.?).

2. This chapter did not discuss foreign acquisitions in detail. Does your country have foreign ownership restrictions? Do you think having a more active international acquisition market can improve the corporate governance environment in your country and worldwide?

3. Do you think hostile acquisitions are going to occur more often in your country? Do you think there should be more hostile acquisitions? Support your contentions.

Endnotes

1. A firm operating in multiple and diversified businesses are known as conglomerates. A good academic article about the economic costs of diversified firms is Phil Berger and Eli Ofek, "Diversification's Effect on Firm Value," *Journal of Financial Economics* 37 (1995):39–65. A good general article about the costs and benefits of diversified firms is Amar Bhide, "Reversing Corporate Diversification," in Donald H. Chew (ed.), *The New Corporate Finance*, 2nd edition (Irwin McGraw Hill, 1999, New York, New York).

2. When two large firms join together, it is often hailed as a "merger between equals." The Daimler-Chrysler merger is an interesting case. It had been highly publicized as a merger between equals, but in fact Daimler bought Chrysler. After the merger, Daimler CEO Juergen Schrempp even stated that he too viewed the merger as a takeover. Kirk Kerkorian, the largest shareholder of Chrysler before the merger, tried to sue Daimler-Chrysler arguing that he had been misled into thinking that it was a "merger between equals" but he lost his lawsuit in 2005. More background details of the story can be found at *http://www.nytimes.com/2006/09/27/automobiles/27daimler.html?_r=1&dlbk*.

3. *http://money.cnn.com/2007/05/01/news/companies/newspapers/index.htm*.

4. *http://en.wikipedia.org/wiki/Yahoo!*

5. *www.microsoft.com/presspass/press/2008/feb08/02-01CorpNewsPR.mspx*.

6. *http://yhoo.client.shareholder.com/press/ releasedetail.cfm?ReleaseID=293129*.

7. *http://yhoo.client.shareholder.com/press/ releasedetail.cfm?ReleaseID=359016*.

8. Information on the aftermath of the merger is summarized at *http://en.wikipedia.org/wiki/Time-Warner*.

9. Information on the legal fight between the three firms is summarized at *www.internetnews.com/bus-news/article.php/2220981*.

10. A good overview of disciplinary takeovers of the 1980s is Michael Jensen, "The Modern Industrial Revolution, Exit, and the Failure of Internal Control Systems," *Journal of Finance* 48 (1993): 831–880.

11. *www.eweek.com/article2/0,1895,1665096,00.asp*.

12. This information comes from *http://www.forbes.com/2005/10/13/newscorp-liberty-malone-murdoch-cx_sc_1013intrepid.html*. Interestingly, News Corp. removed its poison pill and staggered board of directors in 2008.

13. *http://207.36.165.114/Toronto/bizjak.pdf.*

14. Yahoo! Inc. Change in Control Employee Severance Plan, filed with the SEC 2/27/2008 as attachment 10.18 to the 10-K (Annual Report).

15. A good description of this incident is on page 727 in Mark Grinblatt and Sheridan Titman, *Financial Markets and Corporate Strategy*, 2nd edition (Irwin McGraw Hill Publishers, 2001, New York, New York).

16. Grant Gartman, *State Antitakeover Laws* (Washington, DC : Investor Responsibility Research Center, 2000).

17. This information comes from various news clips from *http://news.cnet.com/2030-1012-1018823.html.*

18. A good example of such a study is Gregg Jarrell and Annette Poulsen, "Shark Repellents and Stock Prices: The Effects of Antitakeover Amendments since 1980, *Journal of Financial Economics* 19 (1987):127–168.

19. Sam Szewczyk and George Tsetsekos, "State Intervention in the Market for Corporate Control: The Case of Pennsylvania Senate Bill 1310," *Journal of Financial Economics* 31 (1992):3–23;

Michael Ryngaert and Jeff Netter, "Shareholder Wealth Effects of the 1986 Ohio Antitakeover Law Revisited, Its Real Effects, *Journal of Law, Economics and Organization* 6 (1990):253–262; and Robert Daines, "Do Staggered Boards Affect Firm Value? Massachusetts and the Market for Corporate Control," New York Law School working paper (2001).

20. *http://money.cnn.com/2008/05/03/technology/microsoft_yahoo/?postversion=2008050412.*

21. Julian Franks and Colin Mayer, "Bank Control, Takeovers, and Corporate Governance in Germany, *Journal of Banking and Finance* 22 (1998): 1385–1403.

22. A good illustration of Japanese firms' resistance to foreign hostile takeovers is Koito Manufacturing preventing T. Boone Pickens from getting on its board. The account can be found in Kenichi Miyashita and David Russell, *Keiretsu: Inside the Hidden Japanese Conglomerates* (McGraw-Hill, 1994, New York).

23. *www.businessweek.com/1999/99_48/b3657017.htm.*

The Securities and Exchange Commission and the Sarbanes-Oxley Act

For a while everyone enjoyed a tremendous bull market. Business seemed to be booming. Investors speculated in the stock markets, optimism was high, and some people even pondered early retirement. Then suddenly, quite dramatically, all of it changed. Large corporations went bankrupt. Corporate officers were found to be deceiving the public. Executives became engaged in courtroom battles that grabbed national headlines. As a result, investors were leery of corporations and the stock markets plummeted.

While these events may sound like the late 1990s and early 2000s, they also describe the late 1920s and early 1930s. There are many examples of fraudulent behavior that can be used to illustrate those times, including unethical activities by corporate executives, securities analysts, large investors, and even newspaper reporters who hyped their own stocks. What did the United States do to try to fix the investor confidence crisis during the early 1930s? The government did something quite dramatic; it decided to regulate the securities markets and created the Securities and Exchange Commission (SEC). The SEC would become the investor's advocate, putting investors on equal footing with the corporations in which they invest. When President Franklin D. Roosevelt signed the Securities Act of 1933 into law, he stated, "The Act is thus intended to correct some of the evils which have been so glaringly revealed in the private exploitation of the public's money."[1]

Seventy years later, the nation found itself again in the midst of an investor confidence crisis. In response, the United States again passed a sweeping securities act, known as the Sarbanes-Oxley Act. When President George

W. Bush signed the act into law in 2002, he stated, "corporate corruption has struck at investor confidence, offending the conscience of our nation . . . And today I sign the most far-reaching reforms of American business practices since the time of Franklin Delano Roosevelt . . . The American economy depends on fairness and honesty. The vast majority of businesses uphold those values. With this law, we have new tools to enforce those values, and we will use those tools aggressively to defend our free enterprise system against corruption and crime."[2]

While corporations in the United States are regulated by many governmental agencies at the state and federal level, the primary rules through which the federal government monitors the activities of corporate managers is through the securities laws adopted in the 1930s and in the Sarbanes-Oxley Act. Accordingly, the text that follows discusses how these rules provide monitoring of publicly traded firms, along with enforcement or rules that are intended to prevent abuses by corporate managers.

THE SECURITIES ACTS

There are seven major laws that govern the securities industry, which the SEC oversees. The first is the **Securities Act of 1933**. This act requires firms to register securities intended for public sale. The most common securities registration form is called **Form S-1**. In the registration form, the firm must describe the securities for sale, give an estimate of and state the specific purposes of the sale's proceeds, and describe the underwriting arrangement. In addition, the firm also has to provide a general overview of itself including a description of the nature of its business, balance sheet and operating income information, and details of its management and management compensation. No information can be fraudulent or deceitful. All statements are made publicly available. The information in the registration form helps potential investors make informed investing decisions.

The **Securities Exchange Act of 1934** created the SEC and gave it authority to oversee the securities industry, including large shareholders (defined as shareholders who own at least 5 percent of a firm), brokerage firms, securities dealers, and the stock exchanges. The 1934 act is broader in scope than the 1933 act. As part of the 1934 act, brokers, dealers, and stock exchanges must register with the SEC and file periodic reports. Just as important, public corporations are also required to submit periodic reports under the act, including annual reports known as **10-Ks** and quarterly reports known as **10-Qs**. In a way these reports are updates of the firms' securities registration forms required under the 1933 act. Since 1996, all public firms had to file their 10-Ks and 10-Qs electronically using the Electronic Data Gathering, Analysis, and Retrieval (EDGAR) system. These company filings can be viewed by anyone on the SEC Web site, *www.sec. gov.* Recently, the SEC introduced the Interactive Data Electronic Application (IDEA) system, which is intended to replace EDGAR with a system that uses interactive data.[3]

In addition to the periodic filings, if significant changes or events take place in between the time these files are submitted, then the firm must file update forms known as **8-Ks**. Examples of significant corporate events that prompt these filings include entering or terminating material business agreements, new financial obligations, change in exchange listing status, and sales of unregistered securities. For example, if a firm agrees to settle a lawsuit against it with a cash payment then the firm must file an 8-K describing the nature of the event, the amount to be paid, and the source of the payment. The 1934 act also allows the SEC to govern the proxy process (this is the process used to solicit shareholder votes on director elections or to approve corporate actions) and the reporting of insider trading that takes place among the firm's executives and other inside parties.

The Trust Indenture Act of 1939 applies to the sale and formal agreement between buyer and seller of debt securities. The Investment Company Act of 1940 regulates investment companies such as mutual funds by requiring the disclosure of their financial condition and their investment policies. The Investment Advisors Act of 1940 currently regulates investment advisors who manage more than $25 million or who advise a registered investment company. The Public Utility Holding Company Act of 1935 regulates gas and electric holding companies. Finally, the Public Company Accounting Reform and Investor Protection Act of 2002 (known as the Sarbanes-Oxley Act) expanded regulation of corporate auditors, boards, and executives.

Summary of the Acts

Note that all of the acts taken together, especially the first two (the 1933 and 1934 acts), simply boil down to the following: The acts force corporations to tell the public about themselves and they cannot lie. This allows investors to make informed decisions. In addition, the spirit of the acts is to put investors' interests first. As such, the SEC represents the primary external regulatory body responsible for corporate governance, especially now given that its role in overseeing public accounting has expanded under the Sarbanes-Oxley Act.

ORGANIZATIONAL STRUCTURE OF THE SECURITIES AND EXCHANGE COMMISSION

Headquartered in Washington, DC, the SEC has 11 regional and district offices. These offices are located in Atlanta, Boston, Chicago, Denver, Fort Worth, Los Angeles, Miami, Philadelphia, Salt Lake City, San Francisco, and New York City. The commission consists of four divisions and employs over 3,500 people.

At the top of the organizational chart are the commissioners. Five commissioners each serve a five-year term. The U.S. president appoints these people and the Senate must approve them. Appointments occur annually and there is one appointment per year because the terms are staggered. No more than three commissioners can belong to the same political party. One commissioner serves as chairman, the top SEC executive, and is also designated by the president. The current SEC Chairman is Mary Schapiro who took the helm in January, 2009.

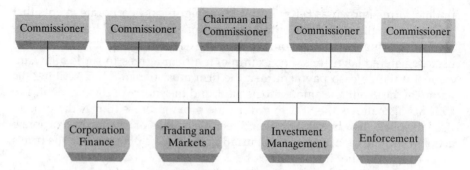

FIGURE 9.1 Securities and Exchange Commission Organizational Structure

Figure 9.1 shows the four divisions that are the pillars of the SEC. The Division of Corporation Finance oversees corporate disclosure, ensuring that the public has all relevant information necessary to make investment decisions. Full corporate disclosure encompasses the registration statements of securities for sale, annual and quarterly reports, proxy materials, and annual reports to shareholders. Because the Division of Corporation Finance reviews the documents required under the 1933, 1934, and 2002 acts, many people tend to think of this Division as being the SEC's primary division.

The Division of Trading and Markets oversees securities markets participants, such as the brokerage firms and their agents, and the stock exchanges under the Investment Advisors Act of 1940. The Division of Trading and Markets is specifically responsible for curtailing securities fraud, for ensuring high-quality securities transactions on exchanges, and for ensuring proper conduct by securities dealers.

The Division of Investment Management assists the SEC with the Investment Company Act of 1940, the Investment Advisors Act of 1940, and the Public Utility Holding Act of 1935. Specifically, the Division of Investment Management is the primary regulator of investment companies. Finally, the Division of Enforcement investigates possible violations of securities laws. The SEC has only civil enforcement authority, but it can also play a crucial role in helping federal agencies pursue criminal charges for severe violations of the law. Each year the SEC prosecutes between 400 and 500 individuals and companies for wrongdoing, with most of these prosecutions being settled out of court. These violations mainly involve accounting fraud, insider trading, and deception regarding securities. A sample litigation release from a recent settlement between Pediatrix Medical Group and the SEC is shown in Example 9.1.

Other SEC offices mostly deal with SEC internal affairs, such as personnel, or serve as advisors (e.g., general counsel and economists) for the divisions and the SEC commissioners. The responsibilities of these offices are varied, including the handling of compliance inspections, investor education, and international affairs. Perhaps the most notable among the offices is the Office of the Chief Accountant, which is the primary advisory office to the SEC on matters of accounting.

EXAMPLE 9.1   Pediatrix Medical Group, Inc., and the Securities and Exchange Commission

Litigation Release No. 20927/March 5, 2009

Securities and Exchange Commission v. Pediatrix Medical Group, Inc., Case No. 09-80366-CIV-RYSKAMP (S.D. Fla.)

Pediatrix Medical Group Settles Charges of Stock Option Backdating

The Securities and Exchange Commission charged Pediatrix Medical Group, Inc. (now known as Mednax Services, Inc.) with backdating stock options grants to executives and employees and with reporting false financial information to shareholders. Pediatrix Medical Group, Inc. ("Pediatrix"), is a physician services provider headquartered in Sunrise, Florida. The Commission's complaint alleges that from approximately 1997 through 2000, Pediatrix, by the actions of a now-deceased former senior financial officer, granted options at below-market prices ("in-the-money" options). Pediatrix has agreed to settle the Commission's charges without admitting or denying the allegations.

The Commission's complaint, filed in federal court in Miami, alleges that on numerous occasions, Pediatrix used hindsight to select favorable exercise prices for employee and officer stock option grants without accurately reporting the financial impact of the grants to investors. According to well-established accounting standards, Pediatrix was required to record an expense for in-the-money options. Pediatrix allegedly avoided those expenses by retrospectively picking dates on which Pediatrix's stock was trading at lower prices and dating and pricing grants of stock options as if they had been granted on those earlier dates.

According to the Commission's complaint, Pediatrix's intentional backdating of stock option grants resulted in material misstatements and omissions in certain of the forms 10-Q, 10-K, registration statements, and proxy statements that the company filed with the Commission. More specifically, the complaint alleges that Pediatrix failed to recognize a total of $8.8 million in compensation expense for the in-the-money value of the backdated stock options, resulting in an overstatement of Pediatrix's pretax income by approximately 6.74 percent in the relevant time period. Moreover, the complaint alleges that Pediatrix's filings contained material misstatements with respect to how it priced and accounted for its stock options.

Without admitting or denying the Commission's allegations, Pediatrix consented to be enjoined from violating Section 17(a) of the securities act, sections 10(b), 13(a), 13(b)(2)(A), 13(b)(2)(B), and 14(a) of the exchange act, and rules 10b-5, 12b-20, 13a-1, 13a-13, and 14a-9 thereunder. The Commission took into account the cooperation that Pediatrix provided Commission staff during its investigation.

NEED FOR THE ACTS AND THE SECURITIES AND EXCHANGE COMMISSION

Opinions regarding the SEC vary. Businesses and the securities industry are not always happy with SEC decisions. In addition, the costs of reporting and following SEC regulations, in general, are tremendous. Byron C. Radaker, CEO of Congoleum Corporation, took his company private in the early 1980s, citing that this would save his firm between $6 and $8 million per year in reporting costs.[4] While companies may not appreciate the SEC, the question that needs to be asked is can investors do without it? In order to consider this we must first think about the thrust of the securities acts.

Many people, especially academics, believe that the stock markets are "efficient." What does this mean? The notion of market efficiency is that current stock prices reflect their fundamentally correct value. To understand this concept, consider this point: Millions of people participate in the stock markets. The average of their beliefs and opinions, based on current and past information, will be reflected in the current stock price. For example, if a stock price is too low, some people out of the millions would recognize this and rush to buy the stock. Because of the buying, the stock price would rise and not be undervalued for long. Millions of market participants continuously process information which, in turn, makes the markets efficient. If markets are efficient then do we really need the SEC?

In the context of market efficiency, if companies do hide facts or lie, then someone will find out because many people are involved, including brokers, analysts, directors, employees, accountants, creditors, investors, and even state regulators. Thus the inevitable revelation of fraud will cause the stock price to plummet. Besides, companies that lie and get caught cannot last anyway. We have always had a climate where consumers and investors have cast a suspicious eye toward large businesses.

Some finance scholars have attempted to assess empirically the importance of SEC regulation to our financial markets. In 1964, George Stigler, who would later go on to win the Nobel Prize in economics, published a famous study in which he compared new securities being issued in the 1920s to those issued in the 1950s, to determine whether the existence of the SEC had improved the securities markets.[5] He found no difference and he contended that SEC regulation did not improve the quality of the securities markets. However, two other professors subsequently countered Stigler's study, citing that securities fraud decreased because of the existence of the SEC.[6] This debate continues today. In 1995, in response to market participants' complaints regarding regulatory costs and excessive regulatory burdens, the SEC formed a committee to study the feasibility of making it less burdensome for established public firms to issue securities.[7] In 1998, the SEC issued such a proposal but it was not enacted.

Overall we may never know for sure if the SEC does make our securities markets better. Perhaps markets would still be efficient without the SEC. However, the very existence of the SEC might contribute to market discipline and thus market efficiency. Consider, for instance, that whenever the SEC makes enforcements actions against public firms for disclosure violations or other securities acts violations, the stock price of those firms decline upon hearing the news. So the SEC at least has some "teeth" as a disciplinarian.[8]

SECURITIES AND EXCHANGE COMMISSION PROBLEM AREAS

Reporting

One issue that people question is the adequacy of quarterly and annual reporting. If the information is to be useful then there may need to be more frequent reporting. We now live in a world where technology permits us to access information, especially up-to-date information, on a continuous basis. Why not take advantage of this? Of course, frequent reporting would cause an outcry by corporate America, which already complains about reporting costs but there may be several viable ways to address this issue. One approach that is perpetually under consideration is to require companies to submit their reports earlier.[9] Instead of providing a deadline of 90 days after the close of the fiscal year for filing of annual reports, it could be 60 days. For quarterly filings the deadline could be shortened to 30 days instead of 45. However, this suggestion might not be ideal. Note that the report frequency may still be the same but the timing would improve. Also, as pointed out in a *Business Week* commentary, this proposal might only add concerns about the haste and thus the accuracy with which companies compile reports.[10] Another way to address the problem of infrequent reporting is to force companies to reveal immediately any material information that investors will deem important.[11] In fact, since March 2004, the SEC has required that 8-Ks be filed within 4 instead of the previous 5 to 15 business days after the triggering event.

Punishment

Others believe that the SEC may be too weak because it cannot pursue criminal prosecution. Note that the SEC has the authority to bring civil charges only. If criminal prosecution can serve as a key deterrent to corporate crime then there may be some truth to the notion that the SEC does not really have the policing power necessary to do its job. However, this problem may not be critical. The SEC can easily persuade prosecutors to bring criminal charges once it has evidence that the case has merit. Also keep in mind that prosecuting corporate criminals is difficult. As pointed out in the July 1, 2002, issue of *Business Week*,[12] securities laws are ambiguous, sophisticated financial concepts that are difficult to grasp and executives have plenty of tricks up their sleeves to absolve themselves of responsibility (e.g., "I didn't know that the books were fraudulent."). Therefore, in light of current difficulties with criminal charges, giving an additional agency, such as the SEC, the additional responsibility of bringing criminal charges might not make sense.

Having civil charge authority only, the primary punishment tool employed by the SEC is to fine companies for wrongdoing. Heavier and heavier fines seem to be levied. Critics argue that when individuals, such as corporate executives, commit fraud, they should be punished. Yet it is often the company that gets fined. Ultimately, those fines are paid by the shareholders because it comes out of the company's profits. Shareholders end up suffering twice—once when the stock price falls as news of the wrongdoing is released and again when the company must pay the fines for the wrongdoing. Indeed, managers often deflect an SEC investigation by offering to pay a fine with the company's money.

Consider that the SEC investigated Bristol-Myers Squibb for accounting fraud in 2002. This led to a 50 percent decline in stock price (a loss of about $40 billion in market capitalization) in the ensuing months and a restatement of earnings in 2003, which included a lowering of reported sales for 1999 to 2001 by $2.5 billion. In August of 2004, after a two-year investigation, Bristol-Myers agreed to settle SEC civil charges by paying a $150 million fine.[13] After seeing their firm lose $40 billion in value because of the accounting fraud allegations, the shareholders will lose another $150 million as punishment for the executives' behavior.

EXAMPLE 9.2 Securities and Exchange Commission Fails to Discover $50 Billion Ponzi Scheme

One activity of the SEC is monitoring investment advisors to ensure they are not misappropriating their clients' funds. Of particular concern is a "ponzi" scheme where an investment advisor does not actually invest his clients' funds but instead arbitrarily reports high profits. These high profits then draw in new clients whose funds are used to pay profits to the original investors. Throughout this process of creating artificial profits, the investment advisor typically embezzles a large portion of the funds.

While it seems like a ponzi scheme would be easy to detect, the SEC failed to uncover the scheme run by Bernie Madoff for more than 30 years.[14] Adding up all client investments, Madoff managed about $50 billion of his clients' money in 2008 (based on the statements he sent them, including years of phony profits). During the market sell-off in the fall of 2008, a large proportion of his investors asked to withdrawal all their money and Madoff was forced to admit he was running a ponzi scheme. Most of the money was gone.

Where did the money go? The SEC is currently working on figuring this out. But the bigger question that many are asking is why the SEC did not catch on to a scheme that was run for so long involving such a large amount of money. All it would have taken is to require that Madoff show he had balances in investment accounts equal to amounts owed to clients. This is a simple test that many assumed the SEC had been doing all along. Further embarrassing the SEC was the fact that there have been numerous tips over the years that Madoff was running a ponzi scheme.[15] As the SEC is the watchdog for investors, this is perhaps the largest failure in the SEC's history. Whether it was Madoff's political connections as past Chairman of NASDAQ or a lack of staffing, the failure to uncover Madoff's scheme cost the SEC a great deal in terms of its credibility as an effective monitor of traders and markets.

Securities and Exchange Commission Resources

Another problem may be that the commission was, and maybe still is, under-funded. Being underfunded has two repercussions. First, the SEC may be hindered in its ability to hire and retain the best staff. One estimate had put the pay of SEC attorneys and examiners at as much as 40 percent less than their peers at comparable federal agencies.[16] In 2001, Congress did give approval to the SEC to pay its lawyers and accountants salaries that are competitive with other government banking agencies, such as the Federal Reserve. The increase in budget from the passage of the Public Company Accounting Reform and Investor Protection Act of 2002 ended up being much larger, more than $300 million, than the previous budget.

For a long time the SEC has had the distinction of being an important stepping-stone for many young ambitious and talented attorneys and account-ants, who usually can count on the experience to command much higher salaries elsewhere. These talented people gain experience and a name for themselves at the SEC and then they are hired by the very law firms that represent companies, auditing firms, and individuals that deal with the SEC. According to one estimate, the SEC employee turnover rate is 30 percent, which is double the rate for the rest of the government. Losing talent shortens the SEC's institutional memory and the average experience of its key employees, while it increases the time and money needed to train new hires.

A second repercussion of being underfunded is being under-staffed. Since 1993, the SEC's workload has almost doubled but staffing levels have been stagnant.[17] Former SEC Commissioner Laura S. Unger once admitted that there were only about 100 lawyers who reviewed the disclosure docu-ments of the 17,000 public firms.[18] An SEC chief accountant stated that only 1 out of 15 annual reports was reviewed. While it may be impossible for the SEC ever to be able to pursue and investigate thoroughly all possible viola-tions, a larger staff would definitely be able to do more. In light of the crisis of the early 2000s, the SEC tripled the number of probes.[19] However, overwork-ing the current staff cannot last forever. Fortunately, the Public Company Accounting Reform and Investor Protection Act of 2002 mandated that the SEC hire hundreds more people.

EXAMPLE 9.3   Arthur Levitt's "I Told You So"

Arthur Levitt served as SEC chairman from 1993 to 2001 and he was often criticized by business—both corporate America and the accounting profes-sion attacked him. This situation is probably why a September 2000 issue of *Business Week* dubbed Levitt the "Investor's Champion."[20]

Levitt was known as a tough regulator whose victories included censur-ing the National Association of Securities Dealers for collusive pricing practices, which resulted in NASDAQ dealers having to pony up more than $1 billion to settle the case. Another was the adoption of Regulation Fair Disclosure, which put an end to corporate officers tipping off analysts. Toward the end of his tenure, one of his main causes was to clean up the accounting profession. In a famous speech delivered at New York University on September 28, 1998, Levitt called for an end to the "numbers game."[21] Levitt felt that corporate managers, auditors, and analysts participated in the process of managing earnings, using a variety of tricks (he called them "nods and winks") to meet earnings estimates, all at the expense of high-quality full disclosure. He felt that this game had to stop and accountants needed to make numbers more reliable and to have the trust of the investing public.

Levitt felt strongly that one way to clean up the accounting profession, which in the late 1990s was facing a slew of accounting scandals, would be to separate the accountant's role as auditor and consultant for the same firm. Levitt felt that there was a huge conflict of interest. Of course there was a tremendous backlash from both corporate America, which claimed that accountants who consult for them are in the best position to audit them and from the accounting industry, which did not want to see profitable consulting practices taken away. Less than two years later, on June 27, 2000, the SEC unanimously approved issuing Levitt's proposal. In the end Congress defeated the proposal. Then two years later, Congress passed most of Levitt's proposals in the Sarbanes-Oxley Act of 2002. Senator Robert Torricelli, a New Jersey democrat, told Levitt on January 24, 2002, "We were wrong. You were right."[22]

SARBANES-OXLEY ACT OF 2002

The **Public Company Accounting Reform and Investor Protection Act of 2002**, a bill drafted by Democratic Senator Paul Sarbanes and Republican Congressman Michael Oxley, was signed into law by U.S. President George W. Bush on July 30, 2002. Overall, the act (usually called the Sarbanes-Oxley Act) created a new oversight body to regulate auditors, created laws pertaining to corporate responsibility, and increased punishments for corporate white-collar crime. The main aspects of this act are as follows:

1. The legislation establishes a nonprofit corporation called the Public Company Accounting Oversight Board, which will operate under SEC discretion, to oversee the audit of public companies and to protect the interests of investors and the general public by improving audit report accuracy.
2. The act attempts to protect investors by breaking the relationships among auditors, consultants, and the public company being audited.
3. The act increases the monitoring ability and responsibilities of boards of directors and improves their credibility by making boards more independent and more responsible for audits.
4. The act tries to make executive actions more transparent to shareholders by requiring the disclosure of "off-balance-sheet transactions" and decreasing the time to two days that an executive has to report company stock (and other equity) trades to the SEC.
5. The legislation makes it easier to prosecute executive criminal behavior in the future by spelling out new or altered definitions of criminal behaviors, by requiring the top two officers of the firm to certify financial statements, and by stiffening penalties.

The 2002 Act's Effect on Accounting Oversight

With the 2002 act's establishment of the Public Company Accounting Oversight Board (PCAOB), the SEC's oversight over public accounting has dramatically expanded. Before the act, the Financial Accounting Standards Board (FASB) and the American Institute of Certified Public Accountants (AICPA) were primarily responsible for governing accounting standards and overseeing audits. In 1973, the SEC appointed FASB, a nongovernment entity made up of members of the accounting, business, and academic professions, to set accounting standards. Its standards are known as generally accepted accounting principles (GAAP). The SEC also required that all public firms be audited by Certified Public Accountants (CPAs) who had to make sure that audited firms complied with GAAP. To oversee this process, the SEC had granted authority to the AICPA to govern external auditors (i.e., public accounting firms) and to set auditing standards. Since the enactment of the 2002 act, however, the AICPA lost its authority to oversee public company audits to the SEC's new PCAOB.

Public Company Accounting Oversight Board

The PCAOB is a nonprofit entity whose financing comes from firms registered with the SEC and from public accounting firms. Under the 2002 act, all public firms have to be registered with PCAOB and meet its standards. The PCAOB oversees the public accounting firms as well. The board consists of five members appointed by the SEC. But while all five members must be financially literate, what is interesting is that only two can be or have previously been CPAs. The duties of the Board are to:

1. register public accounting firms;
2. establish or adopt auditing quality control, ethics, independence, and other standards;
3. conduct inspections of public accounting firms;
4. conduct investigations, disciplinary proceedings, and sanctions of accounting firms were justified;
5. promote high professional standards and improve the quality of audit services;
6. enforce compliance of the rules of the Board, professional standards, and securities laws in regard to auditing; and
7. oversee the budget and manage the operations of the Board.

The five members will be employed full time by the Board and will exhibit independence from the public accounting firms being regulated.

Auditor Independence

The Sarbanes-Oxley Act also tries to ensure auditor independence. This aspect of the act attempts to address one of the core problems with auditors being monitors of the firm (see Chapter 3). To accomplish this goal, the act does the following:

1. prohibits accounting firms from providing both auditing and consulting activities for the same firm;

2. gives the audit committee of the company's board of directors authority over auditing activities;
3. forces the lead audit partner in an audit team to change at least every five years;
4. disallows auditing by an accounting firm if any of the top executives of the public company were employed by the accounting firm within the past year; and
5. requires a study to be conducted that investigates the potential outcomes of mandatory rotation of accounting firms conducting audits.

Corporate Responsibility

The Sarbanes-Oxley Act also attempts to increase the monitoring ability and responsibilities of boards of directors and improve their credibility. Specifically the act does the following:

1. makes the audit committee of the board of directors both more independent from management and solely responsible for the hiring and oversight of auditing services and the accounting complaint process;
2. requires that all directors on the audit committee are independent directors and that one director on the committee be a financial expert;
3. forces CEOs and CFOs (chief financial officers) to certify the appropriateness of the financial statements filed with the SEC;
4. makes it unlawful to mislead, coerce, or fraudulently influence an accountant engaged in auditing activities;
5. forces executives of the firm to forfeit any profit from bonus or stock sales resulting in earnings that needed to be restated as a result of misconduct; and
6. prohibits executives from making stock transactions during the time in which the employee pension plan blacks out employee stock transactions.

Enhanced Financial Disclosures

The Sarbanes-Oxley Act tries to make executive actions more transparent to shareholders. Specifically the act does the following:

1. requires the disclosure of "off-balance sheet transactions" and corrections in reporting identified by auditors;
2. decreases the time an executive has to report company stock (and other equity) trades to the SEC to two days;
3. prohibits the lending of money by public companies to executives, except for the use of home loans;
4. requires increased internal financial controls and review by the board of directors; and
5. encourages a code of ethics for senior officers of the company and report changes and exemptions to the SEC.

Analysts Conflicts of Interests

The role of securities analysts and their failure to monitor the company is detailed in Chapter 5. In recognizing this failure, the act tasks the SEC to develop rules for making sure that analysts are separated from investment banking activities and that any conflicts of interests that analysts may have are fully disclosed.

Securities and Exchange Commission Resources and Authority

One limitation that the SEC has had over the years is that the SEC is small compared to the industry it regulates. The SEC regulates tens of thousands of public companies, investment banks, auditors, and other participants in the stock and bond markets. In order to help it expand its monitoring and investigative capabilities, the act appropriates more money for the SEC and mandates the hiring of at least 200 more employees.

Corporate and Criminal Fraud, Accountability, and Penalties

To make it easier to prosecute executive criminal behavior in the future, the new law spells out new or altered definitions of criminal behaviors and stiffens penalties. For example, the destruction or falsification of documents in a federal investigation or bankruptcy can be punished with a fine and/or imprisonment of up to 10 years. Destruction of audit materials is punishable by a fine and/or imprisonment of up to five years. The statute of limitations for securities fraud is changed to two years after the discovery of the facts or five years after the violation. The bill also protects employee whistle blowers from retaliation by the company or its executives.

    The penalties for committing white-collar crimes were generally increased from a maximum of five years imprisonment to 20 years in most cases. While this pertains to just the *maximum* prison sentence, federal sentencing guidelines were also amended. That is, the intent is for the actual *average* white-collar prison sentence to increase, not just the maximum. Also, the company's principal executive officer (usually the CEO) and principal financial officer (usually the CFO) are required to certify the appropriateness of the financial statements. If they willfully violate the integrity of the disclosures, they can be fined up to $1 million and serve up to 10 years in prison.

WILL THE ACT BE BENEFICIAL?

Note that the Sarbanes-Oxley Act addresses many of the problems outlined in this book. For example, the act addresses problems with auditing, boards of directors, executive behavior, the SEC, and analysts. Thus far, however, it might be fair to say that legal scholars, corporate executives, and, to a lesser extent, large shareholders, have been critical of the act. In general, legal scholars seem to think that the act is either misplaced or repetitive to existing laws.[23]

For example, aside from giving loans to the executives, they argue that Enron would have complied with the governance rules of the Sarbanes-Oxley Act. Yet that did not inhibit Enron from governance failures that caused it to collapse. In addition, many argue that compliance with the act is too burdensome and expensive.[24] Companies report that the average expense for implementing the act was $5.1 million and that the average ongoing annual cost of compliance is $3.7 million.[25]

However, it will probably take some time before the act can be determined a success or a failure. What will make assessing the act especially difficult is that we will not know how much fraud would have been committed had the act not been passed nor will we be able to easily attribute any increase in investor confidence directly to the act. The latter issue is especially problematic as firms can verifiably know the costs of compliance but they *cannot* reliably associate any increase in the firm's value as a result of the act. For this reason the act will probably continue to be a topic of debate for some years.

OTHER REGULATORY CHANGES

In 2002, in light of the burgeoning number of accounting scandals, the SEC chairman called on the New York Stock Exchange (NYSE) and the NASDAQ Stock Market to take a fresh look at their corporate governance listing standards. The markets were challenged to develop and adopt listing standards to address the crisis in investor confidence. Because they developed new governance standards at that same time as the Sarbanes-Oxley Act was being debated, it is not surprising that their new rules are similar to the act's laws. However, there are a few differences that reflect the distinctive types of firms listed on the two exchanges. In November 2003, the SEC approved both the NYSE's and the NASDAQ's changes in listing standards.

The New York Stock Exchange

The NYSE can impose rules on NYSE-listed firms only, which means that its rules do not affect non-listed firms, nor can it impose rules on other members of the business community, such as auditors and financial analysts. We focus here on those rules that were adopted by the NYSE but not adopted by the act.

Most of the new NYSE corporate governance rules have to do with the structure, function, and incentives of the board of directors. Specifically, the NYSE mandates that companies have a *majority of independent directors.* A director is not independent if he or she (or immediate family) has worked for the company or its auditor within the past five years. The board members that are not also executives of the company *must meet regularly* without the presence of management.

The NYSE also requires specific functions of the board. For example, the nominating committee of the board must be composed entirely of independent directors and perform certain duties. This is also true of the compensation committee. Otherwise the executives would have undue influence on their own compensation. As in the act, the audit committee must also be independent and the members of this committee will have an increased authority and responsibility to hire and fire the auditing firm. To handle this expanded responsibility, the audit committee members are to have necessary experience and expertise in finance and accounting. To help maintain the independence of audit committee board members, members are not to receive pay from the company outside of their regular director fees, especially consulting fees.

Lastly, the NYSE will require that shareholders approve all executive equity-based compensation plans. That is, there will be a shareholder vote on whether the CEO gets a certain number of stock options or restricted stock shares. This rule creates more transparency because each shareholder will receive a proxy statement detailing the compensation proposal.

NASDAQ Stock Market

The firms listing on the NASDAQ Stock Market tend to be smaller, on average, than those listing on the NYSE. The NASDAQ also lists a greater proportion of companies in the technology industry than the NYSE. Therefore, NASDAQ adopted rules in the same spirit as those adopted by the NYSE but with differences intended to fit better with its listing firms.

For example, smaller firms often have a smaller number of board members. The Sarbanes-Oxley Act and the new NYSE rules empower independent directors and give them much responsibility. However, the implementation may overwhelm a small number of independent directors serving on a small firm board. Consider a board with only seven directors. Only four independent board members are needed to create a board with an independent director majority. However, having only four independent directors makes it difficult to have independent committees for executive compensation, nomination, auditing, and so on. So instead of having a rule that an independent compensation committee must approve the executive's compensation, they provide an alternative that the independent directors can approve the compensation directly (without being all members of a compensation committee).

While the NYSE requires that shareholders approve all executive equity-based compensation plans, the NASDAQ recognizes that offering "inducement" options to new employees are a common and important practice in the technology sector. The NASDAQ rules allow these offers to new employees without shareholder approval if they are approved by a majority of independent directors and properly disclosed.

INTERNATIONAL PERSPECTIVE

Earlier it was mentioned that we could not know for certain whether or not the United States is better off having the SEC. However, one way we can get some insight into the importance of securities regulation would be to compare countries that have a strong securities regulator and/or regulations to those countries that do not. If stronger regulation is beneficial from a corporate governance perspective, then we should see more successful companies when there is more effective regulations. Two recent academic studies attempt to answer this question.

In one study, the authors examine the quality of securities laws in 49 countries.[26] First, they create a "public enforcement index" that assesses the strength of the countries' public securities regulator (i.e., an institution such as the U.S. SEC) by measuring the regulators' autonomy (i.e., are they free from political interference), by whether or not they are primarily focused on stock markets, by their ability to issue rules, by their ability to investigate potential rule violations, and by their ability to impose sanctions on violators. Second, they create a "private enforcement index" from the countries' quality of disclosure (e.g., on prospectuses of new securities issues, information on compensation, information on ownership structure, etc.) and the relative burden of proof required by investors seeking retribution from firms (in particular, for the omission of material information on prospectuses). Overall they find that countries' quality of public enforcement is unrelated to stock market development. In contrast, countries' quality of private enforcement is strongly related to their stock market development. Their findings suggest that securities laws do matter but probably not as much as many of us would have thought.

The authors of another study use a different criterion to measure the quality of securities laws and find that when law quality is higher the country enjoys a lower cost of equity, higher liquidity for securities, and superior market price efficiency.[27] In other words, this study suggests that securities laws are beneficial. Similarly, evidence from cross-listing of firms suggests that there is a benefit to companies from the increased monitoring of strong regulators such as the SEC. Cross-listed firms are those who choose to list their stock on a foreign exchange in addition to an exchange in their home country. Overall, there is some evidence that cross-listing in a country such as the United States may increase the value of the foreign company because of the resulting increased corporate governance.[28] While corporate scandals were front-page news in the United States and the U.S. Congress was debating the Sarbanes-Oxley Act, countries all over the world were also examining their own corporate governance policies. These actions were also motivated by their own corporate scandals, such as Royal Ahold (of The Netherlands), Parmalat (of Italy), Daewoo Group (of South Korea), Vivendi Universal (of France), and Adecco (a Swiss firm), to name a few. In response to these scandals, many countries adopted changes in their governance system similar in spirit to those adopted under the Sarbanes-Oxley Act. A comprehensive listing of such codes and recent updates is maintained by the European Corporate Governance Institute.[29]

Summary

The SEC's main function is to oversee the federal securities acts, which mandate that public corporations tell the public about themselves and that they do so honestly. The SEC also reviews documents filed in accordance with the acts and investigates potential violations of its acts. The SEC seems to be a powerful and effective monitor, but it has encountered some problems in the performance of its duties. It may be overworked, underfunded, and understaffed. In addition it only has civil powers to punish wrongdoers, not criminal powers. This leads to a focus of levying fines against corporations where executives have been charged with committing fraud. In the end, shareholders suffer from both the wrongdoing itself and the SEC punishment. The Sarbanes-Oxley Act of 2002 gives the SEC more money and power, but will it be enough? The failure to detect Bernie Madoff's $50 billion ponzi scheme or the looming financial collapse of 2008 suggest the effectiveness of SEC monitoring is still problematic.

In response to the corporate and investment community scandals during 2000 and 2001, the U.S. government responded with the enactment of the Sarbanes-Oxley Act. The act established a nonprofit corporation to oversee the audit of public companies, tried to ensure auditor independence, attempted to increase the monitoring ability and responsibilities of boards of directors, tried to make executive actions more transparent to shareholders, tasked the SEC to develop rules for making sure that analysts are separated from investment banking activities, appropriated more money for the SEC, and spelled out new or altered definitions of criminal behaviors and stiffened penalties. Has the act been beneficial? It is hard to say at this point. While scandalous behavior may have been prevented by the act, these benefits are impossible to measure. In contrast, the cost of complying with the act has been criticized widely by legal scholars, business executives, and even large shareholders.

WEB Info about the Securities and Exchange Commission and the Sarbanes-Oxley Act

U. S. Securities and Exchange Commission
www.sec.gov

SEC Filings & Forms (EDGAR)
www.sec.gov/edgar.shtml

Public Company Accounting Oversight Board
www.pcaobus.org/

NYSE Corporate Governance Listing Standards
www.nyse.com/regulation/nyse/1101074746736.html

Review Questions

1. Name and describe the acts that are overseen by the SEC that governs the securities industry.
2. Describe the organizational structure and the primary functions of the SEC.
3. What are the main problems that the SEC has encountered in trying to perform its duties?
4. Describe the major components of the Sarbanes-Oxley Act.

Discussion Questions

1. Do you think we need more or less securities regulation? If more, then do you have any good ideas for additional ones? If less, then which regulations would you eliminate and why?

2. If you were a commissioner of the SEC, would you make any changes in the focus of the SEC in regulating the various parties it monitors? Explain why you would make these changes.

3. As a current or future shareholder, are you happy with the Sarbanes-Oxley Act? As a current or future business employee, are you happy with the act? What has been the general consensus of the Sarbanes-Oxley Act among your colleagues at work, your friends, and in the media?

Exercises

1. Go to the SEC Web site (*www.sec.gov*) and use the EDGAR system to download a 10-Q filing for a large U.S. firm. What does the filing reveal about the firm's operations, its management team, and its financial condition?

2. Find a firm that is currently undergoing an SEC investigation (or has recently settled a suit with the SEC). Describe the issues and circumstances involved. Is, or was, any other government agency, such as the DOJ or New York's Attorney General's Office, involved? If so, then explain their (or its) involvement.

3. Do some research and identify the primary complaints that executives have with the Sarbanes-Oxley Act. Are others complaining about it too? Explain why or why not.

4. Go to the *ecgi.org* Web site. This site contains a link to corporate governance codes from countries all over the world. Provide some thoughts on codes from three different countries and try to explain why there might be differences among the codes.

5. Do some research and find out whether or not firms are reluctant to list on the NYSE because of the new regulations? What about international listings on the NYSE? Have international listings increased or decreased since the passage of NYSE's new regulations? Some people predict that it might increase. Why do you think that they are predicting this?

Exercises for Non-U.S. Students

1. Describe securities regulation in your country. In your opinion, does it impose high quality regulations?

2. Does your country's securities regulator follow through with effective enforcement of its laws? Describe the last time they prosecuted any person or firm for a securities violation.

3. To what extent do you think politics contributes to the quality of securities laws in your country? Explain.

4. Describe your country's corporate code or laws with regard to corporate governance. Also, in your opinion, what are its strengths and weaknesses? Finally, what do you think caused the code or laws to be strong or weak?

5. Identify all Sarbanes-Oxley rules that your country also has and identify those Sarbanes-Oxley rules that your country does not have. Why does your country have and not have these specific rules?

Endnotes

1. Joel Seligman, *The Transformation of Wall Street* (Boston, MA: Northeastern University Press, 1995).

2. *www.whitehouse.gov/news/releases/2002/07/20020730.html*.

3. *www.sec.gov/idea/searchidea/what_is_idea.html*.

4. Cited in Eugene F. Brigham and Michael C. Ehrhardt, *Financial Management*, 10th Edition (Orlando, FL: Harcourt Publishers, 2002), p. 759.

5. George J. Stigler, "Public Regulation of the Securities Markets," *Journal of Business* 37 (1964): 117–142.

6. Irwin Friend and Edward S. Herman, "The SEC Through a Glass Darkly," *Journal of Business* 37 (1964): 382–405.

7. See unpublished paper by Hyun-Han Shin, "The SEC's Review of the Registration Statement and Stock Price Movements during the Seasoned Equity Issuance Process," (Ph.D. diss., Ohio State University, 1995).

8. Mahmoud M. Nourayi, Stock Price Responses to the SEC's Enforcement Actions, *Journal of Accounting and Public Policy* 13 (1994): 333–347.

9. Judy Mathewson, James L. Tyson, and David Evans, "Harvey Pitt: Odd Man Out on Enron," *Bloomberg Markets* (March 2002): 51–56.

10. Mike McNamee, "The SEC's Accounting Reforms Won't Answer Investor's Prayers," *Business Week*, June 17, 2002, 28.

11. Judy Mathewson, James L. Tyson, and David Evans, "Harvey Pitt: Odd Man Out on Enron," *Bloomberg Markets*, March 2002, 51–56.

12. Mike France and Dan Carney, "Why Corporate Crooks Are Tough to Nail," *Business Week*, July 1, 2002, 35–38.

13. Lewis Krauskopf, "Charged with Accounting Fraud, Bristol-Myers Squibb Settles for $150 Million," *Knight Ridder Tribune Business News*, August 5, 2004, 1.

14. David Voreacos and David Glovin, Madoff Confessed $50 Billion Fraud Before FBI Arrived, *Bloomberg News*, December 12, 2008.

15. *www.boston.com/business/articles/2009/01/08/the_whistleblower*.

16. Joseph Nocera, "System Failure," *Fortune*, June 24, 2002, 62–72.

17. Mike McNamee and Amy Borrus, "The Reluctant Reformer," *Business Week*, March 25, 2002, 72–81.

18. Joseph Nocera, "System Failure," *Fortune*, June 24, 2002, 62–72.

19. Mike McNamee and Amy Borrus, "The Reluctant Reformer," *Business Week*, March 25, 2002, 72–81.

20. Cover story in *Business Week*, September 25, 2000.

21. Arthur Levitt and Paula Dwyer, *Take on the Street: What Wall Street and Corporate America Don't Want You to Know*, Pantheon Books, New York, 2002.

22. Judy Mathewson, James L. Tyson, and David Evans, "Harvey Pitt: Odd Man Out on Enron," *Bloomberg Markets*, March 2002, 51–56.

23. Of course, it's difficult to summarize all of the legal literature that has come out against the Sarbanes-Oxley Act, but the interested reader can refer to Roberta Romano, "The Sarbanes-Oxley Act and the Making of Quack Corporate Governance," NYU, Law and Econ Research Paper 04–032; Yale Law & Econ Research Paper 297; Yale ICF Working Paper 04–37; ECGI—Finance Working Paper 52/2004, September 26, 2004, for a thorough overview.

24. In a *Business Week* article, it estimates that compliance to the Act can be as high as $35 million annually for large firms ("Death, Taxes, and Sarbanes-Oxley?" *Business Week*, January 17, 2005).

25. Thirty-first Annual Board of Directors Study, Korn/Ferry International, (Los Angeles, CA, 2004).

26. Rafael LaPorta, Florencio Lopez-de-Silanes, and Andrei Shleifer, "What Works in Securities Laws?" *Journal of Finance* 61 (2006): 1–32.

27. Hazem Daouk, Charles Lee, and David Ng, "Capital Market Governance: How do Security Laws Affect Market Performance?" *Journal of Corporate Finance* 12 (2006): 560–593.

28. For a literature review of the corporate governance effects from cross-listing, see Stephen Ferris, Kenneth Kim and Greg Noronha, "The Effect of Cross-Listing on Corporate Governance: A Review of the International Evidence," *Corporate Governance: An International Review* 17 (2009): 338–352.

29. *www.ecgi.org/codes/all_codes.php*.

Moral Hazard, Systemic Risk, and Bailouts

The financial crisis of 2007 to 2009 showcased the role of the government as the "deep pocket" solution to failures in markets. Why should the government step in and save companies from their own bad decisions? The argument that will be explored in this chapter is that some companies are "too big to fail." In other words, the fear is that failure of a large company such as Citibank or General Motors (GM) would have repercussions throughout the economy. Their failure would start a chain reaction where other companies would fail, hundreds of thousands of people would become unemployed, and the economy would spiral downward. The possibility of one company's bankruptcy causing a chain reaction through an economy is called **systemic risk**. To moderate systemic risk, the U.S. government made loans and bought stock in AIG, previously the world's largest insurance company, totaling more than $170 billion. The goal was to prevent AIG from defaulting on over a trillion dollars in obligations to banks and financial companies around the world.[1] In addition to AIG, hundreds of commercial banks and other key corporations were "bailed out" by governments worldwide to try and avoid a global economic collapse.

From a corporate governance view, the willingness of the U.S. Department of the Treasury and the Federal Reserve to bail out struggling large companies introduces a new aspect of **moral hazard** to an already suspect system of corporate governance. Moral hazard refers to the situation when a decision maker who is insulated from the bad outcomes of the decision may behave differently than one who must endure all consequences of a decision. Those who are insulated from the bad outcomes are more likely to take greater risks with their decisions. In this financial crisis, moral hazard played a role because large financial companies knew the federal government would not allow major bank failures because of their systemic risk. The implicit guarantee of the U.S. government created a situation where managers of financial firms had an incentive to take excessive risks. If those risks paid off, the managers would be rewarded handsomely and firm value would increase. But if a bad outcome occurred, the Federal Reserve and Treasury Department would step in and prevent the bankruptcy of the company. The "heads I win, tails you lose" mentality of this moral hazard has been described by critics of the U.S. government bailout approach as "privatize the gain, socialize the loss."[2] In other words, the benefits of a risky strategy flow to the private company while the costs are borne by taxpayers.

This moral hazard in financial markets should be familiar. It is the same situation as a manager who takes excessive risks with corporate funds. She or he is effectively gambling the shareholders' money for the benefit of management. The difference in the case of firms who are "too big to fail" is that the agency problems between executives and shareholders are exacerbated. An executive of a large bank can risk both shareholders' money and, indirectly, U.S. taxpayer money. If there are good results, the extra risk taken leads to record profits for the firm and correspondingly large incentive compensation for the executive. In the event that the excess risk wipes out the firm, the executive does not have to give back prior compensation. After the government bails out the company, the executive even has a good chance of retaining his or her job.[3]

This chapter will first discuss the history of how systemic risk has triggered government bailouts in past crises. Next, the causes of the financial crisis of 2007 to 2009 and the associated bailouts are examined. Finally, international responses and issues relating to systemic risk and bailouts are discussed. Throughout the analysis, we consider how corporate governance issues and moral hazard affect corporate decisions.

HISTORY OF SYSTEMIC RISK AND BAILOUTS

Most bailouts occur because of government policies enacted during the Great Depression in the early 1930s. The economic effects of the Depression were so severe and lasted so long that economists have carefully studied that period to learn how to avoid such steep economic contractions. While the triggering event was the collapse of the stock market in 1929, most economists have concluded that another cause of the Great Depression was the collapse of the banking system. The period experienced a series of **bank runs**. A bank run occurs when depositors *en masse* take their cash out of the bank. As banks make money by loaning out deposits, there is not much cash on hand and banks can quickly find themselves without enough funds to pay depositors. News of one bank running out of cash creates a panic among depositors of other banks, who then demand cash from their banks. Beyond bank runs, there were also problems with bad loans as the economy fell into a depression. In terms of what economists call the *money supply*, banks play an important role because they act as a multiplier of cash in the system when they make loans. If banks collapse or stop making loans, this causes the money supply to decrease. A decreasing money supply inhibits economic growth. Hence, banks play a critical role in a healthy economy.

Even though there were no bailouts and only limited government intervention in the Great Depression, the events of those years led to increased regulation and a strong effort to avoid another depression. The increased regulation included federal supervision of banks, federal depository insurance to guarantee deposits (to avoid bank runs), securities laws, the creation of the SEC, and other federal laws intended to prevent against the "anything goes" environment that had previously led to fraud, mismanagement, and excessive levels of risk-taking in financial markets. Beyond regulation, the other effect of the Great Depression was to influence a generation of economists to study ways of stopping severe and widespread failure in the banking system. Since then, the U.S. Federal Reserve has monitored financial markets and taken necessary measures to avoid another economic depression.

As the recent research paper discussed in the following text notes, economic crises still regularly occur for a variety of reasons. Economists have not been able to avoid systemic risk entirely. What has changed over the years is that governments now actively manage economic crises. The result is that recessions are typically of short duration and often are contained to individual countries. The tools of this active management by governmental parties has primarily been through the control of interest rates and the power to change rules in financial markets (like the rule temporarily disallowing short selling of financial stocks imposed in September 2008). Figure 10.1 shows recessions since the Great Depression. The average duration is less than a year, which shows the success of government intervention.

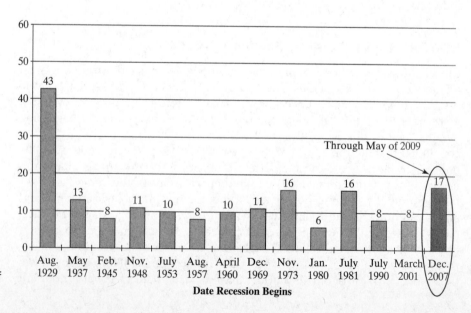

FIGURE 10.1 Months of Recession

The financial crisis of 2007 to 2009, however, has already lasted 19 months as of July 2009, making it the worst recession since the Great Depression. Given its severity, this financial crisis has seen a different method used to avoid further collapse—the "bailout." A bailout occurs when public money is used to support a private business. The argument for bailouts is that it is better to spend public money stabilizing critical parts of the economy than allow a failure that will cause a succeeding chain of failures throughout the economy. In other words, spending public money on private corporations can be in the public's best interest because it avoids another Great Depression.

Bailouts of private corporations by the federal government have taken several different forms over the years. U.S. automobile manufacturers struggled against their Japanese competitors over the period 1979 to 1981. The government responded by providing loan guarantees to entice investors to loan money to Chrysler. They also negotiated a limitation on the number of Japanese cars that could be imported to the United States. In that case, the government did not actually give money to corporations, but instead provided loan guarantees.[4] Similarly, when the hedge fund Long Term Capital Management (LTCM) became insolvent in 1998, the Federal Reserve did not pay cash directly to the fund but instead orchestrated a bailout funded by private investors. Other bailouts have involved direct payment of public money to private corporations. Following the September 11, 2001 terrorist attack, the airline industry received $5 billion in public money and $10 billion in loan guarantees because they were severely impacted by the drop in customers willing to fly.[5]

The bailout examples just described occurred because of a fear that failure of that company or industry would trigger a wider economic collapse. The auto companies employ hundreds of thousands of employees and indirectly support millions of employees including suppliers and dealers. So the failure of an auto manufacturer would trigger a tremendous increase in unemployment and a wide variety of cascading effects throughout the economy. Failure of a hedge fund like LTCM raised fears that a quick liquidation of its positions would cause a drop in prices that would impact investors throughout the financial industry. The airline industry bailout was motivated by fear that a major economy like the United States would be left without a healthy airline industry because the severe decrease in travel after the 2001 attacks on the World Trade Center would bankrupt the industry, impacting the entire economy.

While bailouts may be well intentioned, there are critics who are concerned that it is not a wise policy for the federal government to be deciding which companies survive and which fail. Due to unequal political power, bailouts can be structured to benefit large inefficient companies at the expense of their low-cost competitors. For example in the airline bailout, small airlines that claimed the formula used to determine cash subsidies was biased toward large airlines that had unprofitable business models due to their high costs.[6] Bailouts can also harm consumers. It has been estimated that the restrictions on the importing of Japanese cars during the 1980s cost U.S. consumers $13 billion from the reduced competitive pressures in the automobile market.[7]

Recent Research

How often have banking crises occurred and what methods of intervention were most successful? A recent study collected detailed information about worldwide systemic banking crises over the period 1970 to 2007. The goal of the study was to look at the nature of each crisis, the government solutions implemented, and evaluate the success of intervention. Of interest is whether it has been more successful to focus interventions on long-term structural reforms, accelerating recovery from the crisis, or limiting intervention costs to the government.

In their study, Laeven and Valencia collected information on 42 systemic banking crises from 37 countries. They included an event if the country's corporate and financial sector suffered high defaults and great difficulties in repaying contractual amounts on time. Some events were triggered by bank runs, while others saw sharp increases in interest rates, depressed asset prices or decreased liquidity of capital markets. Each crisis differs somewhat, but one common feature is that the government was faced with the choice whether to subsidize/forgive debt of a bank, take over the bank and restart it under new management, or some combination of these choices. The authors explore multiple dimensions of each crisis to try and answer the question as to the most effective government intervention strategy when faced with a banking crisis.

Overall, the authors do not reach a definitive conclusion as there are too many variables at work. Nonetheless, they do note that reallocating taxpayer funds toward banks and other debtors can lead to distortions in incentives that encourage the abuse of government protections. This is the moral hazard problem discussed throughout the chapter. They also argue that the evidence suggests the choice of government actions should depend on the nature of the crisis. For economy-wide crashes, it is better to leave management in place, while management should be replaced if individual firms collapse due to the managerial decisions.

Source: Luc Laeven and Fabian Valencia, "Systemic Banking Crises: A New Database," International Monetary Fund Working Paper, WP/08/224 (2008).

The temporary propping up of uncompetitive airlines using billions of taxpayer money could be considered a failure. Within five years of the airline bailout, Delta, Northwest, US Air, and United Airlines all filed for Chapter 11 bankruptcy anyway. Was it worth the billions in aid to have four major airlines go bankrupt anyway? And the bailout of the U.S. auto companies was not particularly successful as they asked for another bailout in 2008 and then took TARP funds in 2009 and still Chrysler and GM filed for bankruptcy in 2009.

In addition to concerns about the costs of bailouts to the economy, a related concern is that a history of government bailouts creates a moral hazard for "too big to fail" firms. As discussed next, strategic decisions made by the auto companies and major banks could be partially attributed to increased moral hazard. In other words, why not take extra risks if you know the government will bail you out?

THE FINANCIAL CRISIS OF 2007 TO 2009

From late 2008 through mid-2009, the U.S. government made the boldest intervention in capital markets since the Great Depression to try and avoid a new worldwide depression. Through a variety of investment value guarantees, direct grants, loans and the purchase of preferred stock in banks, the U.S. Treasury Department and Federal Reserve committed the federal government to more than a trillion dollars in aid to banks, financial companies and major manufacturers. This includes the $700 billion Troubled Asset Relief Program (TARP), $200 billion to bail out Freddie Mac and Fannie Mae, at least $130 billion additional support for AIG (beyond TARP funds of $40 billion), $25 billion approved for U.S. automaker support (not including commitments from TARP) and more than $200 billion to support Citibank.[8] The exact dollar figure of the bailouts is a moving target because the money set aside for TARP and automaker bailouts may not all be used and there are potentially other bailouts that may occur. Nonetheless, the intervention by U.S. governmental authorities following the financial crisis of 2007 to 2009 was the largest bailout to date.[9]

What could have happened to trigger the biggest bailouts ever worldwide? The collapse of financial markets resulted from a cascading series of events that began in the United States and quickly spread internationally. The initial trigger was the end of the real estate boom in the United States in 2006 when real estate prices started falling after years of record increases. Figure 10.2 shows housing prices in four states since 1991. Throughout 2007 and 2008, real estate prices fell dramatically in the markets that had experienced the greatest appreciation, like California and Florida. Falling prices led to increased foreclosures, and the failure of mortgage lenders. Due to the interconnectedness of financial firms (i.e., the systemic risk), failures spread to all firms with large investment exposure in the U.S. mortgage industry. Many of these affected firms did not even own mortgages but had instead traded special types of assets called derivative contracts that were based on mortgages. In other words, the interconnected nature of the worldwide

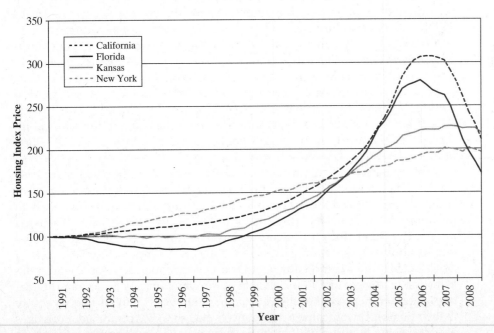

FIGURE 10.2 Housing Prices

financial system meant that a major failure in mortgage lending could spiral into the freezing of credit markets and a worldwide recession. How could one sector of one country's economy pose such global systemic risk? Next we consider the series of events in the mortgage industry that led us to the crisis.

Corporate Governance Failures in the Mortgage Industry

During the booming real estate market of the early 2000s, it was possible for almost anyone to buy any house because banks relaxed lending standards and down payment requirements. This real estate boom led to a big expansion of the mortgage industry and the easing of credit. The rise of "derivative" financial contracts allowed financial markets to readily trade mortgages and mortgage risks in financial markets. In Chapter 6, we discussed how individual mortgage loans were packaged into bonds called collateralized debt obligations (CDOs) that were given artificially high ratings by the bond rating agencies. As a key part of the real estate boom, CDOs expanded dramatically as financial firms worldwide eagerly created, bought and sold CDOs.[10] This increased exposure to the mortgage industry made banks and investment banks susceptible to huge losses when the real estate market crashed.

CDOs were in demand by investors because they paid a higher interest rate than low-risk money-market funds, but were still rated AAA, the highest rating.[11]To fill the demand for mortgage-backed CDOs, banks, mortgage brokers, and other financial intermediaries relaxed standards for qualifying for a mortgage. "Subprime" loans and "Alt-A" loans were made to borrowers who did not qualify for the highest rated "A" loans. In exchange for paying a higher interest rate, subprime and Alt-A borrowers could buy a house without providing verification as to how much income they claimed. These so called "NINJA" loans (No Income, No Job, No Assets) were packaged together into CDOs that carved up interest and principal repayments into separate bonds (called "tranches"). The safest tranches were rated AAA, which meant that low-quality mortgages were magically transformed into the highest quality bonds you could buy. And because AAA tranches of mortgage-backed CDOs paid higher interest rates than other AAA investments, investors worldwide eagerly sought out these investments. Mirroring the boom in the housing industry, CDOs issues grew from $157.4 billion in 2004 to a peak of $520.6 billion in 2006.

In retrospect, it is easy to see that mortgage-backed CDOs had a large risk exposure to a sudden collapse of real estate prices. Another issue was that demand for CDOs led to easy credit and NINJA loans that were more likely to default than "A" loans had done historically. This was the problem discussed in Chapter 6 where the rating agencies mistakenly assumed historical averages would apply in estimating expected defaults. Compounding the risk of default, it became common during this period for lenders to issue home equity loans for 20 percent of a home's value at the same time as issuing traditional mortgages for 80 percent of the value.[12] In other words, buyers had no equity in their homes. The outcome was that even though CDOs contained mortgages at 80 percent of home value, which appeared to have a cushion for house prices falling, there actually was very little cushion for the home owner. For those borrowers who had home equity loans, even a small decrease in housing prices would mean the investor was "underwater" (i.e., owed more on the house than it was worth). Thus the risk of abandoning the house to foreclosure was greater than historical averages suggested.

If the risks were so obvious upon reflection, why would so many financial firms bet their company's survival on the U.S. housing market not collapsing? Failures in corporate governance combined with moral hazard are the most likely explanation for executives disregarding basic principles of risk management. The investment banks Bear Stearns and Lehman Brothers survived the stock market crash of 1929 and the Great Depression, but failed in 2008 because of losses on derivative contracts related to the U.S. mortgage industry. Citigroup, one of the world's most successful banks, had so much risk exposure to mortgage loans that it required a $200 billion bailout and saw its stock price fall from around $50 before the crisis to below $1 at the lowest point.

EXAMPLE 10.1   **Did the Change in Ownership Structure of Investment Banks Contribute to Their Collapse?**

When Goldman Sachs became a public corporation in 1999, it was the last of the major investment banks to convert from the partnership structure of business.[13] All of the major investment banks, which grew to prominence as partnerships run by senior partners, converted to public corporations during a 15-year period from 1984 to 1999. The reason for going public was that this would allow the firms to issue stock to public investors in order to raise funds and for use in acquiring other firms. There was a downside to this move, however. The incentive structure for public corporations is different than that of partnerships because of the separation between owners and managers. As discussed in Chapter 1, in a partnership, the managers of the firm are also the owners. Once a company goes public, however, the managers' portion of ownership begins to decrease. At the IPO, the managers own a significant amount of stock as only part of the company's stock is sold to outside shareholders. Over time, however, the issuance of new stock directly to the public, combined with managers selling some of their stock to diversify their own portfolio of investments, leads to a decrease in the amount of stock owned by managers. This creates the incentive for managers to act in their own interest at the expense of shareholders, as we have discussed throughout this book.

Consider that Bear Stearns and Lehman Brothers were both fully owned by their partners before going public. Documents from the time of their demise indicate that executives and directors owned only 9.7 percent of Bear Stearns and 4.4 percent of Lehman Brothers, respectively.[14] Arguably, this had an effect on the decisions the firms made as compared to the days when managers were also owners. Before it was forced to sell to JP Morgan for $2 a share (later raised to $10), Bear Stearns was a leader in creating the subprime CDO market. Using high amounts of borrowed money, it had amassed a tremendous exposure to mortgage loan risk and the falling real estate market.[15] Would Bear Stearns have taken such risks if the firm was 100 percent owned by the partners who were the firm's managers? The same question can be asked of Lehman Brothers executives. Would they have bet the survival of the firm on real estate prices if they owned the entire firm?

An interesting footnote to the collapse of leading Wall Street investment banks is that the investment banking model is not dead. Instead, small firms are expanding their investment banking operations to try and take over some of the big firms' business.[16] And the small firms, like TM Capital, are wholly owned by their senior management.[17] This suggests one impact of the crisis might be a rearrangement of the industry back toward managers who are also owners.

The failures of banks and investment banks occurred partially due to incentive problems in compensating traders at financial firms and partially due to the failure of executives to monitor the risks these traders were taking. For those few years where CDOs were highly profitable, involvement in creating CDOs or in buying them was a lucrative business. Because traders at financial firms earn bonuses based on the profitability of their activities, it is expected that these traders would seek out opportunities to improve results even if that meant taking extra risks. By itself, this is not necessarily a problem, as it makes sense to reward success. But a problem occurs if no one is monitoring the overall risk of the firm. At AIG, the world's largest insurance company, the actions of the Financial Products Division exposed the company to so much risk that it became severely insolvent.[18] Only the intervention of the U.S. government and more than $170 billion could save AIG from bankruptcy. This was all caused by a few traders in one of their smallest departments.

Similarly, at investment banks, which we discussed in Chapter 5, it was highly profitable to package CDOs and sell the tranches to investors. However, investment banks often could not sell all tranches, so some were retained by the company as assets held in capital.[19] As more CDOs were issued, more unsold tranches were kept and the firms' mortgage industry risk grew. When real estate prices collapsed and foreclosures spiked upward, these retained tranches fell in value, wiping out banks' capital. In this scenario, the corporate governance failure was not in issuing CDOs, because this is the type of service investment banks do as part of their regular business. Instead, the failure was in monitoring the total risk exposure the firm had acquired on its balance sheet.

We have described the excessive risk taken by bailed out firms and bankrupt firms as a failure of corporate governance. Moral hazard is another explanation. Following the bailout of LTCM in 1998, financial firms knew they also were likely to be bailed out if they were large enough to be "too big to fail." Thus, executives recognized they would benefit substantially for good results ("privatize the gain") and would be saved by the government from large losses ("socialize the loss"). The motivation for this attitude is that the only penalty for poor results for executives is a zero bonus. There is generally no requirement that previous bonuses received be returned, called a **clawback**. Consider a firm that would make $100 million from standard operations but, by taking extra risk, had an equal chance of earning $300 million or losing $200 million. If the CEO bonus is 1 percent of earnings, the CEO would normally make $1 million. With extra risk, however, the CEO will earn $3 million in the good outcome and zero in the bad outcome. Over time, this would be an average bonus of $1.5 million per year, 50 percent more than without taking the extra risk. Hence, to the extent that huge losses are not borne by executives, moral hazard can lead to taking extra risk. Example 10.2 discusses how actual behaviors from the financial crisis are consistent with this skewed incentive structure executives face.

EXAMPLE 10.2   Executive Pay and the Financial Crisis

The explanation given for the extremely large pay packages CEOs receive is that they are intended to align the incentives of shareholders and managers. So when the shareholders do well, executives are generously rewarded. Based on this logic, executives should also be penalized for poor results. The results of bonuses paid to firms after the financial crisis suggest that, in practice, the penalty suffered by executives was small. During one of the worst years on Wall Street, the pay packages received by employees of Wall Street firms totaled an estimated $18.4 billion in 2008, the sixth highest on record.[20] Bonuses did fall 44 percent from the previous year, so there was some penalty applied for the poor results. But the fact that positive bonuses were paid at all suggests that incentive compensation is not working as shareholders intended. In practice, pay for performance apparently means executives get large bonuses in good times and get somewhat smaller bonuses if the company nearly fails and requires a bailout.

   In another failure of the executive compensation system, there was reluctance by managers at several companies to participate in bailouts, not because the firm was solvent, but because taking the government's bailout money would limit executive compensation. After public outcry over the bonuses paid by companies benefiting from the September to October, 2008, bailout, political pressure led to limits on executive compensation being included as a condition of receiving bailouts. Executives receiving a bailout for nonfinancial companies were limited to $500,000 in total annual compensation (other than restricted stock that vests after the government is repaid).[21] Similar rules were proposed for financial firms, but the limitation could be lifted by a vote of the shareholders. These stricter pay limitations led to many companies announcing they were going to pay back the government money as soon as possible. Other companies, such as Chrysler Financial decided not to take offered loans once the new executive pay limitations were in place.[22] In other words, companies on the verge of bankruptcy apparently were refusing government bailouts because this would mean reduced executive compensation. The executives would apparently rather see the company fail than have their pay reduced.

The Overreliance of Banks on AIG and Credit Default Swaps

The other financial instrument that played a big role in the financial crisis, particularly for banks and AIG, was the **credit default swap** (CDS). A CDS is essentially a side bet on whether a particular loan will go into default. A CDS acts like an insurance contract because, in exchange for payment of a regular premium, the insuring party agrees to pay the entire amount of the contract if there is a default on the underlying loan.[23] This side bet can be made on any loan, regardless of whether the CDS party has any interest in the loan as lender or borrower. In other words, any financial firm could buy or sell a CDS contract on any loan in existence. Banks typically purchased CDS protection to hedge their balance sheet assets, and AIG was one of the largest sellers of CDS protection. During the time of the financial crisis, the CDS market was unregulated, so there were no limits on the number of contracts banks and other financial firms like AIG could enter into. There was also no guarantee that the seller of CDS protection would be able to pay when the underlying loans defaulted.[24]

In the financial crisis and associated bailouts, the use of CDS contracts as protection for loans played a large role. For banks making large loans, a CDS contract could remove the repayment risk on the loan. If the bank bought a CDS contract that paid if the loan defaulted, then the bank would receive payment on the loan either from the borrower or the CDS contract seller. This ability to reduce risk led to a huge increase in CDS contracts outstanding.

The other reason for the increase was that CDS contracts could be used for purely speculative purposes. Investors could bet on a collapse of U.S. real estate prices using CDS contracts. For both reasons, the CDS market ballooned to over $45 trillion in outstanding contracts before the financial collapse.

While CDS contracts can reduce repayment risk for banks, there is another risk involved called **counterparty risk**. This is the risk that the other party in the CDS will not pay you after the default. As there were trillions in outstanding CDS contracts between and among all the major firms in financial markets, the systemic risk was extremely high. One failure of a loan could cause a firm to be required to pay a large amount, which might cause the firm to become insolvent and unable to make good on its other CDS contracts. This failure would then trigger repayment of CDS contracts written on the failed firm, and so on. This potential for a "domino effect" of default explains why AIG received such special treatment from the U.S. government. On at least three occasions, AIG returned for additional bailout money and was readily granted additional tens of billions in taxpayer money. Why? Because AIG wrote $1.6 trillion in CDS contracts. If AIG was unable to make the CDS payments it owed after the spike in mortgage defaults, it would impact all the financial firms that had hedged their own risks with those CDS contracts from AIG. This could endanger the solvency of those firms.

If AIG went bankrupt and was unable to cover its CDS obligations, its default would be a crushing blow to many large banks who relied on AIG contracts. Banks are required to maintain a capital base of 10 percent of loans outstanding. Through the accounting rules governing CDS contracts, banks are permitted to exclude a loan from their balance sheet if they have CDS protection.[25] This means that banks can increase the amount of loans they make without increasing their capital requirements. Of course, the bank still profits from the loan; it just does not have to reserve capital for losses on it. Given the reliance of banks on CDS contracts, the effect of an AIG bankruptcy would mean that banks who were counterparties to AIG would be forced to put large loans back on their balance sheets and increase their capital accordingly. In other words, an AIG failure would instantly cause many banks to fail because of the lost CDS protection. Hence, government authorities made AIG the first line of defense when trying to limit the spread of the financial crisis.

From a corporate governance perspective, one obvious question is why banks allowed themselves to be in the position where the default of one company, AIG, could cause insolvency of their bank. In other words, why take the high counterparty risk of making a lot of loans backed by CDS protection without reserving capital for losses? One reason is that additional loans increase profitability along with increasing risk. If incentive contracts reward high returns and do not punish low returns, then executives will be tempted to increase risk using CDS contracts. This leads to situations like the current crisis where shareholders and taxpayers bear the brunt of excessive risk taken on by banks and AIG. Whether this was moral hazard or just poor corporate governance, it is hard to separate the two. Similar to the preceding discussion, one-sided incentive compensation contracts (you can win, but you will not lose) can lead to this outcome.

As for AIG, it was mentioned in the preceding text that one small sector of the company brought the company down by writing CDS contracts. This was also a massive failure of corporate governance because AIG, at its core, is an insurance company. If you are a shareholder in the world's largest insurance company, you would expect that executives would actually do a good job of managing risk. After all, that is a basic function of how insurance companies have traditionally earned their money. In the case of AIG, however, the large profits they earned from CDS contracts propped up the bottom line, so top management apparently did not mind the huge risk. Even more surprising for an insurance company, AIG apparently did not set aside any money to cover CDS contracts where payment is required.[26] Traditionally, insurance companies are required to have reserves for expected losses. But CDS contracts are technically not considered insurance, so AIG was within regulatory rules when it decided not to reserve for losses. This is no comfort to shareholders who would have lost everything if the federal government did not step in. Even with the bailout, AIG stock price was down more than 95 percent from its price before the financial crisis. Why would an insurance company allow one division to incur enough risk to bring the company down several times over? AIG has become the symbol for executives taking advantage of both shareholders and taxpayers.

EXAMPLE 10.3 **Poor Governance in Action? The U.S. Auto Companies Return for Another Bailout**

As mentioned in the discussion on bailouts, the U.S. automobile manufacturers were bailed out in 1981 through the negotiation of import quotas on Japanese cars.[27] The reason for the quotas was that gasoline prices spiked in 1979, causing consumers to turn to smaller cars made by the Japanese.

The U.S. companies argued for government help to limit competition from Japan while the U.S. companies restructured and became competitive again.[28] From the auto companies' perspective, the government-imposed limits on Japanese imports worked because the U.S. companies survived long enough to introduce smaller cars and to return to profitability. However, this was not a simple success story because there were two other effects: first, (as discussed earlier in this chapter) consumers were forced to pay higher prices for cars; and, second, moral hazard was introduced into the industry because auto executives learned that the government would not let them fail even if they made bad decisions.

The effect of the moral hazard was seen in the fall of 2008, when the CEOs of the three U.S. automotive manufacturers, GM, Ford, and Chrysler, went to Congress to plead for billions of dollars in bailout money. After years of losses in the billions of dollars, each CEO flew separately on his corporate jet from Detroit to Washington, DC, to plead for government help. These trips turned out to be a public relations nightmare as the CEOs were asked by the press and Congress why they were flying around in private jets while their companies were on the verge of failing.[29] And if they were all going to fly to DC for the same hearings, why didn't they join together on one plane?

Compounding the public relations problem of asking for taxpayer help from your private jet, the auto companies were in financial trouble in part for the same reason they were previously bailed out. Figure 10.3 shows the steady increases in the price of gas from 2004 to 2008 compared to the percentage of pickup trucks, SUVs and vans (jointly called "light trucks") sold by GM and Ford. During this period, GM's and Ford's reliance on the sale of "gas guzzling" larger vehicles was above the industry average and increasing from 2005 to

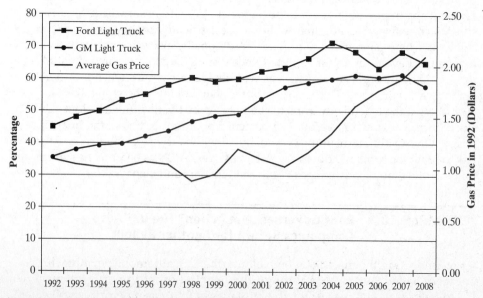

FIGURE 10.3 Light Trucks as a Percentage of Sales

2007. In other words, the companies made the strategic decision to focus on selling large vehicles during a period of rising gas prices.[30] When gas prices spiked over $4 a gallon in the summer of 2008, sales of large vehicles fell dramatically and GM and Ford were soon asking the government for help while they restructured to produce more fuel-efficient cars like hybrids and electric cars.

As this is the second time U.S. auto companies have been burned by a sudden gas price spike, it is hard to argue their executives did not see it coming.[31] A more plausible explanation is that the companies purposely chose to focus on large, gas guzzling vehicles because the vehicles were more profitable. In this way, they took the risk that an increase in gas prices would be catastrophic for their business. How can executives accept such a known risk (and perhaps an inevitable risk given the steady progression in gas prices)? Moral hazard is a likely answer. If you know the government will bail you out, you are free to take a risky strategy. As the cost structure for U.S. companies was higher than their competitors, it appears that the executives decided their only chance for profitability was to sell the largest, most expensive vehicles and hope that gas prices stayed low.[32] This is not a viable long-term strategy given the variability of gas prices. But it would be an expected strategy for a firm where executives were acting in their own personal interest rather than in the interest of shareholders.

Given the history of the auto industry in needing bailouts and the lack of a viable long-term strategy, U.S. President Barack Obama and his advisors apparently decided to force changes so there will not be a third bailout.[33] To receive temporary loans to stabilize their companies, GM and Chrysler had to agree to develop strategic plans that would show how their companies could return to profitability. After deciding the initial plan submitted by GM was inadequate, Obama and his advisors advised GM in March 2009 that they would not provide additional funds unless GM CEO Rick Wagoner resigned.[34] Meanwhile, Chrysler filed for bankruptcy at the end of April 2009 in a Chapter 11 filing supported by $4.5 billion in government loans. GM filed for Chapter 11 bankruptcy on the first day of June, 2009.

INTERNATIONAL PERSPECTIVE

The U.S. financial crisis that started in 2007 from the collapse of real estate prices spread into an international crisis in 2008. Because of the interconnected nature of the financial system, the fall in value of CDS and CDO contracts based on U.S. mortgage loans affected many large foreign banks. As an example of the worldwide systemic risk posed by the collapse in U.S. housing prices, consider that AIG paid over $58 billion of the bailout funds it received to overseas banks to settle CDS contracts, including at least $36 billion to French and German banks.[35] The other impact of the U.S. crisis was that the uncertainty about whether banks were solvent led to a reluctance among banks to lend to each other. This led to a freeze in credit markets worldwide in September 2008, which triggered an economic recession in most countries.

In an effort to avoid a collapse of their own financial systems, governments throughout the world initiated their own bailout plans. In September 2008, central banks injected additional capital into their banking systems totaling more than $200 billion.[36] This was followed in October 2008 by an $850 billion bank rescue plan by the United Kingdom (England), the country hit the hardest by the crisis. China followed suit in November 2008 with a $586 billion economic stimulus plan.[37] The European Union (EU), however, took a different approach and refused to enact a bank rescue plan, despite pressure from other countries to do so. The EU was resisting pressure because they did not want to increase their budget deficits. Many large EU banks also already received an indirect subsidy from the United States through AIG, so perhaps a bailout was not as necessary for those banks.[38]

One country whose banking system did not survive the crisis was Iceland. All three of the country's major banks failed following a bank run that started in the United Kingdom. The effect was that the currency collapsed, the Icelandic stock market lost 90 percent of its value and the economy was plunged into a severe recession.[39] The unfortunate events in Iceland happened quickly as a run on one bank led to a run on other banks. The example of Iceland demonstrates why systemic risk is such a concern to central bankers. Failure of one bank spreads quickly to other banks and financial institutions and an entire economy can collapse quickly.

Summary

In large part, the recent financial crisis was triggered by poor corporate governance. The firms that required bailouts took excessively risky positions that relied on a continuing boom in the U.S. real estate industry. From the shareholders' perspective, a well-run firm would not be in danger of bankruptcy if one sector of the economy collapses. Falling real estate prices would cause some losses but would not put a firm that survived the Great Depression out of business. The reason these failures occurred was that many companies were not well governed. Executives loaded up on risk from one sector of the economy seeking extra profits with little concern for the additional risk. One reason this could happen was the perverse incentives in many executive compensation contracts that reward excessive risk and do not punish failure. As proof of the problem, bonuses were still paid in many firms that required bailouts.

Further compounding the problem is the systemic risk that arises when financial systems worldwide are interconnected. Banks in Europe rely on AIG for CDSs on loans made in Asia. A bank failure in one country can quickly lead to a cascading series of bank failures worldwide. This systemic risk leads to bailouts which lead to moral hazard. Add moral hazard on top of poor incentive contracts and you find executives betting on their companies in the hopes of obtaining higher personal bonuses. If the bet pays off, the executives earn huge bonuses. And if there are catastrophically poor results, taxpayers will save the company (and perhaps even allow the executive to keep his or her job). Of course, shareholders will be wiped out or nearly wiped out, not the result they would like from the executives they put in charge.

WEB Info about Moral Hazard, Systemic Risk, and Bailouts

Department of the Treasury: Financial Stability
Plan Web page
www.financialstability.gov

Federal Reserve: Banking Information & Regulation
www.federalreserve.gov/bankinforeg/default.htm

Review Questions

1. Describe systemic risk and how high systemic risk can lead to bailouts.
2. How do bailouts create moral hazard?
3. What are examples of how moral hazard might affect the decisions of executives?
4. What caused the financial crisis of 2007 to 2009?
5. How did the Federal Reserve and Department of the Treasury respond to the crisis?
6. Explain how failures in corporate governance contributed to the financial crisis.

Discussion Questions

1. What would you expect to happen if the U.S. government refused to bailout any firms after a crisis like the financial crisis of 2007 to 2009?
2. Should governments try to discourage firms from becoming "too big to fail"? Would this help avert a future financial crisis? In this chapter, we discussed the costs of "too big to fail" firms. What are the benefits, to society, of such large firms? Do you think the benefits outweigh the costs?
3. What corporate governance changes would help to avoid financial meltdowns like the recent financial crisis?
4. What, if any, strings would you attach to government assistance if you were in charge of bailouts?
5. How would you decide which firms should be bailed out and which firms should be left to go bankrupt? How would you decide which industries should be bailed out and which industries should be left to go bankrupt? For both questions, is there a consistent policy supporting your answer or are you deciding on an ad hoc basis?

Exercises

1. This chapter mentioned several firms that were bailed out or that went bankrupt in the current financial crisis. Identify one firm not mentioned in the chapter that was bailed out and one firm that was not bailed out and was allowed to go bankrupt. Analyze why the government authorities made different bailout decisions.
2. In reviewing the choices made by executives before and during the financial crisis, identify two decisions (other than those in the chapter) that represent moral hazard caused by being "too big to fail."
3. Identify a large financial firm that was not severely affected by the financial crisis. What was different about the policies and operations of this firm as compared with those that were bailed out?
4. Find two different proposed reforms of financial markets whose purpose is to avoid future financial crises. For each proposal, identify how the changes suggested would affect the monitoring of corporate executives and otherwise improve corporate governance.

Exercises for Non-U.S. Students

1. How was your country affected by the meltdown in U.S. real estate prices and the associated collapse of financial products based on the U.S. mortgage loan industry? Explain.
2. Do you have financial firms that are "too big to fail" in your country? Did your country provide assistance to any of these banks in the recent crisis? Explain.
3. How has your country responded to economic crises in the past? Did the response always work?

What government interventions seem to work in your country?
4. Can executives in your country increase a firms' exposure to one sector of the economy as easily as financial firms in the United States? What differences or similarities in corporate governance systems lead to this result?
5. Do you see examples of moral hazard in your country among firms that are "too big to fail?" Provide examples.

Endnotes

1. Michael Gray, "AIG Saves U.S. $1.6 Trillion," *New York Post*, March 22, 2009.
2. *www.washingtonspectator.org/articles/20080801GSEs.cfm.*
3. As of March 2009, it appears that only six CEOs (Citigroup, Bank of America, AIG, Fannie Mae, Freddie Mac, and GM) were replaced as a condition of receiving a bailout even though hundreds of firms participated.
4. *www.heritage.org/research/energyandenvironment/EM74.cfm.*
5. *www.businessweek.com/magazine/content/01_41/b3752735.htm.*
6. *www.usatoday.com/money/biztravel/2001-11-26-airbailout.htm.*
7. *www.perc.org/articles/article416.php.*
8. For a summary of the size of recent bailouts including the financial crisis of 2008 to 2009, see *www.propublica.org/special/government-bailouts.*
9. Oxfam has estimated the worldwide bailout to equal $8.42 trillion considering all forms of assistance provided to private companies by governments. See *www.oxfam.org/en/pressroom/pressrelease/2009-04-01/bank-bailout-could-end-poverty.*
10. *http://en.wikipedia.org/wiki/Collateralized_debt_obligation.*
11. Roger Lowenstein, "Triple-A Failure," *New York Times*, April 27, 2008.
12. *www.fdic.gov/bank/analytical/regional/ro20063q/na/2006_fall01.html.*
13. *http://money.cnn.com/magazines/fortune/fortune_archive/1999/05/10/259534/index.htm.*
14. These figures are obtained from proxy statements filed by the companies with the SEC.
15. *www.answers.com/topic/bear-stearns.*
16. *http://news.efinancialcareers.com/newsandviews_item/newsItemId-15234.*
17. *www.tmcapital.com/principals.html.*
18. Gretchen Morgenson, "Behind Insurer's Crisis, Blind Eye to a Web of Risk," *New York Times*, September 27, 2008.
19. *www.realestatejournal.com/buysell/mortgages/20071228-ng.html.*
20. Ben White, "What Red Ink? Wall Street Paid Hefty Bonuses," *New York Times*, January 28, 2009.
21. "Treasury Announces New Restrictions on Executive Compensation," Release TG-15, U.S. Department of the Treasury, February 4, 2009.
22. David Cho, Peter Whoriskey, and Amit R. Paley, "Pay Rule Led Chrysler to Spurn Loan, Agency Says," *Washington Post*, April 21, 2009.
23. *http://en.wikipedia.org/wiki/Credit_default_swap.*
24. In March 2009, one of the reforms that followed the financial crisis was that most CDS contracts began trading through a clearinghouse that guarantees payment and removes counterparty risk. A list of the largest outstanding CDS contracts is maintained at the following link: *www.dtcc.com/products/derivserv/data/index.php.*
25. *www.federalreserve.gov/boarddocs/srletters/1996/sr9617.htm.*
26. See Endnote 19.
27. See Endnote 6.

28. Eduardo.Porter, "Detroit Can't Count on Government Help," *International Herald Tribune*, April 15, 2006.

29. Dana Milbank, "Auto Execs Fly Corporate Jets to D.C., Tin Cups in Hand," *Washington Post*, November 20, 2008.

30. Eduardo Porter, "A Chicken in Every Garage," *New York Times*, September 12, 2008.

31. *www.autoobserver.com/2008/06/gms-wagoner-defends-suv-reliance.html*.

32. *http://money.cnn.com/2006/01/07/news/companies/detroit_autoshow_preview/index.htm*.

33. *www.entrepreneur.com/localnews/1802990.html*.

34. "GM CEO Wagoner Forced Out as Part of Gov't Plan," *Associated Press*, March 31, 2009.

35. *www.businessweek.com/the_thread/economicsunbound/archives/2009/03/german_and_fren.html*.

36. *http://en.wikipedia.org/wiki/Global_financial_crisis_of_2008%E2%80%932009*.

37. *http://en.wikipedia.org/wiki/China_Stimulus_Plan*.

38. Some may argue that it was not a subsidy for AIG to pay funds that were legally due to French and German banks. However, without U.S. backing of more than $170 billion, AIG would have been bankrupt and the foreign banks would have received pennies on the dollar in bankruptcy court.

39. *http://en.wikipedia.org/wiki/2008%E2%80% 932009_Icelandic_financial_crisis*.

Corporate Citizenship

The previous chapters discuss corporate governance from the perspective of agency theory. As described in the first chapter, agency theory focuses on the separation of ownership and control. Shareholders (owners) are the central point of concern. From this perspective, corporate governance is mainly about the incentive systems and monitors designed to protect shareholder interests. The primary goal of the firm is to create wealth for these shareholders.

However, this is not the only perspective from which to consider corporate governance. Many believe that companies should have a greater responsibility to society. Proponents argue that companies have unique opportunities to improve society. This *stakeholder* view of the firm describes the firm as having many different groups with legitimate interests in the firm's activities. Corporate governance is then defined as the mechanisms that ensure corporations take responsibility for directing their activities in a manner fair to all stakeholders. Strategic management concepts argue that this is based on creating positive relationships with stakeholders. Through creating these positive relationships, firms can create sustainable economic wealth.

In particular, agency theory has been an important perspective for formulating governance rules, laws, and policy in the United States. However, many other countries have operated under the idea that large corporations have a greater responsibility in society than just maximizing shareholder wealth. Their governance rules tend to be influenced to a greater extent by this duty to an expanded set of stakeholders.

If U.S. firms believed they had a social obligation to be good citizens, then this sense of responsibility for the greater good could serve as yet another governance device. However, do firms have a sense of social responsibility? Some might say that they do not, but others may argue that they should. We discuss the stakeholder view of the firm and we also describe problems with the view, which make it difficult to use this view to ensure good governance.

STAKEHOLDER VIEW OF THE FIRM

A company must maintain relationships with several groups that affect or are affected by its decisions.[1] Stakeholders are identified as people or groups with legitimate interests in various aspects of the company's activities. Note that stakeholders are defined by their interest in the corporation, not whether the corporation has any interest in them. Companies have varying responsibilities to each of their stakeholders. While some relationships may be more valuable (or important) than others, no one group should be able to dominate all of the others. These relationships between managers and stakeholders are based on a moral or ethical foundation.

Clearly groups, such as stockholders, employees, and creditors have a strong interest in the firm. But what other groups might be considered stakeholders? Figure 11.1 shows the different types of groups that might be considered stakeholders of the firm. The primary stakeholders (sometimes called contractual stakeholders) have direct, contractually determined relationships. While the stockholder is considered a very important stakeholder, other groups are also important. Company employees have short-term interests in the firm in the form of pay and working conditions and long-term interests

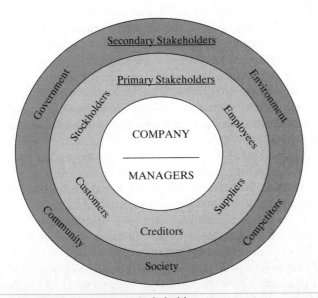

FIGURE 11.1 Company Stakeholders

in the form of pension and health care. Employees often have labor unions to manage their relationship with the firm. Creditors, customers, and suppliers also have legitimate interests in the organization. The secondary (or diffuse) stakeholders are impacted by the firm's actions but have limited contractual connection to it. Examples of secondary stakeholders may be its competitors and environmental activists. Certainly, local communities, governments, and all of society may be affected by the company's decisions.

The figure shows just one way to categorize the different stakeholders of a firm. Other distinctions could be made. For example, groupings can be based on the various activities of the firm and those that they impact. It can be based on a resource view, or industry structure, or by social and political affiliations. Or these stakeholders can be grouped by institutional, economic, and ethical interests. There is no consensus on how these stakeholders should be categorized. However, all the stakeholder views illustrate a much different perspective than agency theory—companies have responsibilities to groups other than to stockholders.

A stakeholder view of the firm places its executives at the center of managing relations with each stakeholder group. The managerial objective in this view is to maximize sustainable organizational wealth (all stakeholders' utilities) by optimizing these relationships. Many companies now have an organizational unit tasked with communicating with stakeholders. These units may have camouflaged names like "corporate communication department" or "public affairs department." Others use more direct names like "sustainability group" or "corporate social responsibility committee."

EXAMPLE 11.1   Wal-Mart's Battle with Stakeholders

Wal-Mart operates over 4,100 discount stores in the United States (Wal-Mart, Super Centers, and Sam's Clubs). The firm generates over $13 billion in profits per year. The company is the largest corporate employer in the United States, with 1.4 million employees and plans to open about 200 new stores every year.

But Wal-Mart seems to be coming under increasing pressure from different social groups for its business practices. Coalitions of community groups have worked to keep Wal-Mart from coming to their towns. Hundreds of communities have been successful. A recent class-action lawsuit was filed against Wal-Mart on behalf of female employees, arguing that they were being paid less than their male counterparts. Many politicians have noticed that a large percentage of Wal-Mart's employees end up on public health care assistance. The firm has endured allegations of child labor law violations, the hiring of illegal immigrants, and violations of worker rights.

Wal-Mart's view is much different. It claims that its low prices help everyone in the community. Also by giving $296 million to charity last year, it is the largest corporate cash contributor in the United States. Wal-Mart targets 90 percent of its charitable contributions at the local level where Wal-Mart customers and associates live and work.

Whether Wal-Mart has been a good corporate citizen or not is being actively debated. However, one thing seems obvious—Wal-Mart has done a poor job of actively engaging many of its stakeholders to optimize their mutual interests. Having adversarial relationships with employees, potential customers, politicians, and civil rights activists do not seem like wise business choices.

Legal Foundations

The legal underpinnings of the stakeholder view of the firm stems from property rights. This may seem ironic because it is the stockholders who own the firm. If stockholders are the owners, do not they have the property rights? Not necessarily. The definition of property can be expressed as a "bundle" of rights, which may be limited.[2] Owners of property have the right to engage in a limited set of activities.

Consider a landowner. Building a home requires a building permit. The government agency that grants the permit must first approve the building plans. The building must meet adequate safety and appearance criteria. Land is also zoned for specific uses. These laws and procedures protect citizens who may go on the property (safety) and the landowners in the area (appearance and use). Although they are not owners of the land, these citizens and nearby property owners are stakeholders of this land. They also have rights.

The U.S. government, various state governments, and courts have formalized the rights of stakeholders in corporations. Many states have adopted statutes that extend the concern of corporate boards beyond that of the shareholders to other stakeholders, such as employees, creditors, suppliers, customers, and communities. The determination of which rights are held by the corporation (and its owners) and which rights belong to various stakeholders continues to evolve.

Corporate Social Responsibility

The modern evolution of the stakeholder view of the firm advocates that management develop specific relationships with stakeholder groups. Proponents of this view argue that companies have a social obligation to operate in ethically, socially, and environmentally responsible ways. This active approach is referred to as corporate social responsibility[3] (CSR) or corporate citizenship.

What is a company's responsibility to society? Archie Carroll has offered a four-part taxonomy of CSR that lends itself to corporate citizenship from a managerial perspective. A firm should conduct its business in a manner that meets its economic, legal, ethical, and philanthropy expectations:[4]

Level I: Economic—the first and foremost social responsibility of a firm is economic. The firm must survive by producing goods and services at a profit.

Level II: Legal—society expects firms to operate their business within the legal framework.

Level III: Ethical—these responsibilities are those over and above the ones codified in laws and are in line with societal norms and customs. They are expected, though not required, by society even though they may be ill-defined. This could include things such as environmental ethics.

Level IV: Philanthropy—corporate giving is discretionary, although increasingly desired by stakeholder communities.

The economic responsibilities (Level I) have the highest priority. A firm must be efficient and survive over the long term, in order to be useful to society. However, it must execute its business activities in a legal (Level II) and ethical (Level III) way. Philanthropy (Level IV) is the least important priority. Reconsider the Wal-Mart example through this model of CSR. Corporate social responsibility proponents might argue that any failure of Wal-Mart in higher-priority responsibilities, such as legal and ethical considerations, cannot be to offset through greater participation in lower-priority responsibilities, such as corporate giving.

While corporate citizenship might include charity or philanthropy (Level IV), the concept focuses more on engagement with stakeholders to achieve mutual goals (Levels II and III). Proponents of CSR argue that the main drivers of the citizenship trend include the following:

- globalization, the worldwide expansion of business and market economies;
- greater power of global firms should fill the activities formerly left to governments;
- pressure from assertive social activists;
- an increasingly popular environmental movement; and
- a rising desire in the capital markets to punish firms not meeting ethical standards.

Some corporations have responded to this trend by including CSR-oriented statements in their corporate values and goals. These statements recognize that CSR has value in a code of conduct or ethics, a commitment to local communities, an interest in employee health and education, an environmental consciousness, and recognition of social issues (e.g., diversity, social fairness, etc.).

By embracing citizenship goals, advocates claim corporations will insulate themselves from many activist actions, establish stakeholder confidence in management, enhance the firm's reputation, and demonstrate an emphasis on prevention rather than corrective actions.[5] As a result of these perceptions, firms may find that their goodwill opens doors to new communities and additional sales.

However, social responsibility is a dynamic process. It stems from the making of decisions balancing the interests of all stakeholders. But these decisions can only be made from an ongoing conversation among affected parties. For this to occur over time, social awareness must become an integral part of the corporate culture. Ethical considerations become central to this process.

When Enron executives were falsifying revenue and taking excessive risks, they not only hurt their shareholders but other stakeholders as well. Enron hurt their customers who now have to find other vendors, suppliers who depended on Enron's orders, employees who could have worked elsewhere, and the future local economy as current and future jobs have now been taken away. In addition, because the government spent millions investigating and prosecuting Enron executives, society as a whole is harmed as well, as that money could have been spent elsewhere for a greater good. For these Enron executives, where was their sense of corporate citizenship? Can citizenship, or a sense of corporate responsibility to society, be considered a type of monitor?

EXAMPLE 11.2 Corporate Citizenship at American Express

American Express is the world's largest travel agency and a large issuer of credit cards. It has a presence in 160 countries and more than 40 percent of its 84,000 employees work outside the United States. The firm has had "company values" long before the term became vogue. American Express values:[6]

- developing relationships that make a positive difference in their customers' lives;
- providing outstanding products and unsurpassed service;
- upholding the highest standards of integrity in all actions;
- working together across boundaries, to meet the needs of their customers and to help the company win;
- valuing employees, encouraging their development, and rewarding their performance;
- being citizens in the communities in which employees live and work;
- exhibiting a strong will to win in the marketplace and in every aspect of the business;
- being personally accountable for delivering on commitments.

Note that only three of the eight values can be clearly identified as relating to the business bottom line of the firm. Many of these values are clearly grounded in moral and social objectives.

These values are far more than just statements for the company coffee mug. American Express ensures that these values become an integral part of mainstream operations by surveying each employee on how the company has performed with respect to these values. The results of this survey are then used as one of several measurements used to determine compensation issues of managers. Social goals can really only be effective in the long run when objectives can be measured and when progress success or failure is tied to managerial compensation.[7]

GOVERNANCE AND STAKEHOLDER THEORY

Can stakeholder theory play a role in corporate governance? In the agency theory view of the firm, governance is about aligning managerial incentives and providing monitoring of management behavior. In the stakeholder view of the firm, how can management be forced to internalize the welfare of stakeholders?

Managerial incentives can be provided by rewarding management on the basis of some measure of the welfare of the stakeholders.[8] This process requires clear objectives and performance measurements. Defining acceptable, multiple missions suitable to all stakeholder groups can be tricky. Another key problem to be overcome is whether a measure of stakeholder welfare is available. It is harder to measure the firm's performance to its employees, customers, and so on than to its stockholders. There is no *accounting* measure (like earnings) or *market* value measure (like stock price) of the impact of past and current managerial decisions on stakeholder welfare. The result is that aligning managerial incentives with multiple stakeholder groups and measuring overall performance can become a noisy and chaotic process.

To date, there is no consensus on how to measure and report on changes in stakeholder welfare. Ideas that have supporters are the balanced scorecard[9] approach and the "triple bottom line."[10] The balanced scorecard measures performance in four perspectives: customer, internal processes, employee learning and growth, and financial success. Triple bottom line accounting expands the traditional company-reporting framework to take into account financial, environmental, and social outcomes. While both systems are used by some companies, neither has been generally adopted.

Regardless of the overall measurement of outcomes, organizational theory states that the firm will only value CSR goals if the company executive exhibits strong leadership in instilling corporate responsibility within the company's culture. The values of the culture influence the processes by which the company will try to solve a problem.[11] Executives signal which values are important through both employee incentives and through organizational structure.[12] The primary means is that of setting the criteria for recruitment and promotion. CSR goals are best executed when individual employees have promotion criteria incentives tied to those goals. A secondary means are the design of organizational structure and procedures that are aligned with the values. Mission statements, which reflect CSR goals and organizational units tasked with interacting with stakeholders, are examples of structural means of promoting culture values. The values set at the top of the company filter down throughout the organization. Therefore, leadership in corporate responsibility is critical to its adoption by a firm.

CRITICISMS

The authors, researchers, and practitioners of the stakeholder view of the firm use the concepts in different ways and often use contradictory evidence and arguments to support the theory. For example, some characterize stakeholder theory as a **descriptive theory**. It is used to describe what firms are doing and how they are doing it. Others use stakeholder theory from an **instrumental perspective**. This approach provides principles and practices that should be implemented to achieve (or avoid) certain results. They portent that if corporate performance results A, B, and C are desired, then the firm should implement standards and practices X, Y, and Z. Lastly, the stakeholder view is used to advocate how firms should behave based on ethical and philosophical principles. Advocates of CSR or corporate citizenship use this **normative approach**.

Is the stakeholder view correct? Should we view firms from a stakeholder perspective? If so, then how can we operationalize it? Because the stakeholder view is not a well-defined theory, it is difficult to assess. As an example, consider one of the primary stakeholders—employees. Providing employees with high-quality health care seems consistent with the tenets of the stakeholder view of the firm. The descriptive approach might ask how many companies are providing quality health care. The instrumental approach would be interested in how the providing of quality health care impacts the firm's stock returns and operating performance. The normative approach advocates that firms should provide quality health care because it is the moral thing to do. However, none of these provide the chance to accept or reject the validity of the stakeholder view.

Since the stakeholder view of the firm is difficult to empirically validate or reject, can it be philosophically criticized? Even critics of corporate citizenship agree that companies should act responsibly and should be seen doing so. After all, this is often good for business. However, that is different than aggressively pursuing the CSR doctrine advocated today. Indeed, critics argue that deviating too far from the profit-maximizing role of companies would be harmful to society.

The critics' argument stems from the experience that economic progress comes from profit-related activities. The primary role of business in society is to act as a vehicle for economic development. In a market-oriented economic system, economic progress results from entrepreneurial opportunities and competitive pressures. Successfully introduced new or improved products enhance profits while increasing the quality of life in society. Competition forces business to continually work to provide goods and services more effectively and more efficiently.

When managers have to take into account a wider range of goals and involve themselves in stakeholder engagement activities, higher costs and impaired business performance are likely to follow. When trying to serve "many masters," managers often become ineffective in achieving any of the goals.[13] Indeed, more exacting environmental and social standards will bring more regulation. Overregulation exacts an enormous cost on society in the form of limiting competition, narrowing opportunities, and worsening economic performance. History shows that when the economy is intentionally focused on social goals, such as employment, production, and so on, society becomes worse off. The poor economic performance of the former Soviet Union, Cuba, and China (before its more recent move toward a market-based economy) shows this.

EXAMPLE 11.3 Dow Jones STOXX Sustainability Index

One way to measure the success of firms engaged in corporate citizenship activities is to form a stock index of such firms. The SAM (sustainable asset management) Group measures a company's "corporate sustainability" and forms an index of the best companies (in cooperation with Dow Jones Indexes and STOXX Limited).

The SAM Group purports that "corporate sustainability is a business approach that creates long-term shareholder value by embracing opportunities and managing risks deriving from economic, environmental, and social developments." Specifically, the SAM Group quantifies the quality of a company's strategy and management in dealing with economic, environmental, and social opportunities. Competence is measured in areas such as strategy, financial performance, customer relationships, stakeholder engagement, governance standards, and employee satisfaction.

The Dow Jones STOXX 600 Index is designed to provide a broad representation of the European market, by including 600 firms from Austria, Belgium, Denmark, Finland, France, Germany, Greece, Ireland, Italy, Luxembourg, the Netherlands, Norway, Portugal, Spain, Sweden, Switzerland, and the United Kingdom. The narrower Dow Jones STOXX Sustainability Index (DJSI) tracks the performance of the top 20 percent (in terms of sustainability) of the companies in the Dow Jones STOXX 600 Index. This index started at the beginning of 1999. As of March 27, 2009, the DJSI STOXX included 161 companies.

Figure 11.2 shows both the DJ STOXX Index and the DJSI[14] since the creation of the DJSI. The DJ STOXX Index was scaled to 100 on January 1, 1999

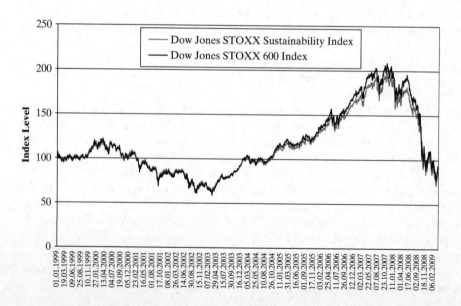

FIGURE 11.2 DJ STOXX 600 Index and DJSI, Since January 1, 1999

to equal the DJSI. Notice that performance of both indexes is nearly identical. In late 2001 and 2002, the sustainability index seems to be higher than the broader index. However, this reverses in 2004 as the sustainability index lags behind by a small amount for the next few years. This evidence does not seem to support the argument of corporate citizenship critics that companies serving multiple masters often become ineffective at achieving any of the goals. Neither does the evidence support proponents' argument that corporate citizenship maximizes company wealth. The sustainability index performs no better than the broader index.

INTERNATIONAL PERSPECTIVE

Corporate citizenship has different historical roots in different regions of the world and therefore is viewed with different perspectives. For example, CSR in the United States derived from the conflict between stockholder-focused managers and social activists. This unenthusiastic relationship between companies and some activist groups created a negative attitude toward stakeholder theory in the business community. Over the past few decades, many U.S. business groups have slowly began to embrace CSR ideas. In the United Kingdom and Europe, corporate citizenship has been viewed less negatively and is currently a more holistic concept. In India, the lack of government efficacy in the provision of social welfare has caused corporations to step into the role of helping society. Stakeholder concern is integrated within the firm and is based on family values.

A stakeholder view of the firm is also reflected in many laws internationally. In the United Kingdom, company directors are mandated to include the interests of employees in decision-making (the United Kingdom's Companies Act of 2006). In Germany, employee representation is required on one of the two-tier boards (codetermination laws). The European Union (EU) permits corporations to take into account the interests of employees, creditors, customers, and potential investors (harmonization laws). In Japan, after World War II, corporations were tasked with the responsibility for rebuilding the Japanese economy. The same was true for Korea after the Korean War in the 1950s. Korean companies that focused on exporting were even given tax breaks to help them bring capital into Korea.

How actively are managers engaging stakeholders? This is a difficult question to assess. The Conference Board surveyed over 700 companies on the issues of corporate citizenship between 2000 and 2001.[15] The firms tended to be very large (over 95 percent of the firms surveyed recorded over $1 billion in sales annually). The companies that respond to such surveys are those that have a positive attitude toward corporate citizenship. Instead of declaring a negative attitude, managers that do not value CSR simply do not complete the survey. Therefore we should consider the survey responses as a survey of firms actively engaged in CSR.

In the surveys, CEOs were asked what their firm's role would play in creating good business and good society. They were given the choices of

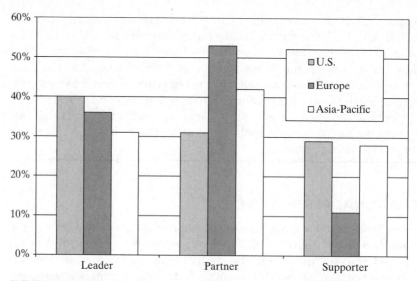

FIGURE 11.3 What Role Will Your Company Play in Increasing Good Business and Good Society?

Data Source: Corporate Citizenship in the New Century: Accountability, Transparency, and Global Stakeholder Engagement, The Conference Board. Research Report # R-1314-02-RR, July 2002.

being a leader, a partner, or a supporter. Results are shown in Figure 11.3 by geographical region for the companies completing the survey. Note that the most frequent answer from U.S. managers was to be a leader. European managers and those in the Asia-Pacific region most often chose to be partners. In general, managers from Europe and Asia-Pacific generally believed that the government should assume the leadership role in designing social good standards and activities.

The surveys also asked managers about how effective they were in implementing standards, codes, and programs that will result in achieving their corporate citizenship goals. Figure 11.4 shows that these companies believe they still have much room for improvement. Keep in mind, however, that it is more difficult to achieve higher-standard goals than lower goals. Nevertheless, there appears to be a large difference between U.S. and European firms and those in the Asia-Pacific. Over 50 percent of the firms from the United States and Europe responded as being either extremely effective or somewhat effective in their efforts. Only 20 percent of the Asia-Pacific firms believed they were so effective. Any lack of effectiveness may arise from not having a structured program to engage stakeholders on a regular basis. Only 60 percent of the responding firms have a structured program. Nevertheless, many companies are learning how to deal with this new area of corporate accountability.

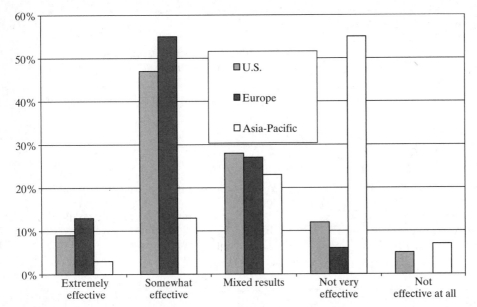

FIGURE 11.4   How Effective Are Your Efforts Today to Address the Citizenship Factors That Will Assure Your Success Tomorrow?

Data Source: *Corporate Citizenship in the New Century: Accountability, Transparency, and Global Stakeholder Engagement*, The Conference Board. Research Report # R-1314-02-RR, July 2002.

Summary

The stakeholder view of the firm does not focus on the maximization of shareholder wealth but rather on the optimization of the sustainable economic wealth of all stakeholders. Stockholders, employees, customers, communities, and the environment are just some examples of stakeholders. Their legitimate interest in the firm arises from the perspective that these stakeholders have property rights in the firm. Corporate stakeholder relationships have different historical roots in different regions of the world and therefore are viewed with different perspectives.

The modern evolution of the stakeholder view of the firm, called CSR or corporate citizenship, advocates that companies have a social obligation to operate in ethically, socially, and environmentally responsible ways. By embracing citizenship goals, corporations may insulate themselves from activist actions, enhance the firm's reputation, and find that their goodwill opens doors to new communities and additional sales. Therefore, a sense of corporate citizenship potentially represents another way to affect business people's behaviors and actions. In this sense, it can be considered a monitor. But is the CSR concept good for society? It is difficult to do well while doing good. A company can fail in its social goals and still succeed as a business, but it cannot fail as a business and still succeed in its social goals. In addition, how do we create a governance system based on this sense of citizenship?

WEB Info about Corporate Citizenship

The Conference Board
www.conference-board.org

CSR Europe
www.csreurope.org

The Corporate Citizenship Company
www.corporate-citizenship.co.uk

Review Questions

1. Name and describe as many stakeholders of the corporation as you can.
2. Describe the differences between agency theory and stakeholder theory.
3. Name and describe the four levels of CSR.

4. What are the criticisms of a profit-maximization focus?
5. What are the criticisms of the stakeholder view of the firm?

Discussion Questions

1. Do you think corporations should have a responsibility to society in general? Explain.
2. Let's say companies should be good citizens. How can this be measured? How can it be enforced?

3. How should we solve a stakeholder crisis? Who would be the monitors? Who should be the monitors? What regulations can be imposed?

Exercises

1. Report on the latest developments of CSR as described by The Conference Board (*www.conference-board.org*).
2. Go to *www.wakeupwalmart.com*. Describe the current stakeholder problems with Wal-Mart. Also go to *www.walmart.com* and determine what Wal-Mart is doing to engage the stakeholders.

3. How might corporations engage environmental activists in a productive and legal way?
4. Investigate and report on the standards of corporate social responsibility issued by the Social Venture Network (*www.svn.org*).

Exercises for Non-U.S. Students

1. Does your country subscribe to an agency view or the stakeholder view of the firm? Explain.
2. In what ways are firms in your country viewed differently from U.S. firms? Are they seen as contributors to the national economy? Are corporate executives looked upon as greedy or as important social leaders?

3. What is your overall opinion of the role of your country's firms in your country? Is it good for the long run? What criteria (profits, environment, etc.) should be applied?

Endnotes

1. An early organization of the stakeholder theory concepts is provided in E. R. Freeman, *Strategic Management: A Stakeholder Approach*, (Boston, MA: Pitman, 1984).

2. Thomas Donaldson and Lee E. Preston, "The Stakeholder Theory of the Corporation: Concepts, Evidence, and Implications," *Academy of Management Review* 20, no. 1 (1995):65–91.

3. Andrew Carnegie is generally credited with creating the term *corporate social responsibility* in his 1889 essay entitled "The Gospel of Wealth."

4. See Archie B. Carroll, "A Three-Dimensional Conceptual Model of Corporate Performance," *Academy of Management Review* 4 (1979):497–505 and Archie B. Carroll, "Corporate Social Responsibility: Evolution of a Definitional Construct," *Business & Society* 38, no. 3 (1999):268–295.

5. Paine, Lynn S., *Value Shift: Why Companies Must Merge Social and Financial Imperatives to Achieve Superior Performance* (New York: McGraw-Hill, 2003).

6. See *www.americanexpress.com*.

7. For an example of American Express's commitment to corporate responsibility, see "Recognizing Responsibility: American Express Company 2007/2008 Corporate Citizenship Report" at *http://home3.americanexpress.com/corp/gb/cresp/pdf/cresp.pdf*.

8. See Jean Tirole, "Corporate Governance," *Econometrica* 69, no. 1 (2001):1–35.

9. Robert Kaplan and David Norton, *The Balanced Scorecard: Translating Strategy into Action* (Harvard Business School Press, 1996).

10. John Elkington, *Cannibals With Forks: The Triple Bottom Line of 21st Century Business* (New Society Publishers, Stony Creek Creek, Connecticut, 1998).

11. Diane Swanson, "Toward an Integrative Theory of Business and Society: A Research Strategy for Corporate Social Performance," *Academy of Management Review, 24* (1999):506–521.

12. Edgar Schein, *Organizational culture and leadership*, 2nd ed. (San Francisco, CA: Jossey-Bass, 1992).

13. Michael Jensen, "Value Maximization, Stakeholder Theory, and the Corporate Objective Function," *Journal of Applied Corporate Finance* 14, no. 3 (2001): 8–21.

14. Data is from *www.sustainability-indexes.com*.

15. Sophia A. Muirhead, Charles J. Bennett, Ronald E. Berenbeim, Amy Kao, and David J. Vidal, *Corporate Citizenship in the New Century: Accountability, Transparency, and Global Stakeholder Engagement* The Conference Board, Research Report # R-1314–02-RR, July 2002.

INDEX